IMAGES
of America

THE BIG DUCK
AND EASTERN LONG ISLAND'S DUCK FARMING INDUSTRY

ON THE COVER: THE BIG DUCK AND BIG DUCK RANCH, C. 1958. This image shows the Big Duck and the layout of farm buildings on the east side of Flanders Road (New York State Route 24) in Flanders while owned by the Desson family (from 1951 to 1971). (Courtesy of Leonard Desson.)

IMAGES
of America

THE BIG DUCK AND EASTERN LONG ISLAND'S DUCK FARMING INDUSTRY

Dr. Susan Van Scoy

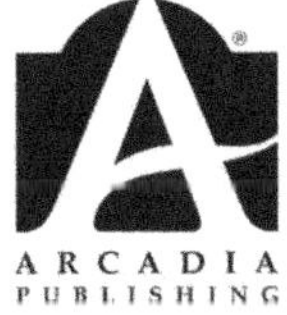

ISBN 978-1-4671-0282-7

Published by Arcadia Publishing
Charleston, South Carolina

Library of Congress Control Number: 2018953455

For all general information, please contact Arcadia Publishing:
Telephone 843-853-2070
Fax 843-853-0044
E-mail sales@arcadiapublishing.com
For customer service and orders:
Toll-Free 1-888-313-2665

Visit us on the Internet at www.arcadiapublishing.com

To my three ducklings—Lillian, Annabel, and Hazel—and to my husband, Brian

To the duck farmers on the East End—your hard work and ingenuity set the stage for the thriving farm industry on Long Island today

Contents

Acknowledgments

I would like to thank Richard C. Martin, director of Historic Services, Suffolk County, who welcomed this project enthusiastically and granted me access to the Big Duck's records. A huge thank-you to Janice Jay Young, Big Duck docent and secretary of the Flanders Village Historical Society, who put me in contact with crucial sources for photographs.

Because there is no central archive of Long Island duck farm photographs, this book would not have been possible without the generosity of those who loaned me their personal photographs. Specifically, I wish to thank Leonard Desson for sharing never-before-seen images and providing detailed information. Dean Colombo and Mac Titmus also provided me with original photographs. A special thank-you goes to Douglas Corwin, of Crescent Duck Farm, for giving me access to his family archive and a tour of the farm in Aquebogue.

I am grateful to Eric Woodward for granting access to his vast collection of postcards and to Ronald Bush and Meghan Bush for their hospitality at the Bush Farm Museum. Thank you to Dr. William F. Dean, Cornell University Duck Research Laboratory; Thomas Williams, The Post-Morrow Foundation; and Martin Van Lith for their photographs.

Gina Piastuck, Long Island Collection at East Hampton Library; Caren Zatyk, Long Island Room at the Smithtown Library; and Kristen J. Nyitray, Special Collections, Stony Brook University Library, helped me with my research. Many thanks go to Susan Strange, independent researcher, and Kaitlyn Enriquez, Still Picture Reference Team, the National Archives.

Erin L. Vosgien, acquisitions editor, and Caroline Anderson, title manager, at Arcadia Publishing provided me with helpful advice and answered countless questions.

Thank you to Emily Morgan, Iowa State University, whose SECAC (formerly Southeastern College Art Conference) panel "Beastly Spirits and Spirited Beasts" first inspired me to research the Big Duck and to Prof. Donald Kuspit for helping develop the connection between the Big Duck and Freud. Thank you to St. Joseph's College for rewarding me with two faculty small grants and to my colleagues for their encouragement: Dawn Lee, S. Pat Manning, Wendy Turgeon, and Anna Malzone and the Council for the Arts. Finally, thank you to my family for their love and support.

Introduction

Most white-tablecloth dining establishments have featured "Long Island duckling" on the menu. The Pekin duck, chosen for its quick birth to slaughter weight time and tender, savory meat, has become inextricably linked to the Eastern Long Island region, despite not being native to the area. The multimillion-dollar Long Island duck industry was hatched from one drake and three ducks, which were brought over to New York from China in 1873. Long Island's sandy terrain, vast waterfront, temperate climate, and proximity to New York City markets made it an optimal environment in which to breed and raise ducks. After much experimentation with the Pekin breed, duck farms were established all along the coastline of Long Island with the greatest concentration between Eastport and Riverhead, and the Pekin duck population exploded on Eastern Long Island.

Initially, raising ducks was labor-intensive and required many human hands. Duck farmers raised their own breeding stock and hatched their own eggs. Pekin ducks stood out amongst other duck breeds available because they were good breeders, usually laying about 150 eggs a year. Farmers would choose good breeder specimens by sight and touch, looking for a well-shaped head and wide-set breasts. Four weeks were needed to hatch an egg, and the first were hatched with "setting hens" until kerosene heated incubators were introduced. The ducklings were stored in young brooder houses and fed a homemade fattening mixture of bran, meal, flour, beef scrap, rye, wheat, alfalfa, and other green vegetables. Farmers devised a track system with trains that delivered the feed to the ducklings. At about six weeks, the ducklings were sent to the waterfront until they reached market weight. The "day of reckoning" came at about 10 to 12 weeks. The ducks were slaughtered on the farm, by a knife to the jugular when hanging upside-down in a stockade. They were then plucked by female pickers, packed in vats of ice, and transported to New York City markets.

Modern innovations, such as electric incubators, food pellets, and a duck growers' cooperative marketing association founded in 1921, were gradually introduced to the duck farming industry. After setting hens, farmers relied on hot water incubators until the first electric incubator was introduced on Long Island in 1928. The electric incubators cut down on the risk of fire and maintained a stable temperature during the hatching period, turning the eggs three times a day to prevent the embryos from sticking to the shells. Other modern improvements soon followed, including water pumps, radiant heated floors, and germicidal lamps, which cut down on airborne diseases and reduced labor needs on the farms.

From the 1930s to the 1950s, Long Island duck farms' activity peaked. Throughout the 1940s, Long Island produced about six to eight million ducks annually, and the number of farms expanded to around 100. This eventually led to overproduction, and in 1959, most farms began to lose money. In 1960, a total of 44 farmers formed the Long Island Duck Farmers Cooperative to fix prices, centralize processing, and create promotional campaigns. However, by the mid-1960s, the number of duck farms dwindled to 48. In 1974, there were 27 duck farms left on Long Island producing seven million, or 70 percent of the ducks in the United States per year. In the 1960s and

1970s, stricter New York state environmental regulations were implemented, specifically focusing on water pollution in the South Shore bays and inlets. Farmers were forced to invest millions of dollars into wastewater treatment plants, moving their ducks inside. Faced with increasing property taxes and higher costs of grain, rather than invest heavily in updated farm facilities, many of them chose to sell their valuable real estate to developers. In 2009, only three duck farms remained. One longstanding holdout, Chester Massey & Sons closed in 2015, making Douglas Corwin's Crescent Duck Farm in Aquebogue the last remaining duck farm on Long Island. The farm produces around one million ducks annually, or four percent of the nation's duck supply. Crescent Duck Farm and Martin Maurer's Big Duck are the strongest enduring vestiges of the once-thriving duck farming industry on Long Island.

The Big Duck, an 18-foot-tall-by-30-foot-wide ferroconcrete building in the shape of a Pekin duck, was first conceived by duck farmer Martin Maurer in 1931 as a retail shop for duck eggs and poultry, in the Upper Mills section of Riverhead, Long Island. Since then, it has been the subject of much wonder, consternation, and controversy—children yearn for the sight of the "duck building" out of their car window. It is a wonderful example of American "roadside architecture." It has escaped destruction by developers numerous times, and it stands as a monument to the once-active duck farming industry on the eastern end of Long Island. The Big Duck has carved its place in popular culture. It is featured in a cartoon by Saul Steinberg on the cover of the *New Yorker*, comic strips, and countless artists' reproductions and continues to enjoy a strong following with organizations such as "Friends of the Big Duck" and the annual holiday duck lighting.

The Big Duck has also been criticized and dissected in academia and architectural history books. In 1964, Peter Blake included it in *God's Own Junkyard: The Planned Deterioration of America's Landscape*, or what Blake called "a deliberate attack upon those who have already befouled a large portion of this country for private gain, and are engaged in befouling the rest [no pun intended]." Blake called out those who ruined the landscape through the billboard industry as well as the "little people" who had no ties to the landscape or town in which they lived.

The Big Duck was most famously celebrated by architects Robert Venturi and Denise Scott Brown in their influential 1972 book, *Learning from Las Vegas*, in which they used the term "duck" to classify any building that was a symbol, that took the shape of its function, or "where the architectural systems of space, structure, and program are submerged and distorted by an overall symbolic form," as opposed to a "decorated shed," or a shelter that "applies symbols." Subsequently, in 1972, architect James Wines proposed the DDT, or Duck Design Theory, and claimed that architecture like the Big Duck introduced play, fantasy, and whimsy into otherwise humdrum, everyday experiences.

After Maurer's retirement in 1951, the Desson and then the Colombo families operated the Big Duck as a poultry retail shop until the 1980s. In 1982, the Duck was purchased by Kia and Pouran Eshghi, Iranian immigrants who had come to the United States in 1962. Kia, a sculptor, and Pouran had plans to turn the land into an artists' commune, but they could not overcome the zoning restrictions. The farm sat unused and fell into disrepair until 1987, when the Eshghis sold the land to developers and donated the Big Duck to Suffolk County to save it from demolition. In 1988, the Big Duck was moved a few miles southeast to the 1,000-acre Sears Bellows County Park and remained there for 19 years, re-opening as a gift shop and East End welcome center in 1993. During this time, the site of Maurer's Big Duck Ranch on Route 24 remained undeveloped and the Town of Southampton purchased it in 2001. The Big Duck was returned to its previous location in 2007 and continues to operate as a gift shop and welcome center. The Big Duck receives approximately 10,000 visitors a year, not including the countless numbers who stop to take a "selfie" in front of the Big Duck. Besides Crescent Duck Farm and the Big Duck, many other reminders of the famous Long Island duck farming industry persist such as the Long Island Ducks minor league baseball team, Duck Walk Vineyards, and a resurgence of small family-run poultry farms on the East End of Long Island, particularly on the North Fork. Despite the lack of duck farms that used to dominate Eastern Long Island, like Idaho potatoes and Maine lobsters, Long Island duck will continue to persist on menus and in the minds of people everywhere.

One

Establishment of Long Island Duck Farming

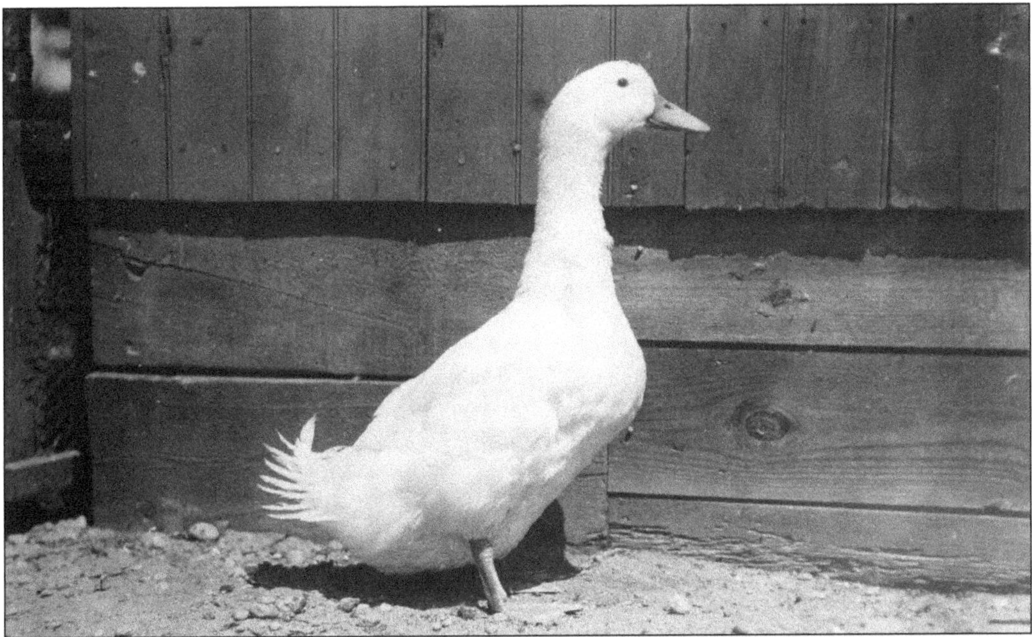

Drake, Eastport, June 1920. On a trip to Shanghai, China, in 1872, James E. Palmer of Stonington, Connecticut, witnessed ducks from the Imperial City of Peking so large that he thought they were geese. He immediately sought to acquire some "Pekin" ducks to bring back to America. (Courtesy National Archives, No. 17-P-16-05.)

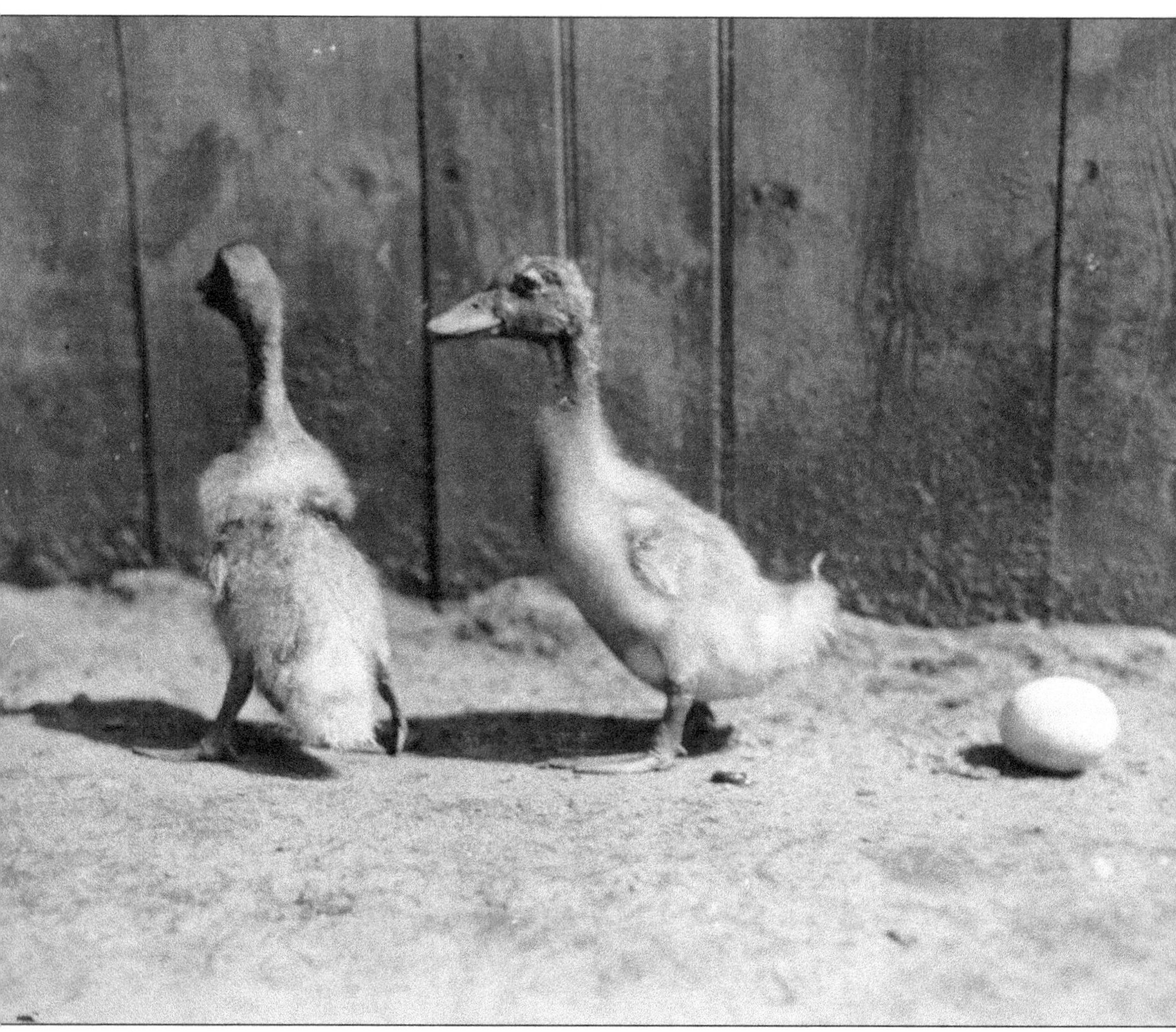

THREE-WEEK-OLD PEKIN DUCKLINGS AND ONE EGG FOR COMPARISON, CENTER MORICHES, JUNE 1920. Palmer arrived back in the United States in 1873 and brought one drake and three ducks to his farm. To his pleasant surprise, they started laying eggs after two weeks. He began breeding them and selling them around the country. It is uncertain how Pekin ducks "migrated" from Palmer's farm in Connecticut to Long Island; however, they landed here sometime between 1873 and 1883. Before the Pekin ducks arrived, many farmers were raising Western breeds like Muscovy. Washington Warren Hallock, who had raised Muscovy ducks since 1858, is likely one of the first recipients of the Pekin breed at his Atlantic Duck Farm in Speonk. By 1886, Eugene Wilcox of Speonk had 67 Pekin ducks. (Courtesy National Archives, No. 17-P-16-60.)

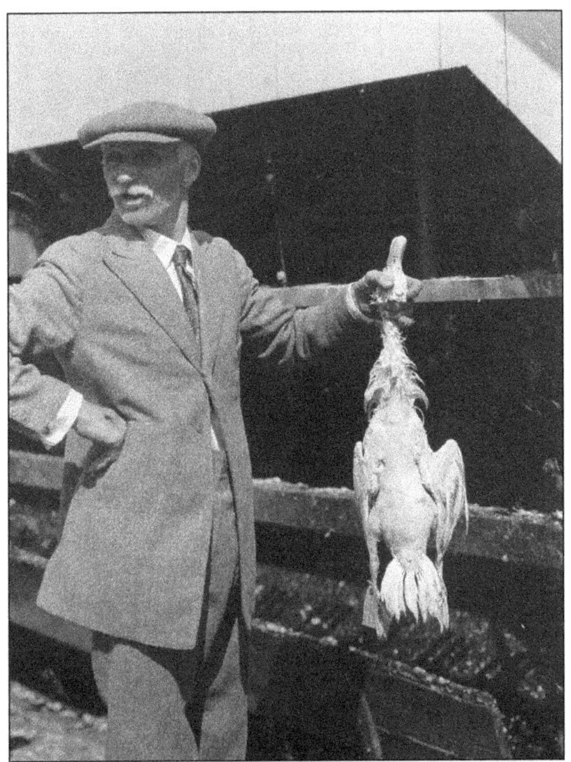

Pekin Duck Held by W.W. Lukert, "New York Dressed," Center Moriches, 1920. In 1894, William Lukert started Lukert Farm in Moriches on the Forge River. Duck growers soon began to favor Pekin for its marketability and profitability—a Pekin is ready for market in 10 to 12 weeks, contrasted with the five to six months needed for Western breeds. Pekin meat is also tender, juicy, and can fetch a higher price per pound. (Courtesy National Archives, No. 17-P-16-168.)

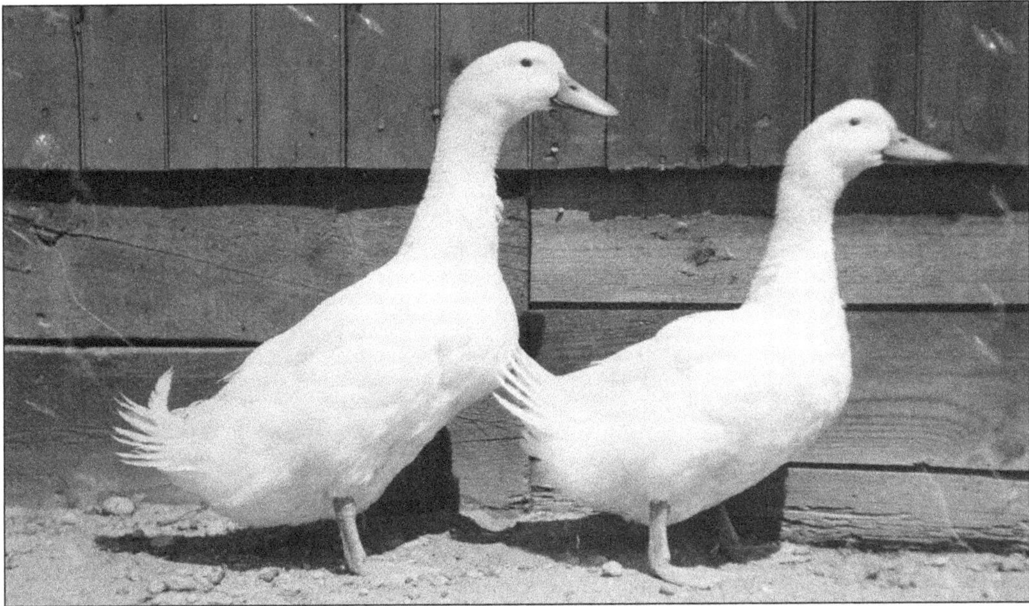

Two Breeders, about 12 Weeks Old, Eastport, June 1920. Pekin ducks were good breeders, usually laying about 150 eggs a year. Farmers chose breeder specimens by sight and touch looking for a well-formed head and wide-set breasts. Female breeders would produce eggs when they were only seven months old. Four weeks were needed to hatch an egg, and the first were hatched with "setting hens" until kerosene heated incubators were introduced. (Courtesy National Archives, No. 17-P-16-08.)

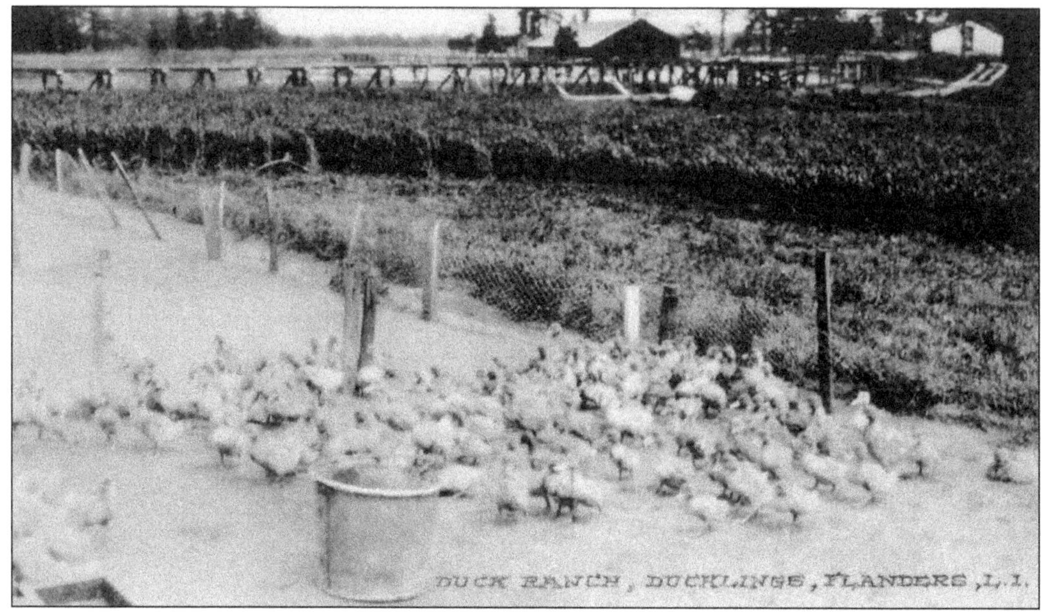

DUCK RANCH, DUCKLINGS, FLANDERS, NEW YORK. Long Island's sandy terrain, abundant waterfront, temperate climate, and proximity to New York City markets—replete with a diverse population of duck-meat consumers—made it an optimal environment for breeding and raising ducks. (Courtesy Collection of Eric Woodward.)

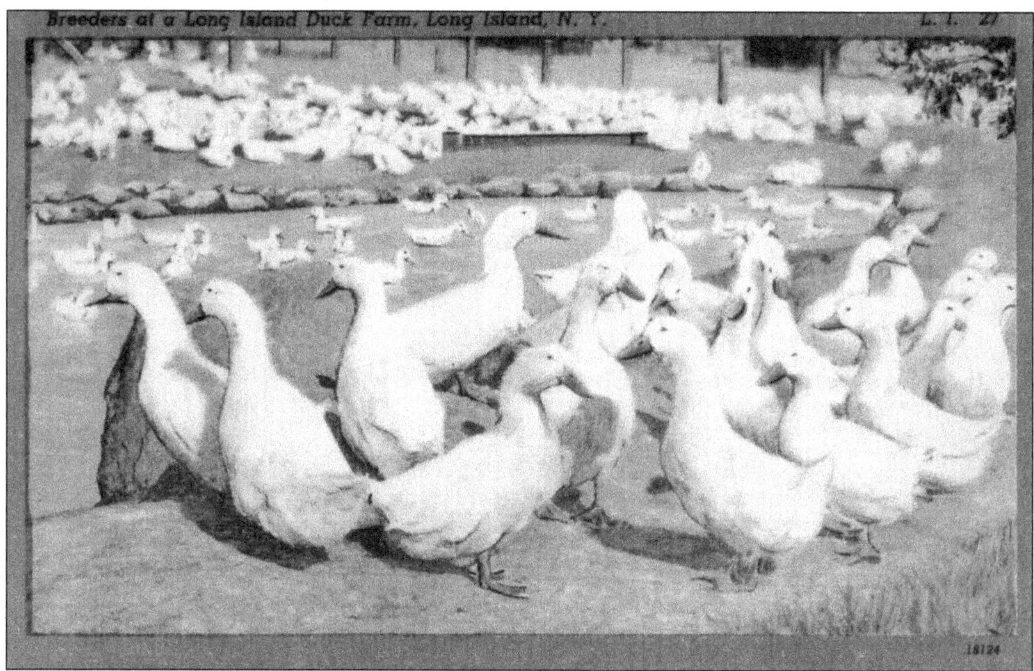

BREEDERS AT A LONG ISLAND DUCK FARM. After much experimentation with the Pekin breed, duck farms sprouted up all along the waterfront of Long Island, though the greatest concentration was between Eastport and Riverhead. Some of the earliest farms were Hallock's Atlantic Duck Farm (1858); Wilcox's Sea Side Ranch, subsequently named Oceanic Duck Farm (1883); Lukert Farm (1894); and Asa Fordham/A.B. Soyars Duck Farm (1902). (Courtesy Collection of Eric Woodward.)

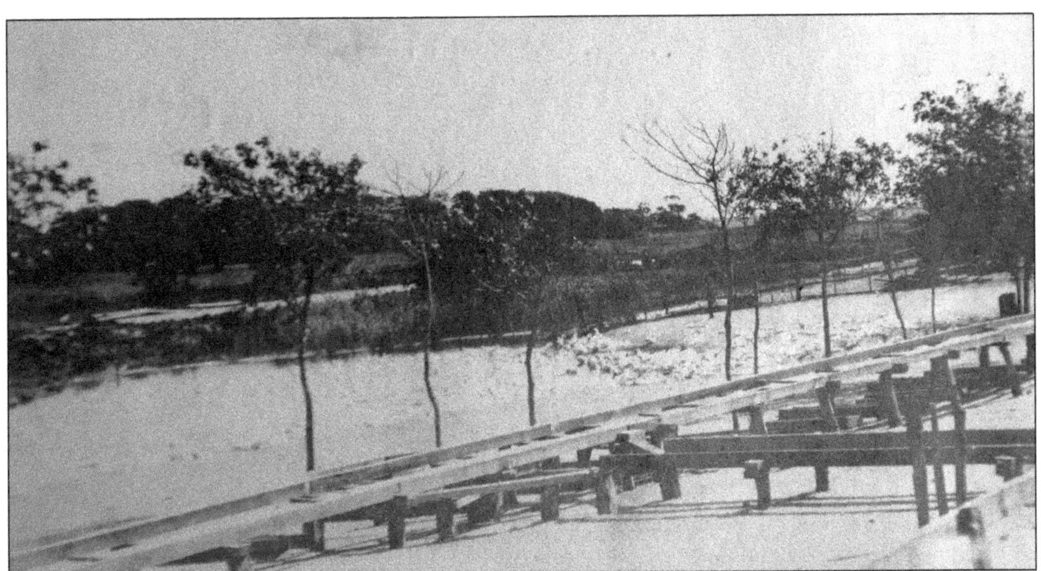

A.J. Hallock Farm, Speonk, 1905. Hallock was one of the oldest-running duck farms, established by Warren Hallock, who settled in Brushy Neck in 1838. By 1858, Hallock was producing 5,000 ducks annually on a farm near the Speonk River. In 1892, Warren died and passed the business to his son, Arthur J. who renamed it W.W. Hallock & Son, also known as Atlantic Farm. In 1900, the farm hatched 28,000 ducks. Unfortunately, in 1938, a hurricane destroyed much of the farm. (Courtesy National Archives, No. 17-P-16-85.)

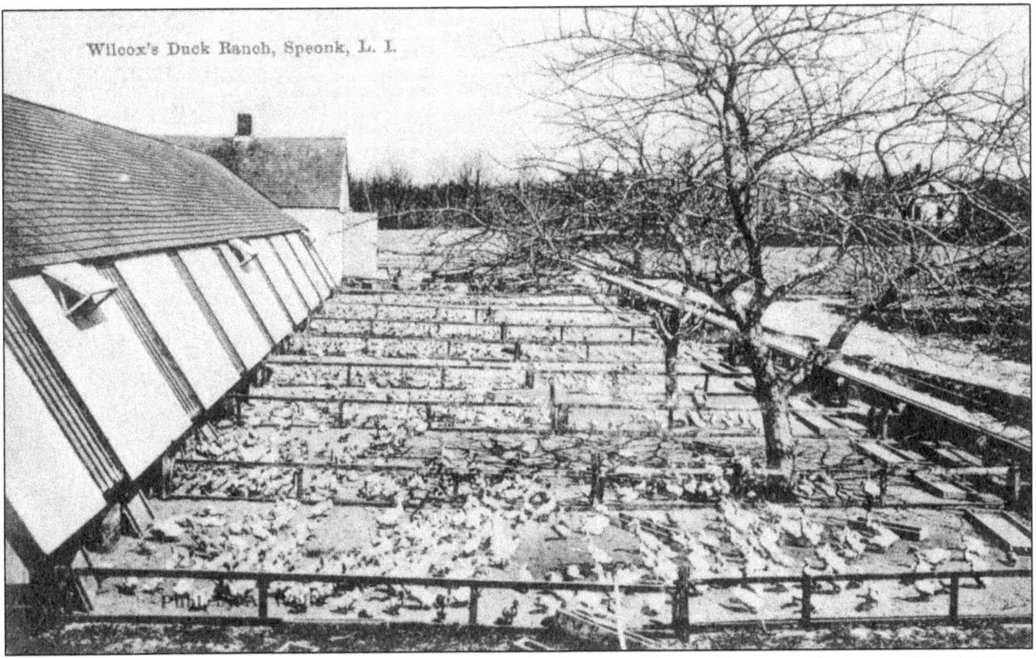

Wilcox's Duck Ranch (Oceanic Duck Farm), Speonk, Long Island. Oceanic Duck Farm was started by E.O. Wilcox in 1883. According to LeRoy Wilcox in his 1949 history of the duck farming industry, E.O. Wilcox produced 775 ducks in 1883, his first year in business; 1,101 in 1884; 1,566 in 1885; and 3,466 in 1886. By 1887, about 200,000 ducks were produced by Long Island farms. (Courtesy Collection of Eric Woodward.)

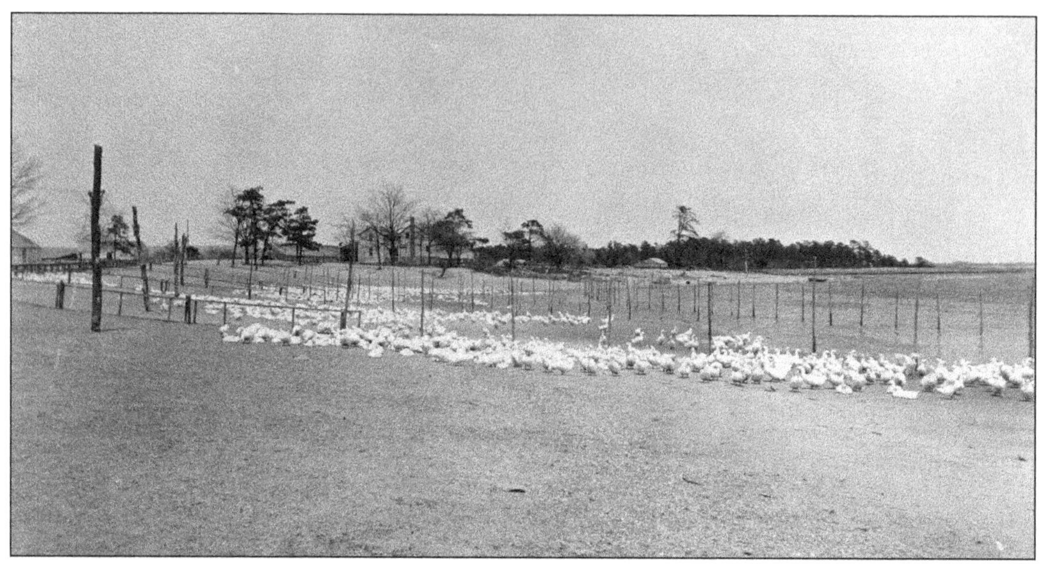

A.B. Soyars Farm, Riverhead, 1920. A.B. Soyars purchased the farm from Asa Fordham in 1902 in Riverhead. Based on the banks of the Peconic River, it became one of the larger duck farms. (Courtesy National Archives, No. 17-P-16-102.)

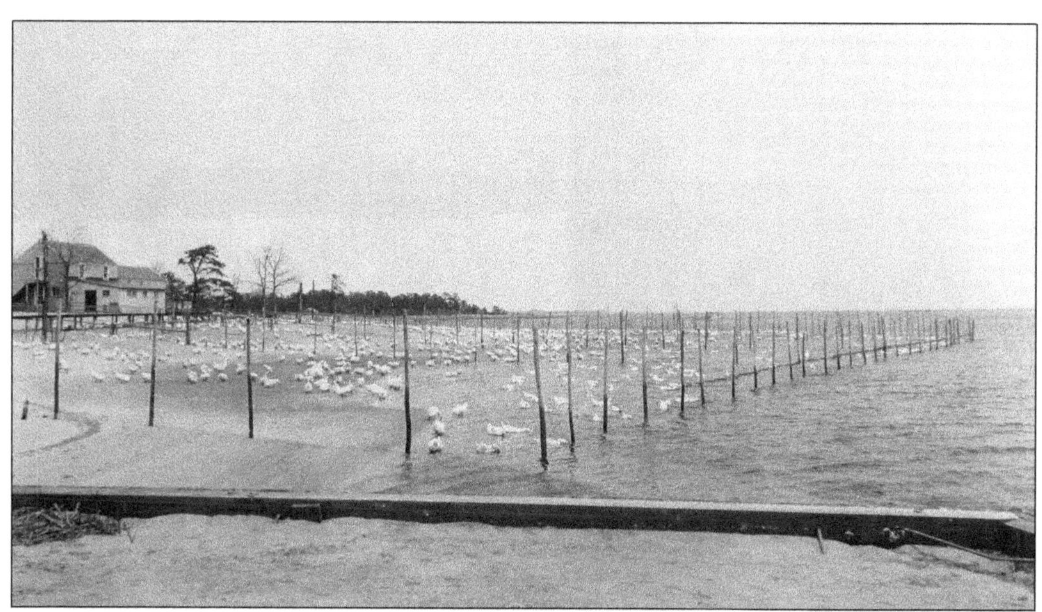

Breeding Yards, A.B. Soyars Farm, Riverhead, 1920. During the early years of duck farming, it was widely accepted that breeders increased their fertility by swimming and benefitted from having access to water for drinking and cleaning their feathers; however, there were a few duck breeders who had success on dry farms. As a result, most duck farms were located along freshwater streams on the south shore that fed into bays. (Courtesy National Archives, No. 17-P-16-103.)

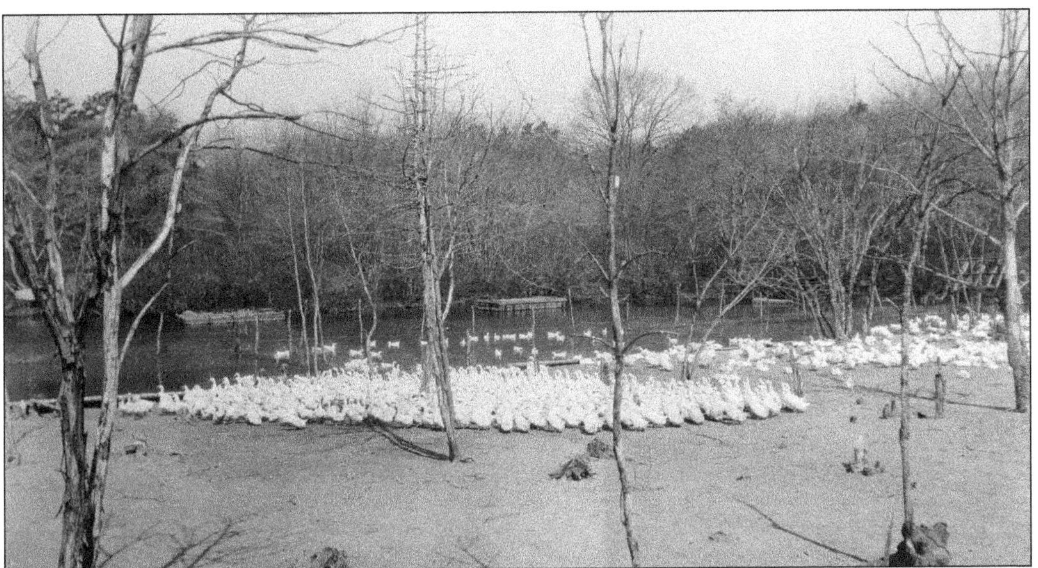

Breeding Ducks, R.A. Tuttle's Farm, Center Moriches, 1920. R.A. Tuttle, son of Brewster Tuttle, started a farm in Center Moriches, on West Senix Creek in 1912, in partnership with Clifford Bowditch until 1919. (Courtesy National Archives, No. 17-P-16-111.)

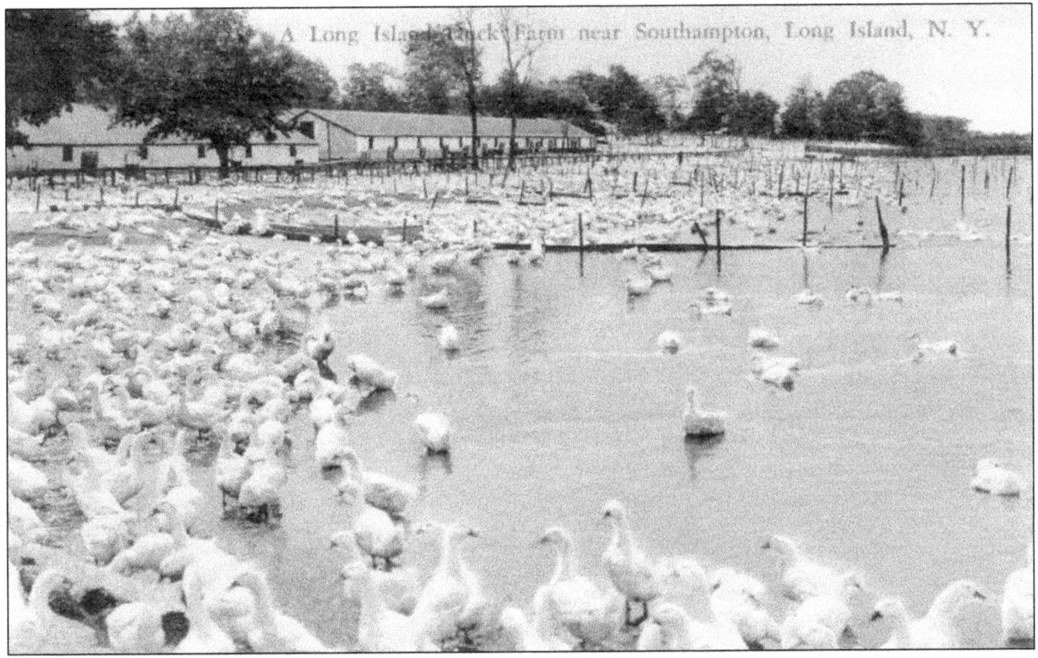

A Long Island Duck Farm near Southampton. Early Pekin duck raisers were in Massachusetts and Long Island; however, Massachusetts employed "dry duck farming." Conversely, Long Island duck farmers allowed their ducks to have free reign over ponds, bays, and streams. In 1949, out of 77 duck farms, only one was located "upland" in Moriches. The water pollution, however, is what would become a major factor in the Long Island duck industry's downfall. (Courtesy Collection of Eric Woodward.)

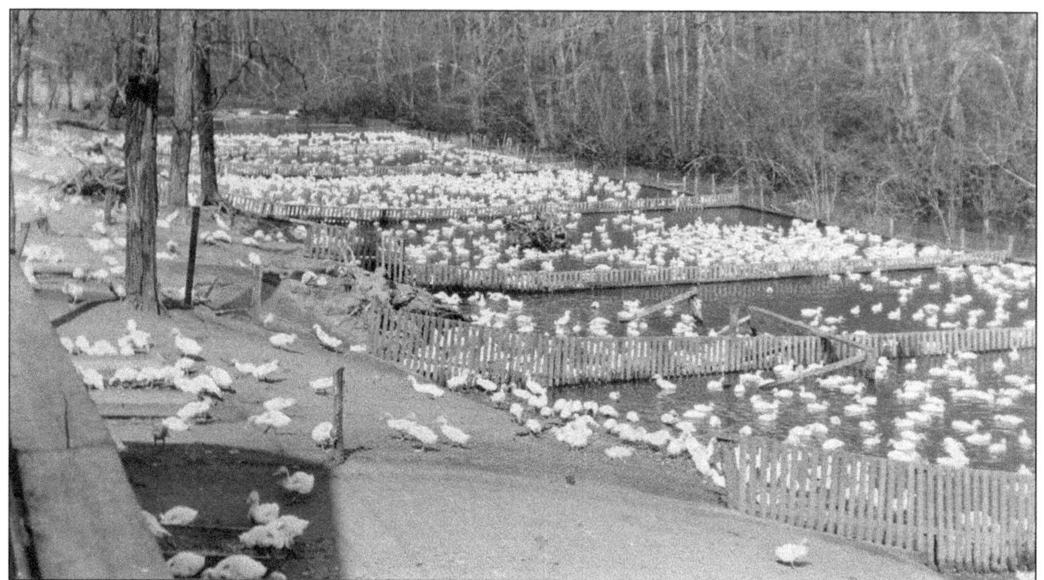

View of Ducks in Water Yards, W.W. Lukert, Center Moriches, 1920. Surprisingly, Pekin ducks are not born knowing how to swim; they must learn. As such, they are kept on land for their first few weeks. At about six weeks, after they grow feathers, the ducklings are sent to the waterfront where they can swim initially for short periods of time lest they become too waterlogged and drown. Once they adapt to being in the water by preening and oiling their feathers, then they can swim for longer amounts of time. Mating usually occurred in the water. (Courtesy National Archives, No. 17-P-16-128.)

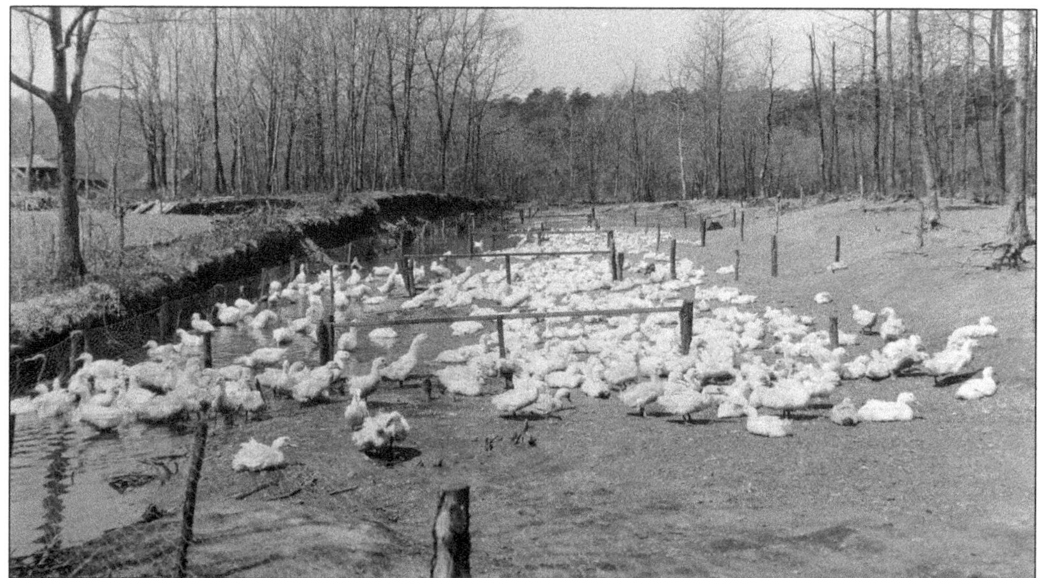

Canals, R.A. Tuttle's Farm, Center Moriches, 1920. If the duck yards did not run naturally into a stream, farmers took great pains to dig artificial canals from the stream to the yards so that their birds would have access to clean water. (Courtesy National Archives, No. 17-P-16-114.)

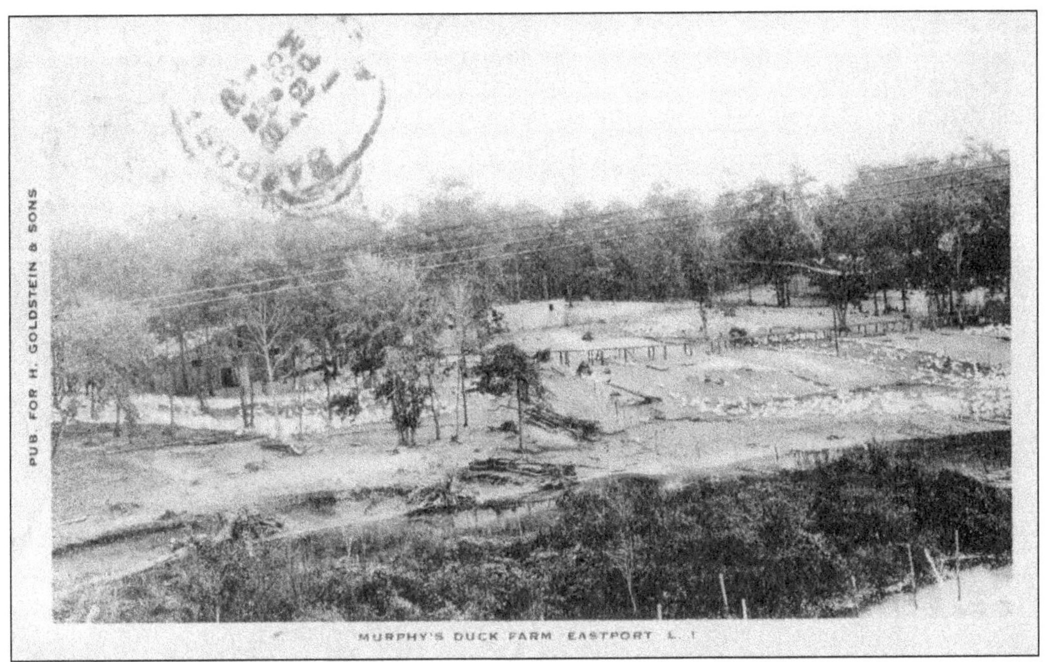

VIEW OF WATER YARDS, MURPHY'S DUCK FARM, EASTPORT, 1930S. Murphy's Duck Farm was started by Hugh Murphy in 1912. It was located on the east side of the east creek and south of the Long Island Railroad. (Courtesy Collection of Eric Woodward.)

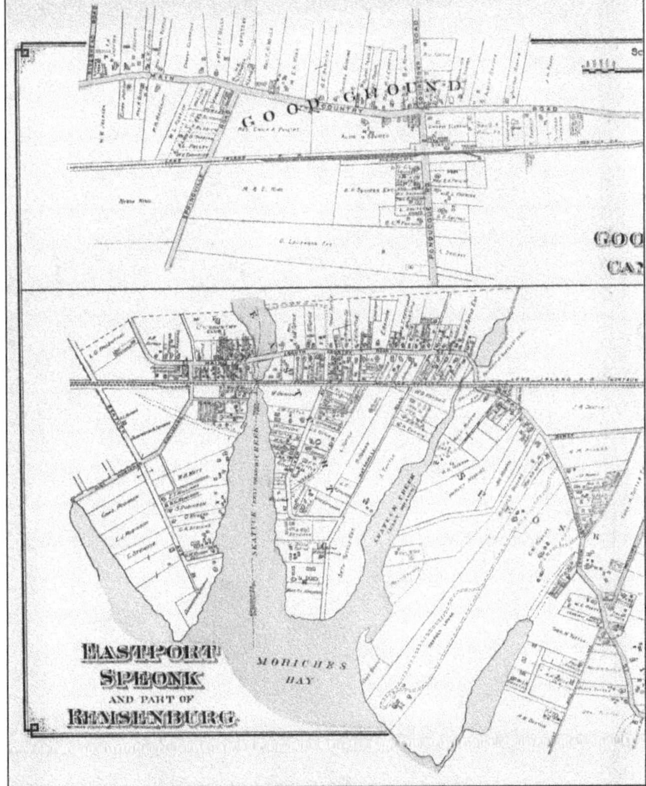

EASTPORT, SPEONK, AND PART OF REMSENBURG, *ATLAS OF A PART OF SUFFOLK COUNTY, LONG ISLAND, NEW YORK: SOUTH SIDE–OCEAN SHORE* (1916), PLATE 12. The West and East forks of Seatuck Creek boasted a great concentration of duck farms. Prominent duck farmers in Eastport shown here include Seaman, Murphy, Frey, Pye, Gordon, Tuttle, and Edwards, to name a few. (Courtesy the Long Island Collection, East Hampton Library.)

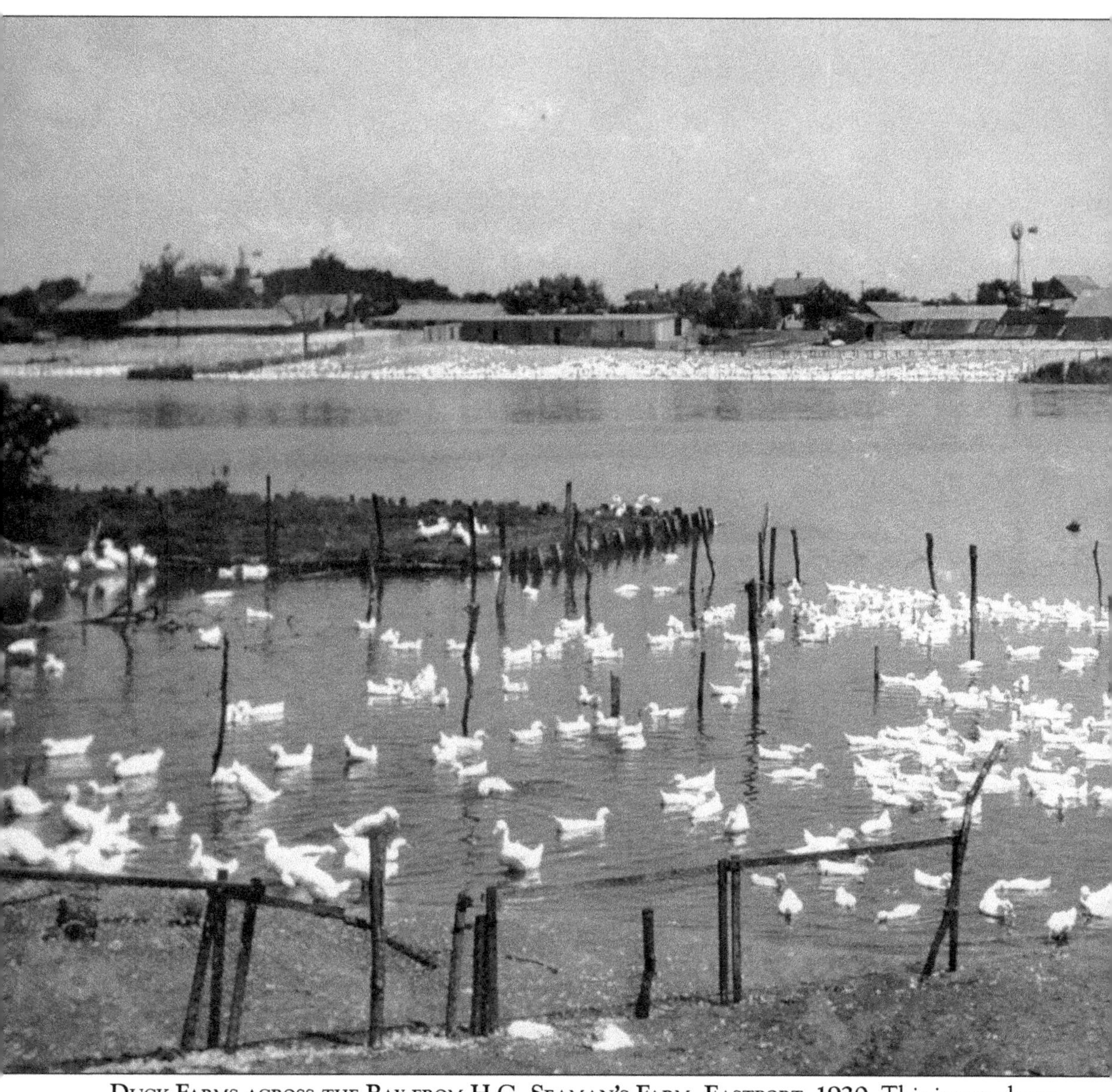

Duck Farms across the Bay from H.G. Seaman's Farm, Eastport, 1920. This image shows the concentration of duck farms in Eastport along the east side of the river; Seaman's was next to Murphy's Duck Farm and across from Pye's and Tuttle's Duck Farm. South of Murphy's, Capt.

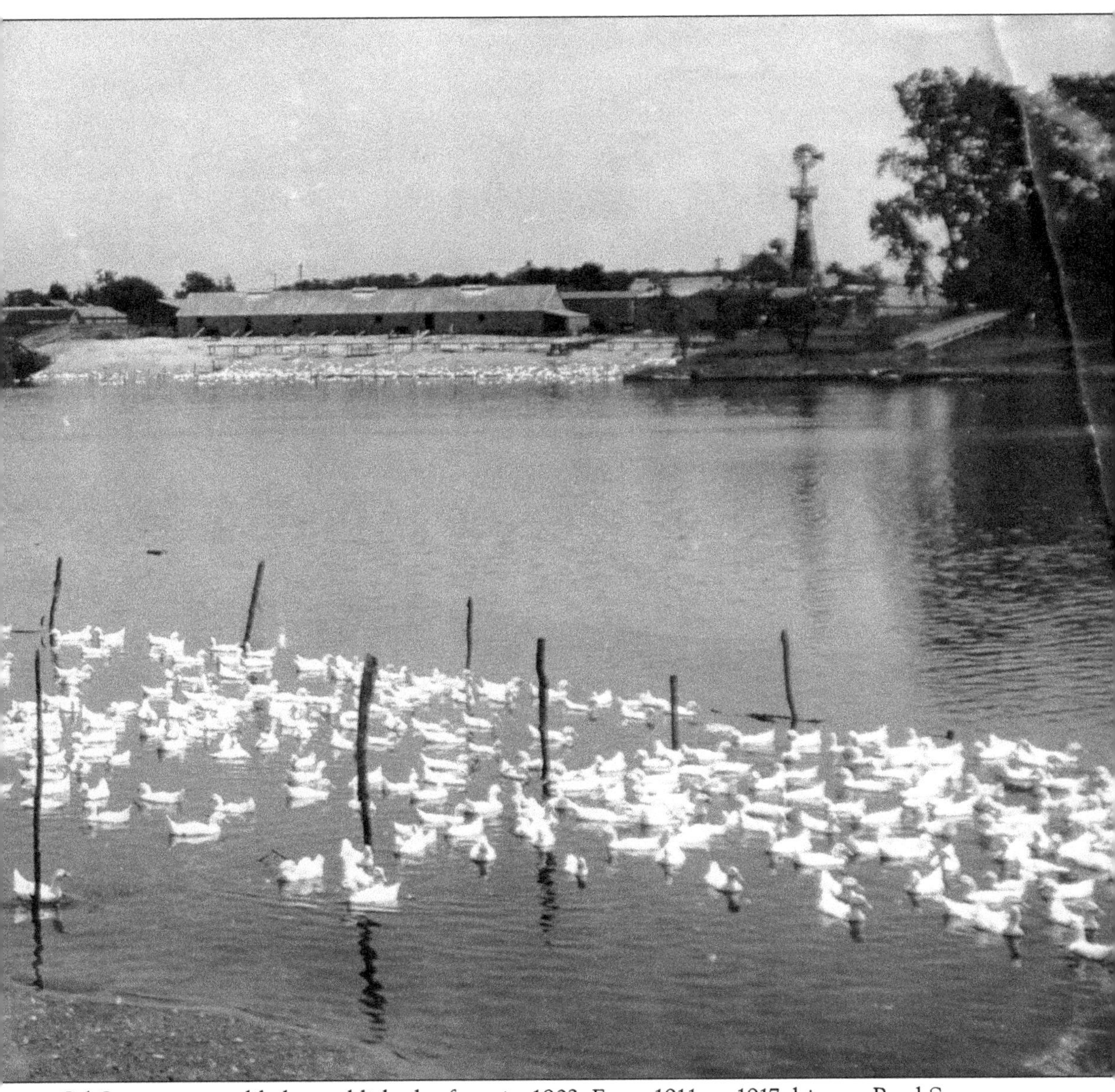

Gil Seaman most likely established a farm in 1903. From 1911 to 1917, his son Brud Seaman operated a farm with Chester A. Pitney on the west side of the east creek in Eastport. (Courtesy National Archives, No. 17-P-16-88.)

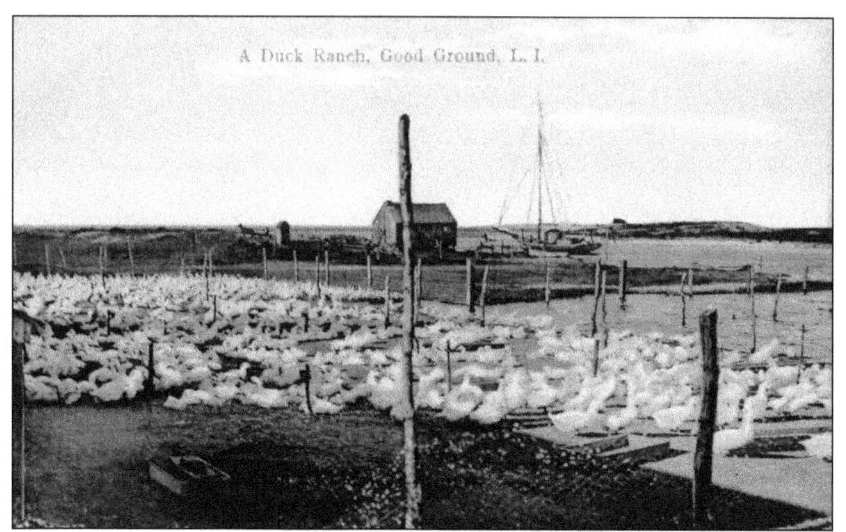

Duck Farm Good Ground. Good Ground, a hamlet settled in 1740, became known as Hampton Bays in 1922. Here, ducks enjoy their water yard. (Courtesy Collection of Eric Woodward.)

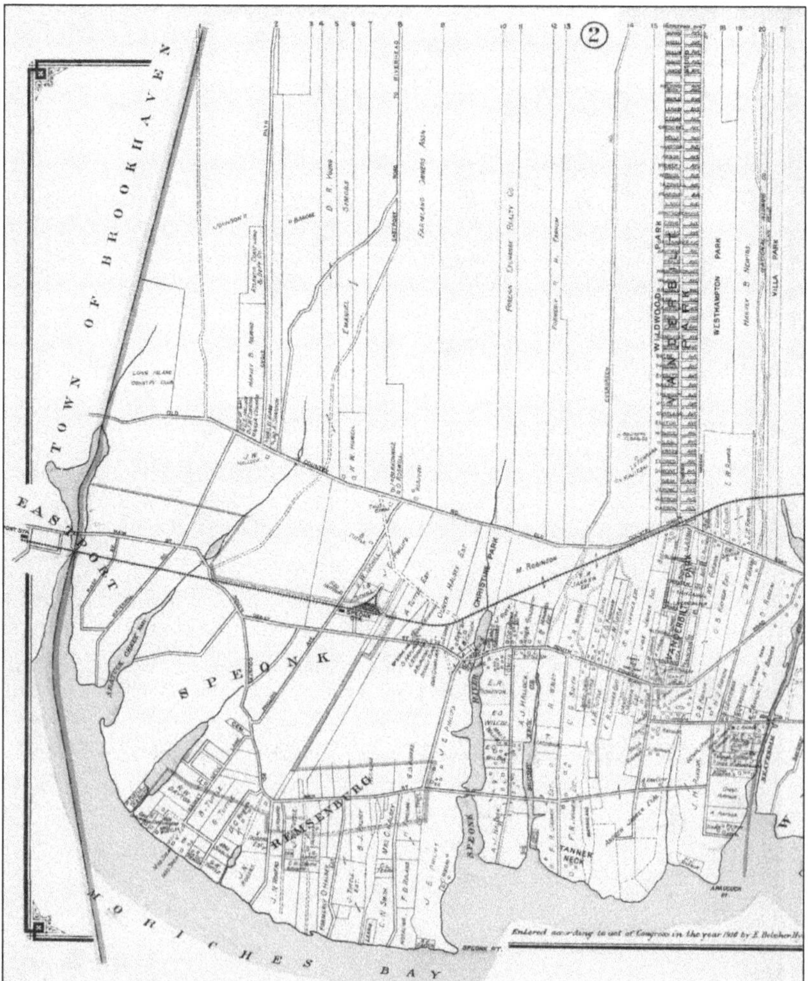

Speonk and Remsenburg, *Atlas of a Part of Suffolk County, Long Island, New York: South Side–Ocean Shore* (1916), Plate 1. Two large farms—Wilcox's and Hallock's—were located on the Speonk River and Brushy Neck Creek. (Courtesy the Long Island Collection, East Hampton Library.)

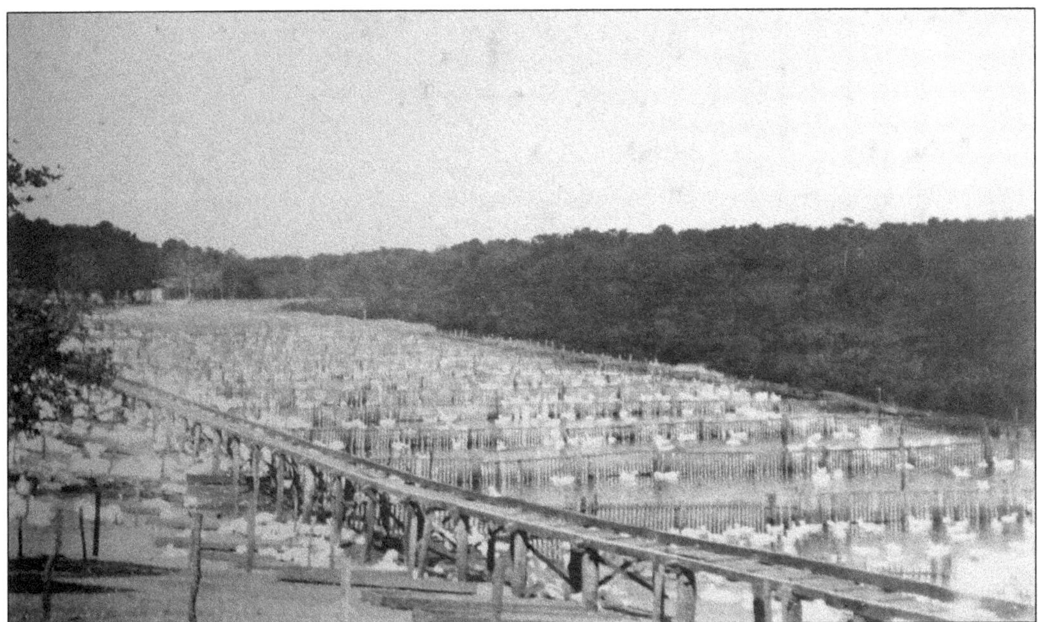

WATER YARDS, A.J. HALLOCK, SPEONK, 1905. Ducks are highly versatile in water. Most farms were located on freshwater streams, but when closer to the bay, the water was more brackish. Older ducks could exist in salt water; however, farmers had to provide supplemental fresh drinking water for younger ducklings. (Courtesy National Archives, No. 17-P-16-84.)

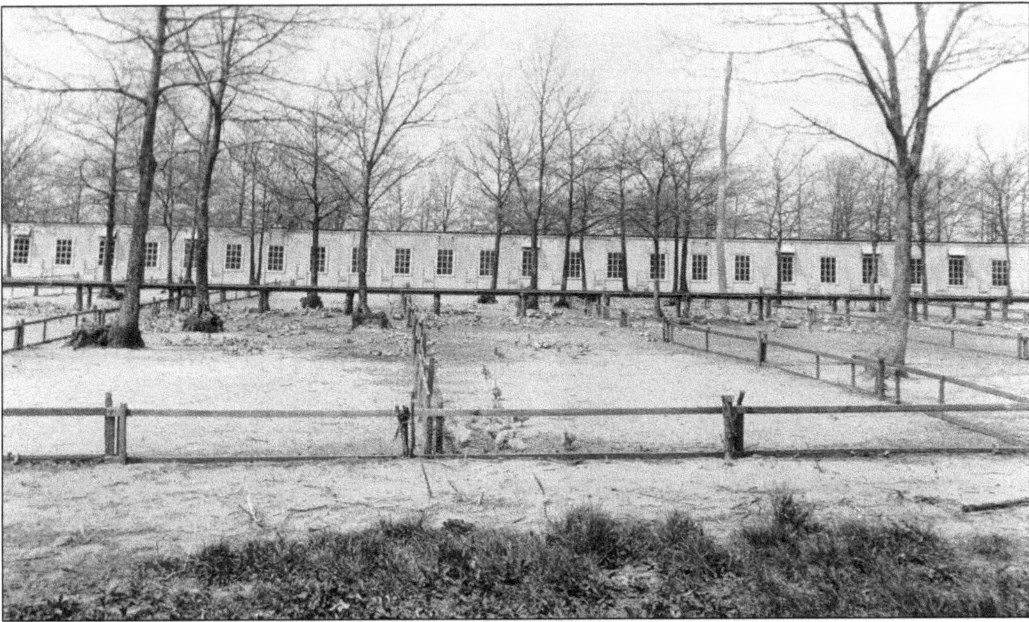

BROODER HOUSE WITH FOOD TRACKS, A.B. SOYARS FARM, RIVERHEAD, 1920. Duck farms required considerable investment and some structures to run, though the low-slung buildings were constructed by the farmers themselves and could be knocked down without a trace. Brooder houses were oriented north to south with windows on the sides for ample sunlight. Most were constructed on a concrete foundation with dirt floors built up higher than the surrounding ground to prevent water from entering. (Courtesy National Archives, No. 17-P-16-100.)

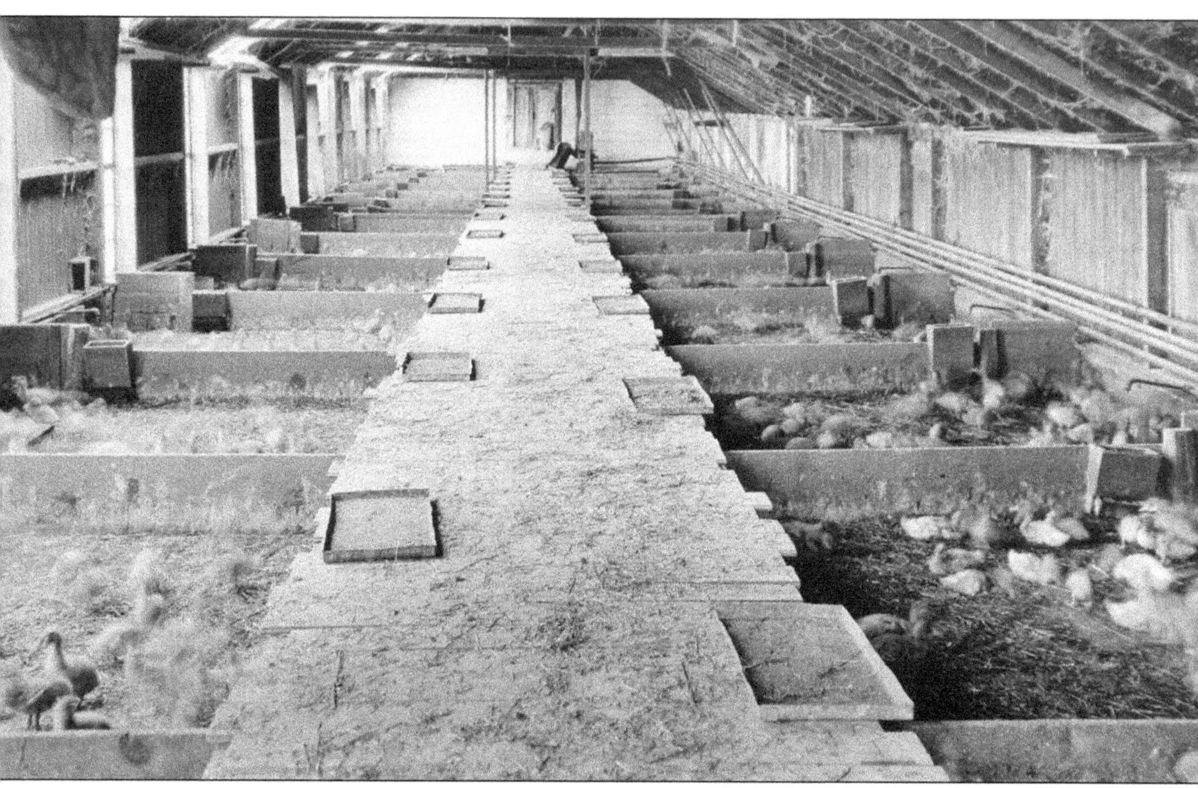

Interior of No. 1 Brooder, R.A. Tuttle's Farm, Center Moriches, 1920. In order to grow ducks, three brooder houses were recommended to house the young ducklings at controlled temperatures. In brooder house No. 1, temperatures were kept at 65 to 70 degrees with covered areas, or hovers, at 80 to 90 degrees. The setup seen here optimized the space, allowing pens on each side of the alleyway. Heat was provided by the heater in the back and by the pipes that ran along the sides. The newcomers were kept closest to the heaters and then were ushered to the next pens with a broom. Ducks were kept in brooder house No. 1 until they were two to three weeks old and then moved to brooder house No. 2. (Courtesy National Archives, No. 17-P-16-141.)

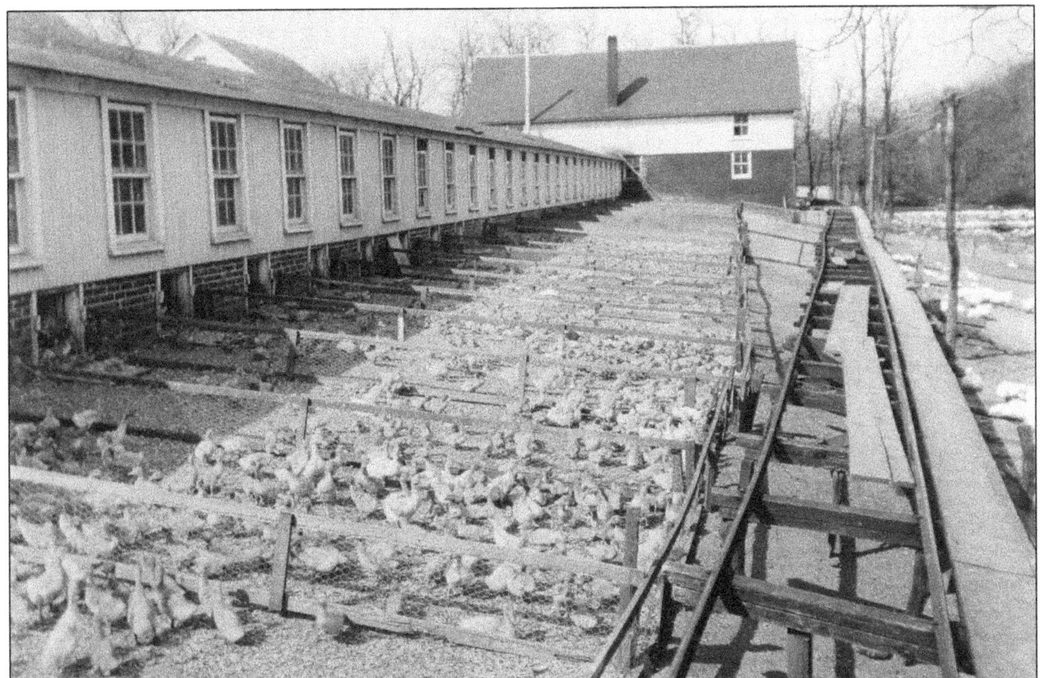

One-Week-Old Ducks in Brooder House Yard, W.W. Lukert's Farm, Center Moriches, 1920. Sliding doors underneath the windows allowed the one-week-old ducklings to roam outside in their pens and to eat outside in the warmer weather. (Courtesy National Archives, No. 17-P-16-117.)

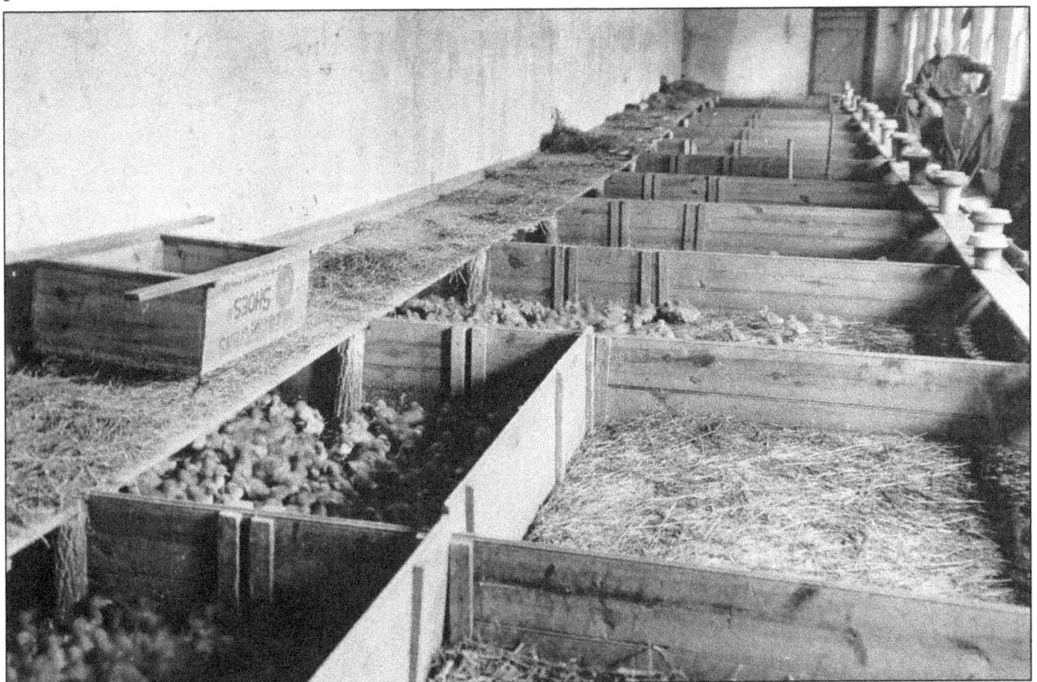

Interior of Brooder House, A.B. Soyars Farm, Riverhead, 1920. Baby ducks gather near the end together. The crate on top of the hover was used for transporting ducklings. (Courtesy National Archives, No. 17-P-16-142.)

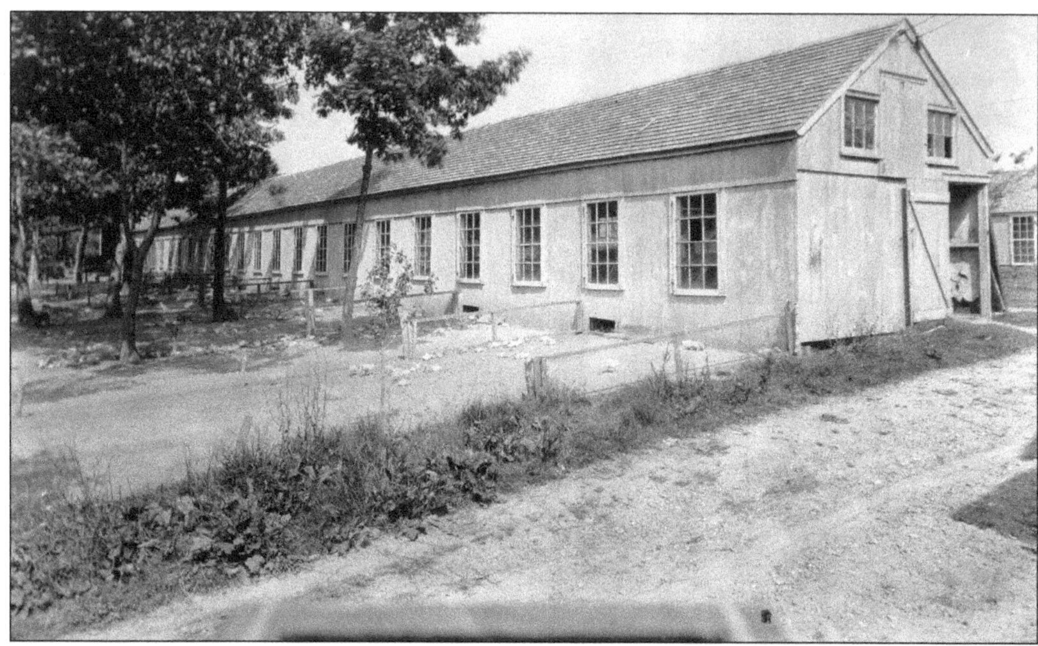

Brooder House No. 2, R.A. Tuttle's Farm, Center Moriches, 1920. The second brooder houses were kept at a temperature of 60 degrees. Ducklings usually spent about two weeks in brooder house No. 2. (Courtesy National Archives, No. 17-P-16-115.)

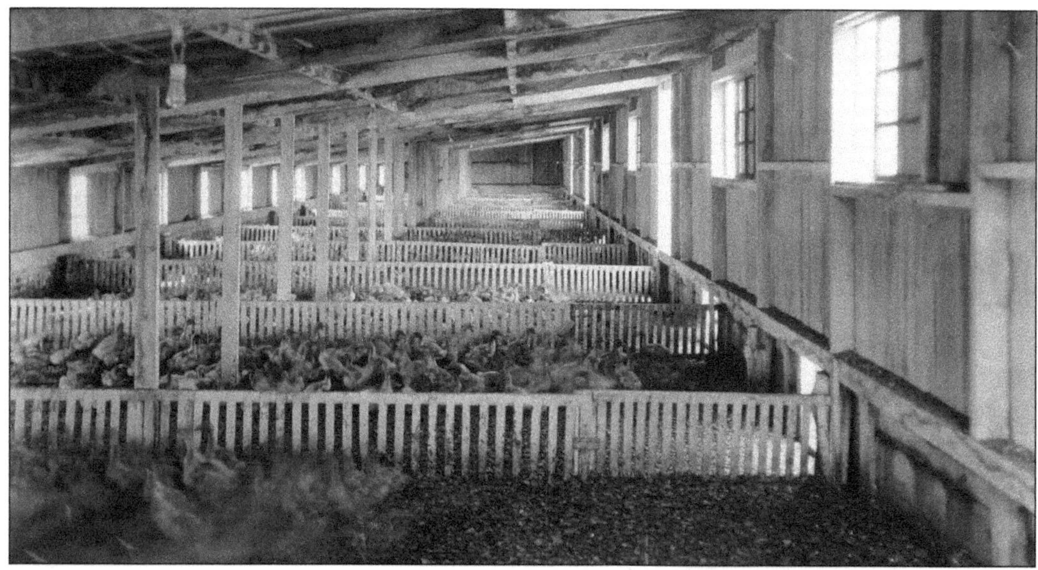

Three-Week-Old Ducks in Cold Brooder House No. 3, W.W. Lukert's Farm, Center Moriches, 1920. Brooder house No. 3 was a cold house without any additional heat that was reserved for older ducklings about five to eight weeks old. In addition to bedding, water, food trays, and pens, brooder houses were equipped with electric lights kept on all night to avoid stampedes, especially during rainstorms. (Courtesy National Archives, No. 17-P-16-145.)

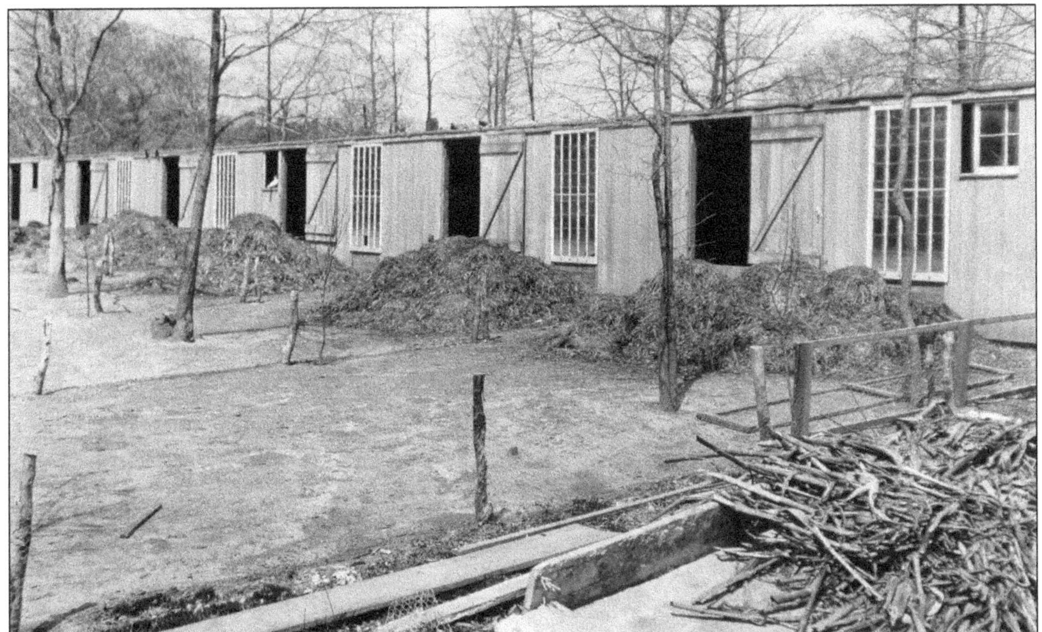

Piles of Manure outside No. 3 Brooder House, R.A. Tuttle's Farm, Center Moriches, 1920. Cleanliness was key and would cut down on the rate of disease and improve the quality of the ducks, so layers of bedding were added every other day to keep the interiors dry. Any time the ducks were moved, houses would be cleaned out by shoveling the bedding out and then dispersing it on the land for fertilizer. (Courtesy National Archives, No. 17-P-16-125.)

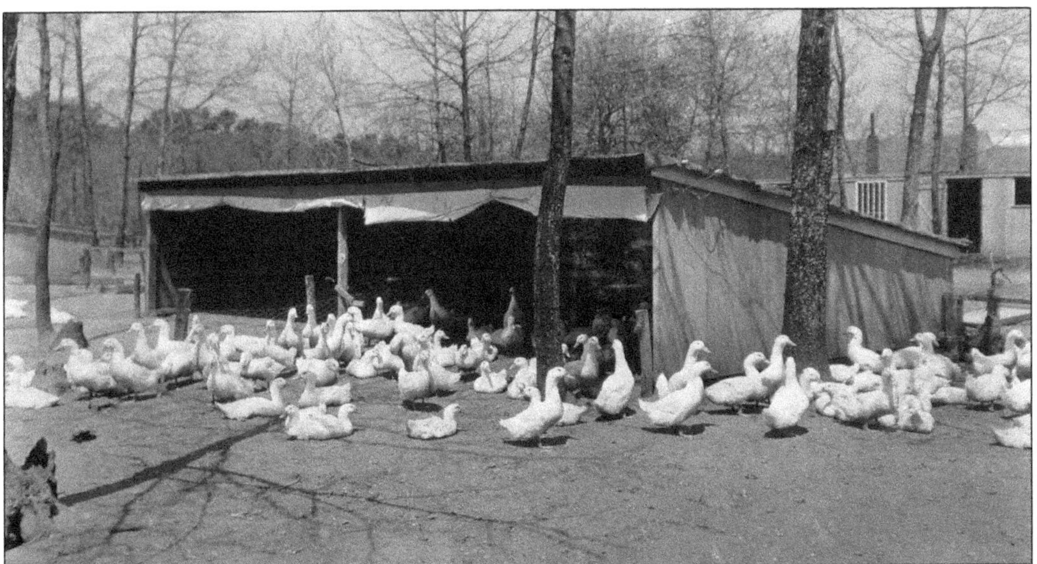

Fattening Ducks and Houses, R.A. Tuttle's Farm, Center Moriches, 1920. After the ducklings turned eight weeks old, they were able to withstand weather conditions outside and were moved from the brooder houses to the yards until they reached market weight. Farmers provided these sheds with open fronts for the "yard ducks" as temporary shelter for them at night or during a storm. (Courtesy National Archives, No. 17-P-16-122.)

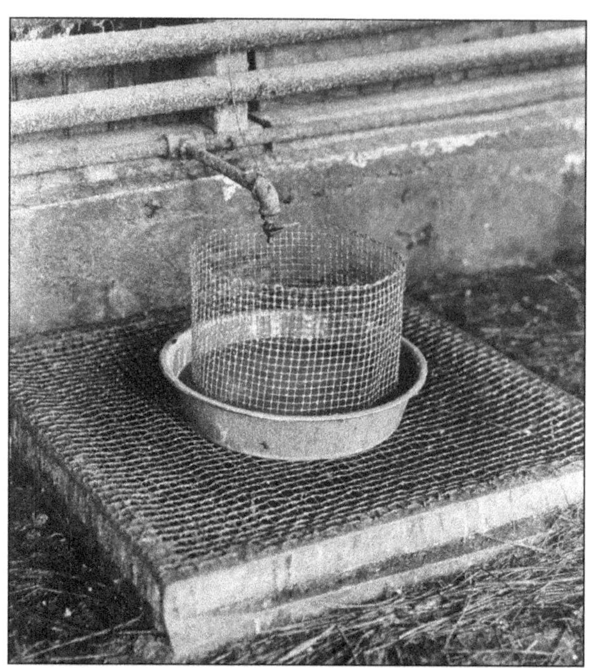

Waterer, R.A. Tuttle's Farm, Center Moriches, 1920. The mesh of the water dispenser was important to prevent the ducklings from drowning. It had to be small enough to prevent their beaks from getting stuck in addition to containing the water in order to prevent the hay from getting soggy. (Courtesy National Archives, No. 17-P-16-149.)

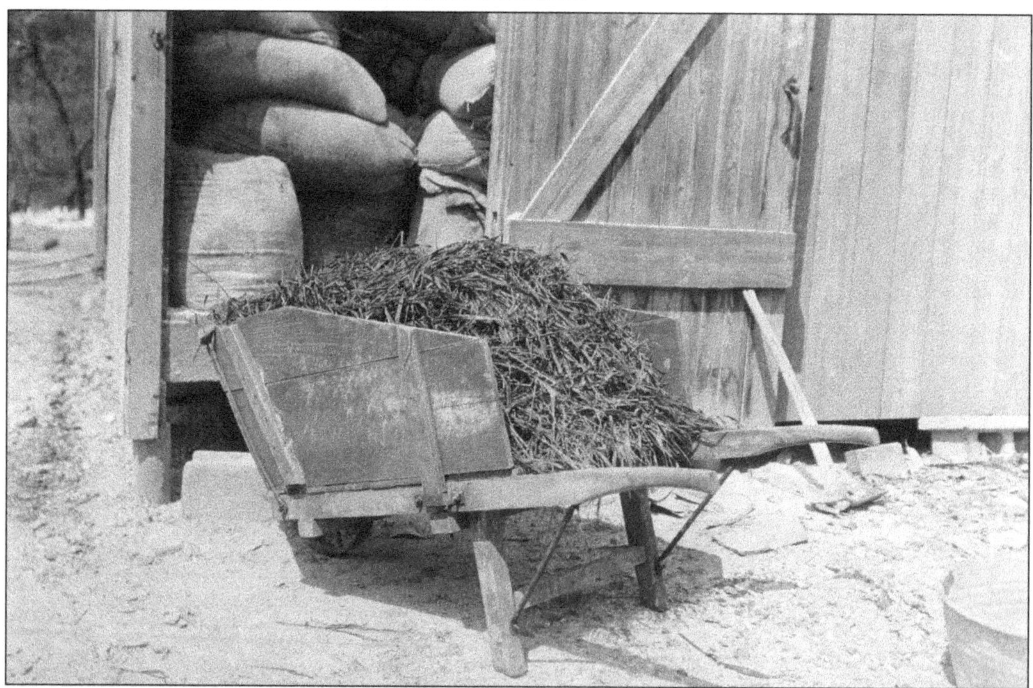

Wheelbarrow of Green Feed for Ducks, R.A. Tuttle's Farm, Center Moriches, 1920. Before food pellets became commercially available, farmers would concoct their own recipe for feed for optimal duck performance. Breeders were fed twice a day a special mixture of bran, flour, corn, green feed, vegetables, beef, and fish that encouraged egg laying and prevented the ducks from getting too fatty. Sand was also added to the feed to aid with digestion if the ducks could not access it outside. Fields on the duck farms were used for growing oats or rye that was chopped and added to the mixture. (Courtesy National Archives, No. 17-P-16-150.)

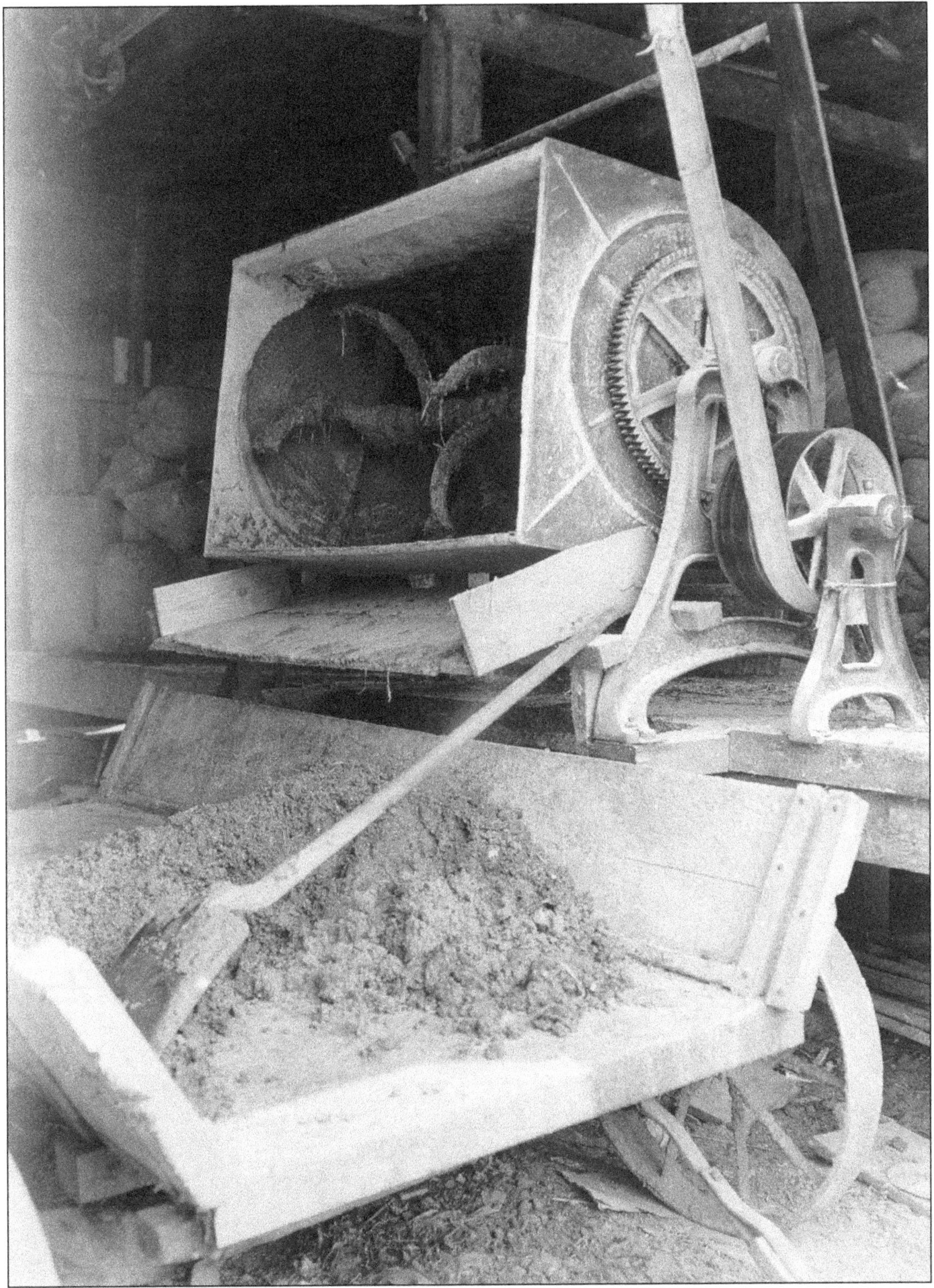

Mixer for Duck Feed, R.A. Tuttle's Farm, Center Moriches, 1920. The feed mixture would be mixed with water in a power mixer to a moist yet crumbly texture. The feed would be transferred to horse-drawn wagons or train cars to be delivered to the ducks. (Courtesy National Archives, No. 17-P-16-147.)

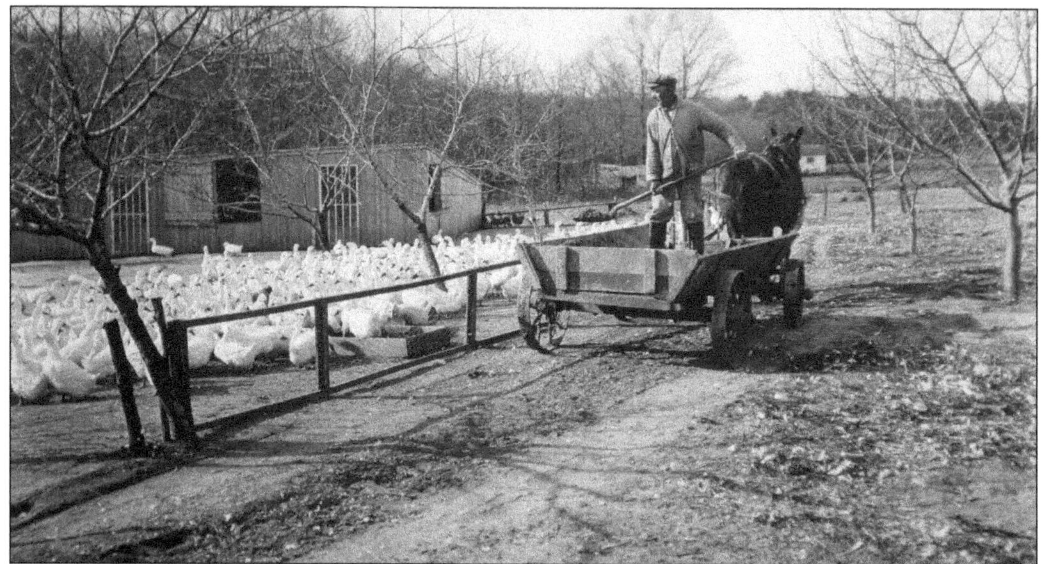

SHOVELING FEED FROM HORSE-DRAWN FOOD WAGON, R.A. TUTTLE'S FARM, CENTER MORICHES, 1920. Once loaded onto the wagon, the feed was driven around the yards and then shoveled into the flat food troughs on the ground. The breeders needed to be fed consistently in the same place. Pekin ducks were known gluttons; they would eat everything that was set before them. (Courtesy National Archives, No. 17-P-16-124.)

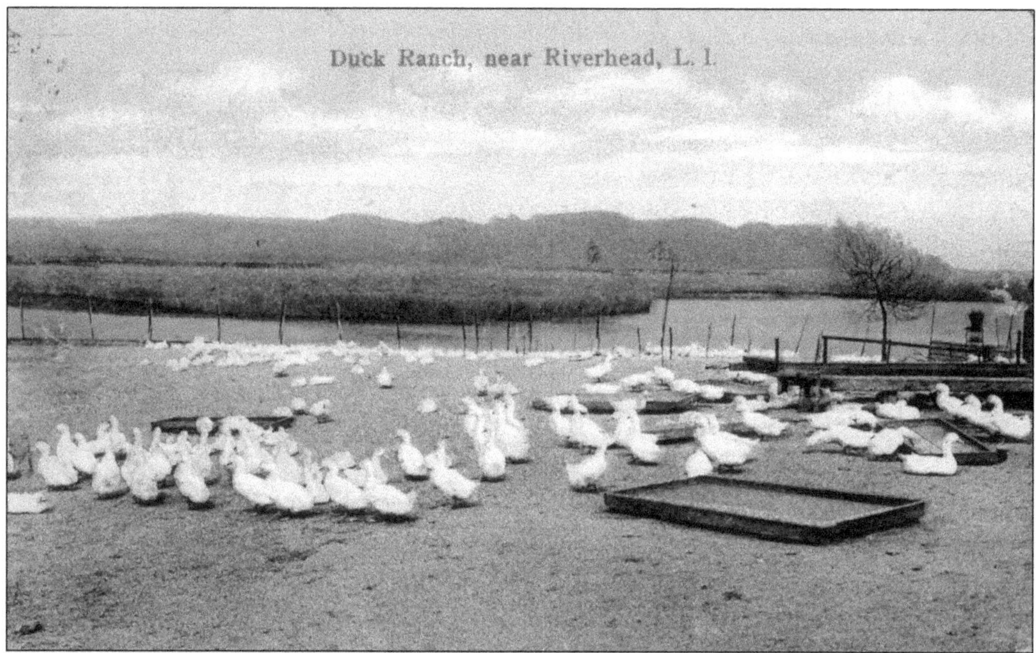

DUCK RANCH NEAR RIVERHEAD. Ducks are eating from food trays without the help of a feed track. Feeding was labor intensive, and it was important to disperse the right amounts to avoid excess because old feed would spoil and make the ducks sick. (Courtesy Collection of Eric Woodward.)

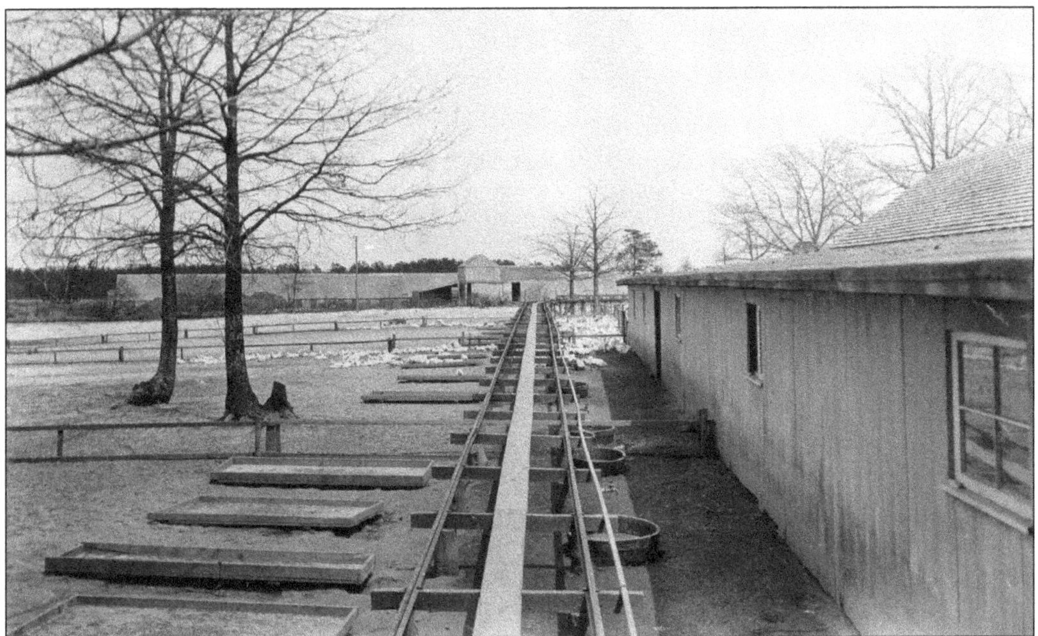

FEED TRACKS, A.B. SOYARS FARM, RIVERHEAD, 1920. Eventually, on the larger farms, farmers devised a track system with a cart on wheels to ameliorate the labor involved with feeding. Carts would be loaded with feed and pushed along the tracks, and the feed would be shoveled into the troughs. (Courtesy National Archives, No. 17-P-16-107.)

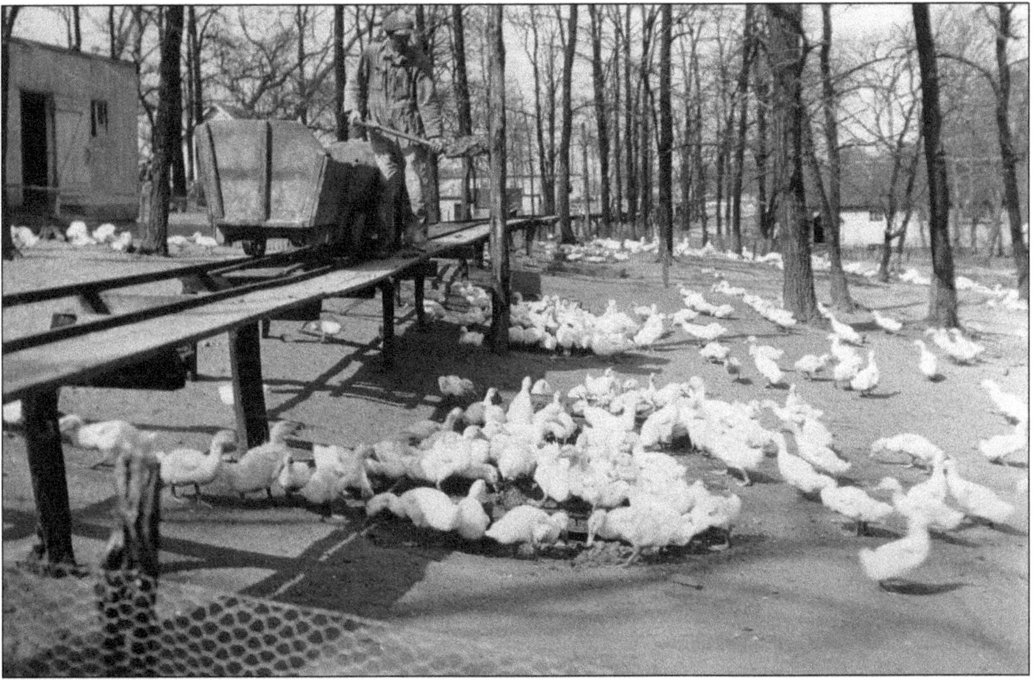

FEEDING FROM FEED TRACKS, W.W. LUKERT, CENTER MORICHES, 1920. Here, a worker shovels feed into the feed troughs from the raised tracks for the breeders. Tracks needed to be level and able to withstand the heavy weight of the feed mash. (Courtesy National Archives, No. 17-P-16-131.)

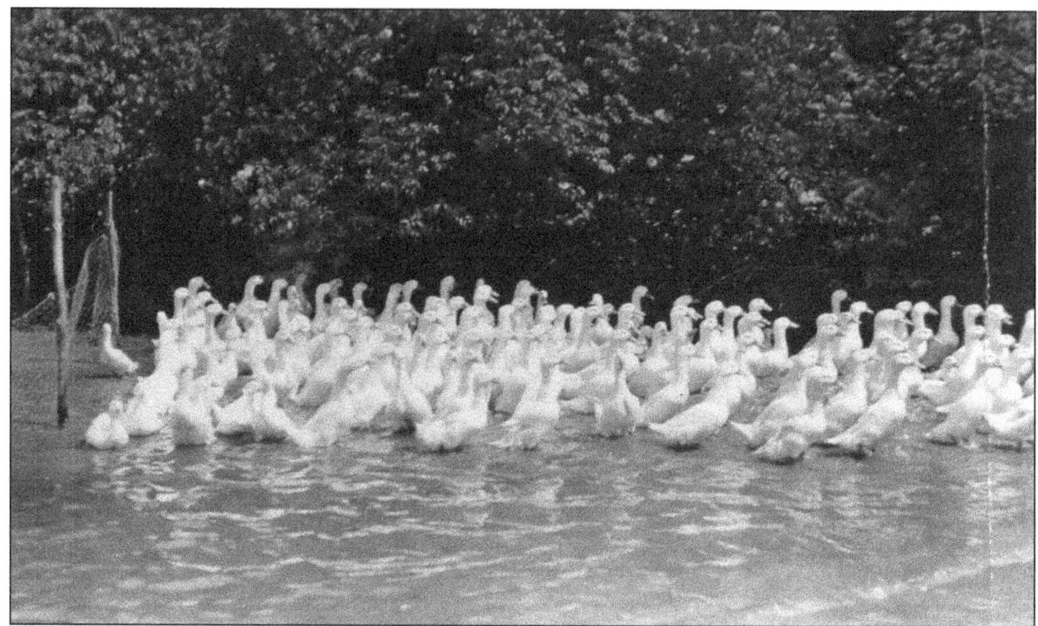

DUCKS READY FOR MARKET, MR. LITTLE'S FARM, EASTPORT, 1920. Long Island ducks grew to market weight of five and a half to six pounds in 10 to 12 weeks. At this time, they began to lose feathers around their neck and breast and had to be marketed within one week from molting lest they get too thin and farmers would have to wait six more weeks for new feathers. (Courtesy National Archives, No. 17-P-16-57.)

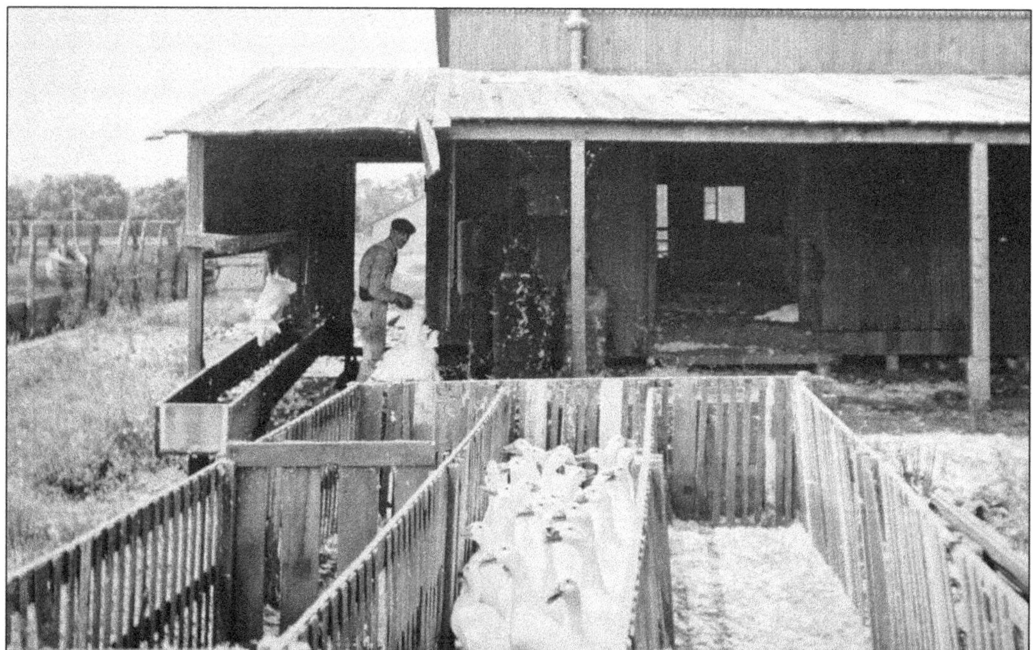

DUCKS IN THE KILLING PEN, H.G. SEAMAN'S FARM, EASTPORT, 1920. After they were deemed ready for market, ducks were driven or carried to the killing pen, where they were examined for defects. If the breastbone was not sticking out and it had no visible defects, then it was suitable for market. (Courtesy National Archives, No. 17-P-16-156.)

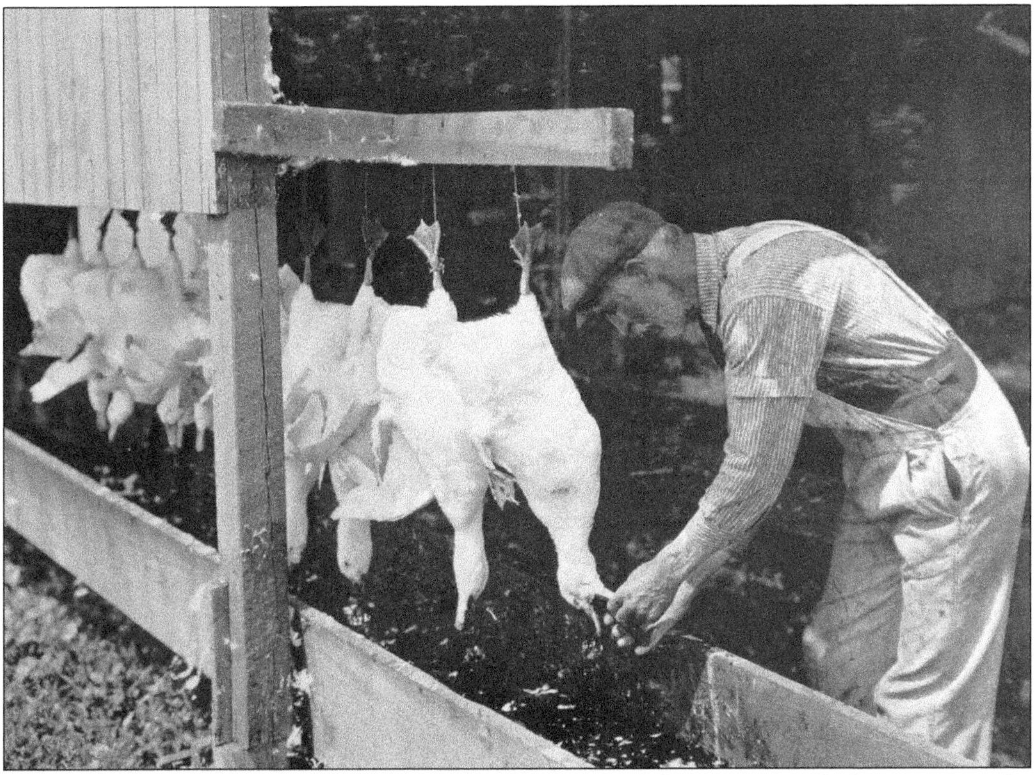

DUCK KILLING, H.G. SEAMAN'S FARM, EASTPORT, 1920. Selecting 10–12 ducks at a time, the ducks would be hung upside-down by their feet with their beaks weighted down with a can to catch their blood or fastened with a hook. (Courtesy National Archives, No. 17-P-16-159.)

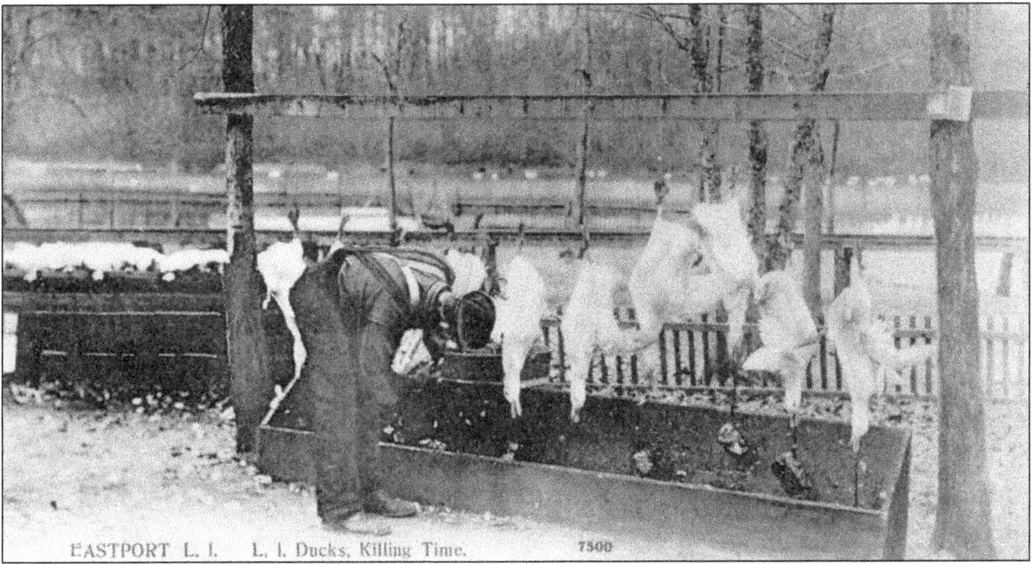

KILLING STOCKADE, EASTPORT, C. 1910S. To strike the final blow, a worker with a sharp knife would cut the veins inside the duck's mouth at the back of their throat that would cause free bleeding. The blood would collect in the blood can attached to the beak or down into the trough underneath. (Courtesy Collection of Eric Woodward.)

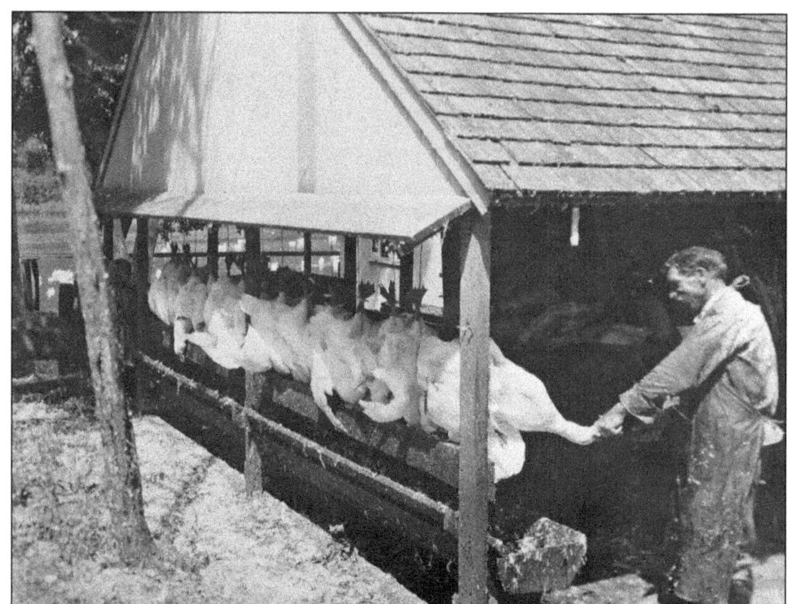

KILLING STOCKADE, WILCOX'S FARM, EASTPORT, 1920. The ducks hang there until the blood runs dry. Then they are taken down, washed, and replaced with another set of live ducks. (Courtesy National Archives, No. 17-P-16-157.)

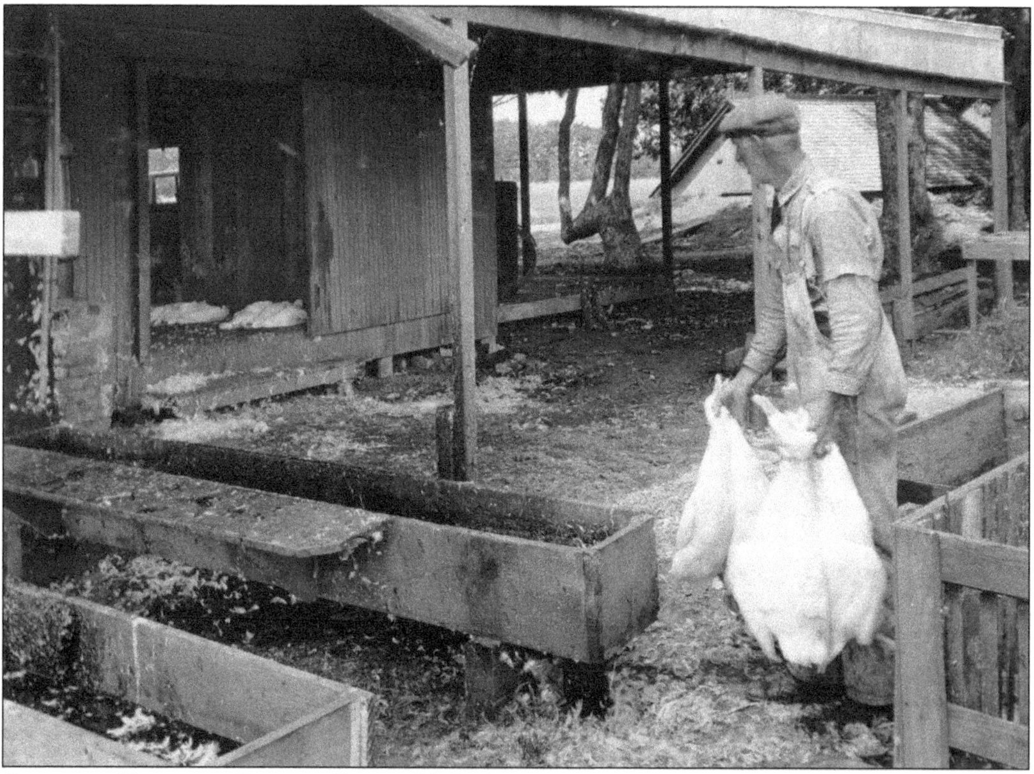

CARRYING DUCKS TO PICKING ROOM, H.G. SEAMAN'S FARM, EASTPORT, 1920. After they had been killed and washed, a worker carried the ducks to the picking room. Almost all parts of a duck were used except for the blood—the intestines and heads would be sent to the minx farms for food, and the feathers were highly sought after for pillows, sleeping bags, jackets, and insulation. (Courtesy National Archives, No. 17-P-16-160.)

SCALDING DUCKS BEFORE PICKING, H.G. SEAMAN'S FARM, EASTPORT, 1920. Until 1900, ducks were picked dry for 5¢ each. After 1900, most farms would scald the ducks in hot water with care to avoid submerging the feet and head for fear of discoloration, until feathers came out more readily. (Courtesy National Archives, No. 17-P-16-164.)

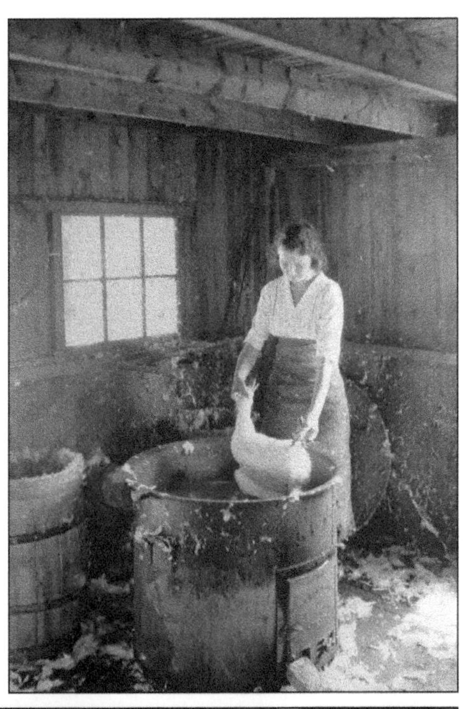

SIX WOMEN PICKING FEATHERS, H.G. SEAMAN'S FARM, EASTPORT, 1920. Mostly female pickers would pluck about 50 to 100 ducks per day, with some experts picking up to 150 birds each day. In 1937, feather-picking machines were introduced to Long Island duck farms. (Courtesy National Archives, No. 17-P-16-163.)

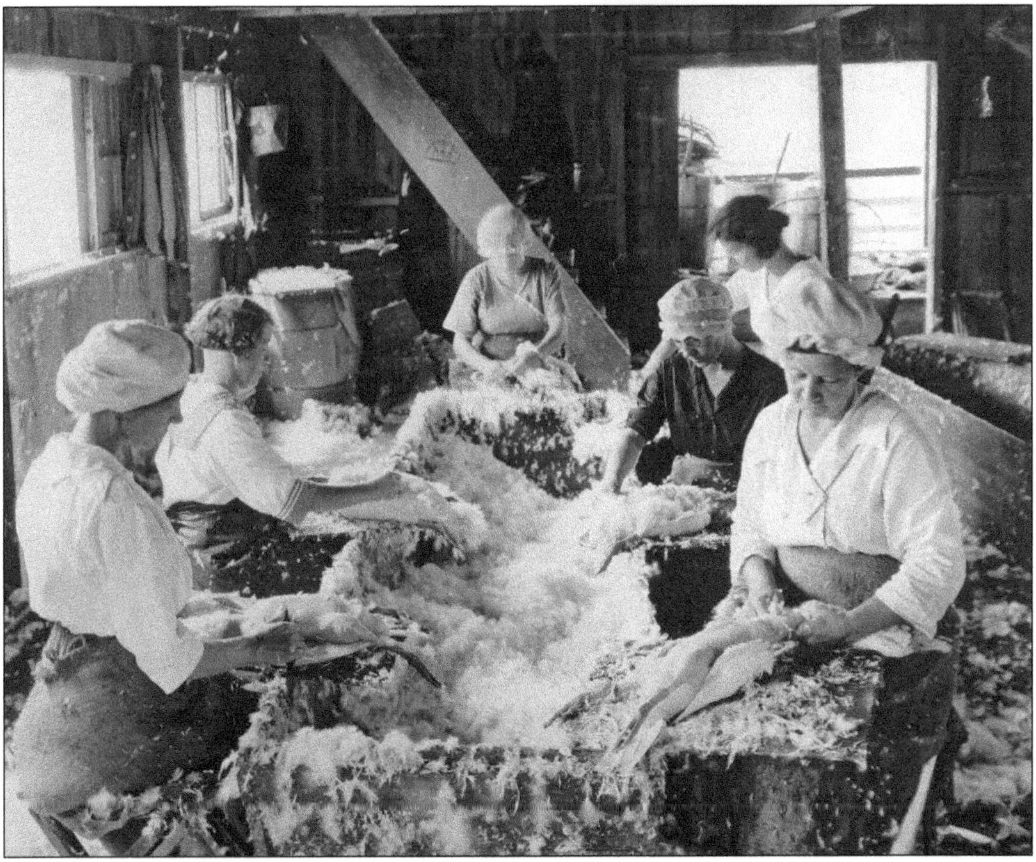

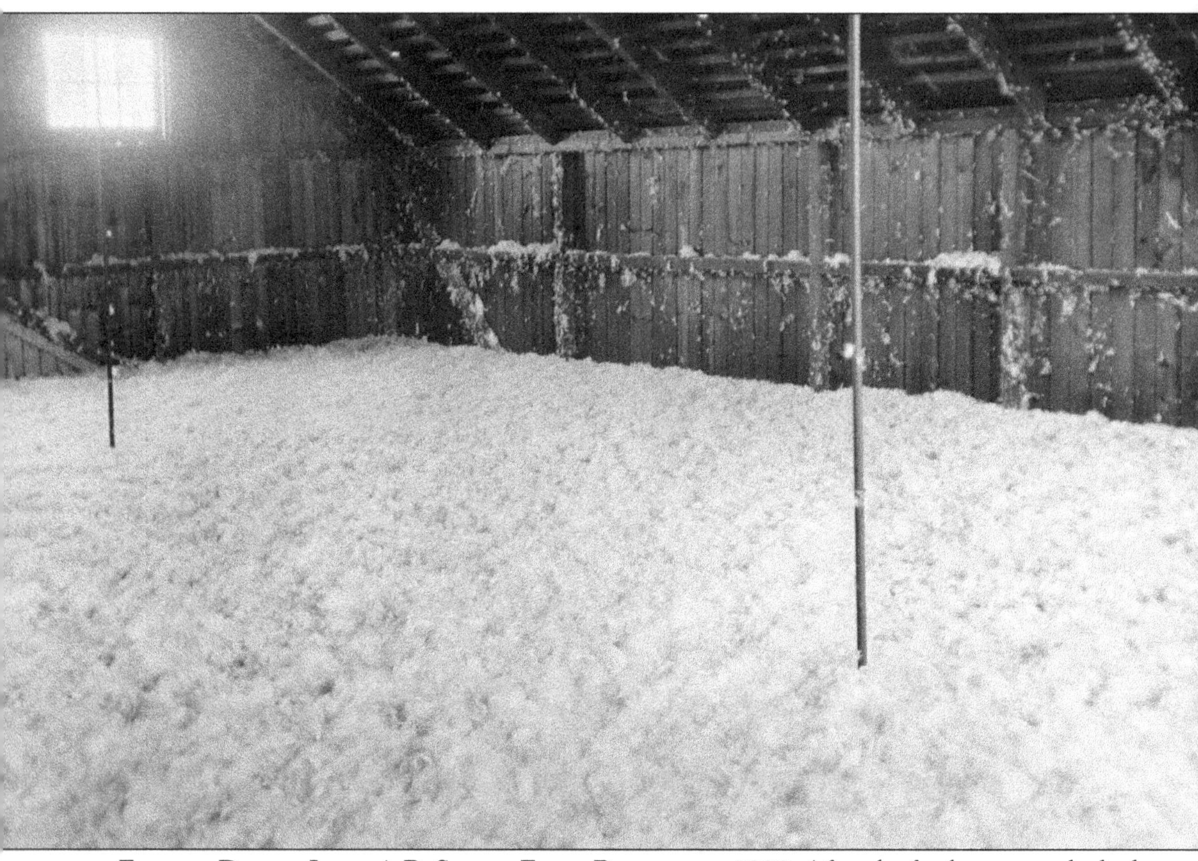

Feather Drying Loft, A.B. Soyars Farm, Riverhead, 1920. After the feathers were plucked, they were placed in wringers to remove any excess moisture before being transferred to feather lofts. In the loft, feathers would be thrown or shaken twice a day for two weeks until they were completely dry and then sold to feather dealers. The cost of picking, which was a necessity to prepare the ducks for market, was slightly less than the sale price of the feathers. Dry-picked, soft body feathers fetched up to 50¢ per pound. (Courtesy National Archives, No. 17-P-16-151.)

Clean Ducks after Picking, H.G. Seaman's Farm, Eastport, 1920. After picking, ducks would be packed in wooden barrels with layers of ice and driven to New York City markets. (Courtesy National Archives, No. 17-P-16-165.)

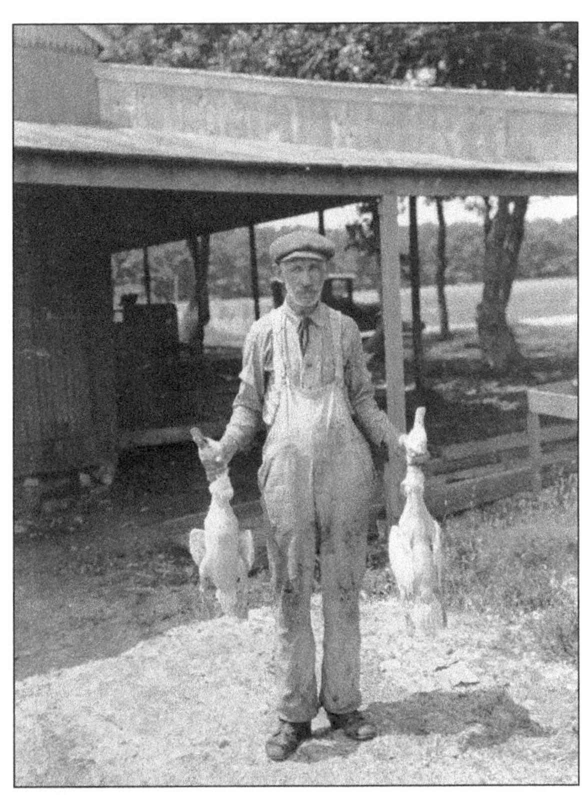

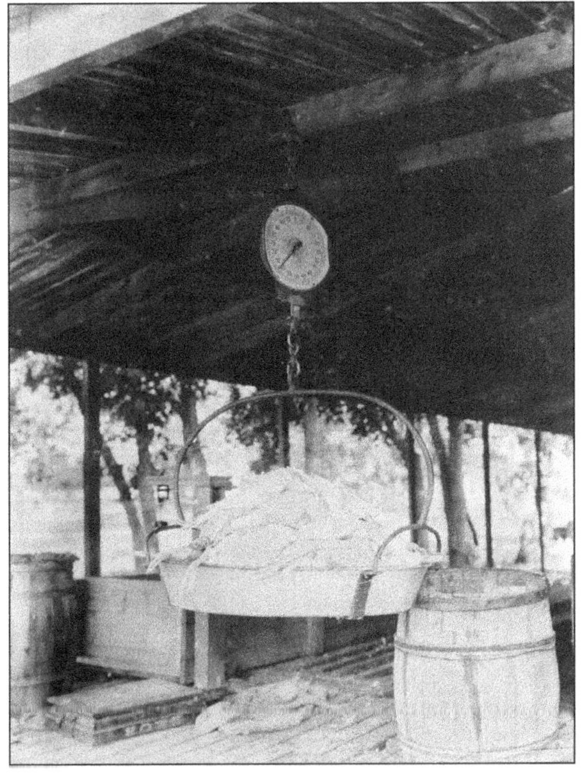

Weighing Ducks for Market, H.G. Seaman's Farm, Eastport, 1920. After having been thoroughly cooled and cleaned, workers would weigh ducks to determine prices and pack them into the barrels. Prices for ducks fluctuated depending on the season; prices were highest in spring and dipped in the summer months due to greater supply. In 1920, Long Island duck prices ranged from 35¢ to 45¢ per pound. (Courtesy National Archives, No. 17-P-16-166.)

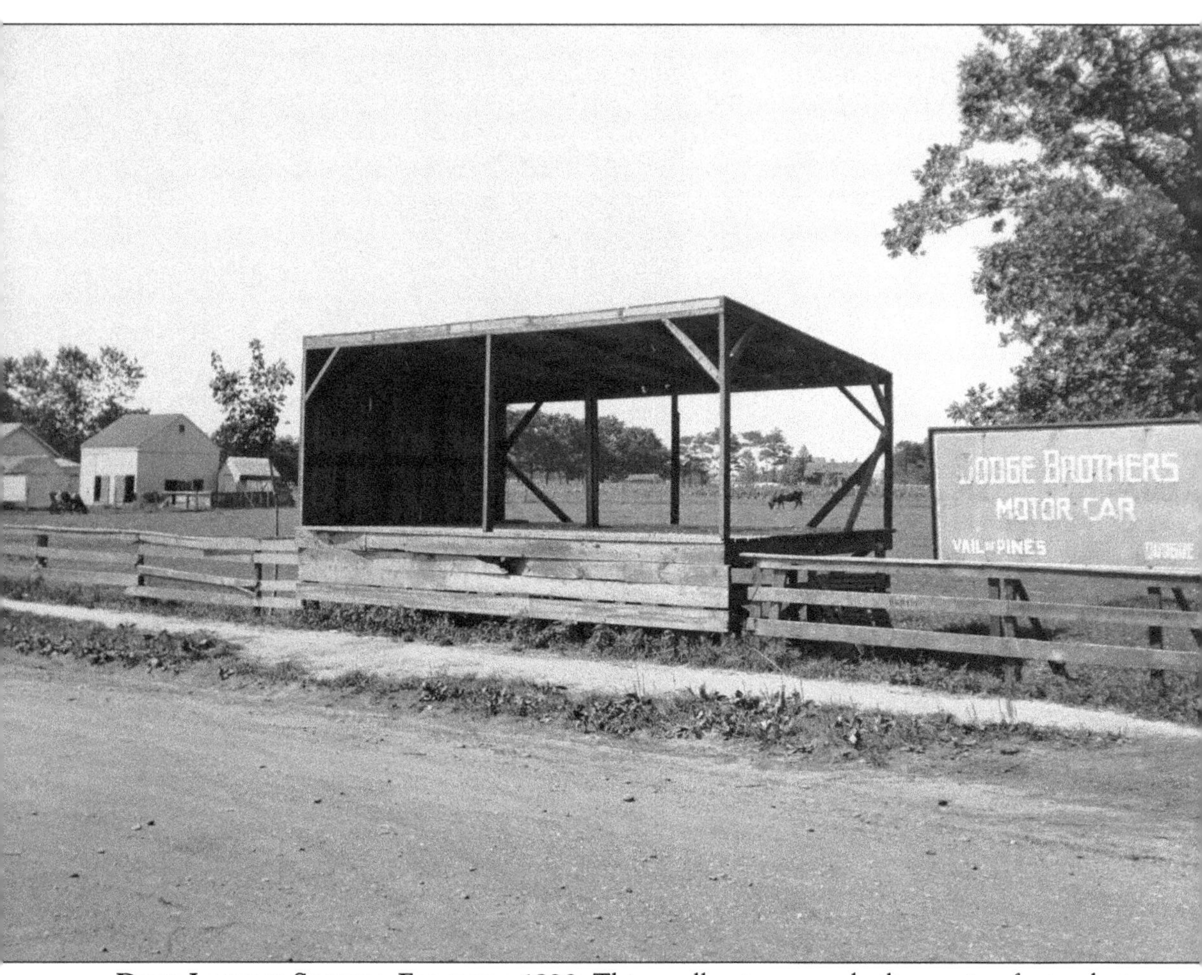

Duck Loading Station, Eastport, 1920. This small outpost was built as a stop for trucks to pick up the packed barrels of freshly killed ducks on ice and transport them to New York City markets. (Courtesy National Archives, No. 17-P-16-153.)

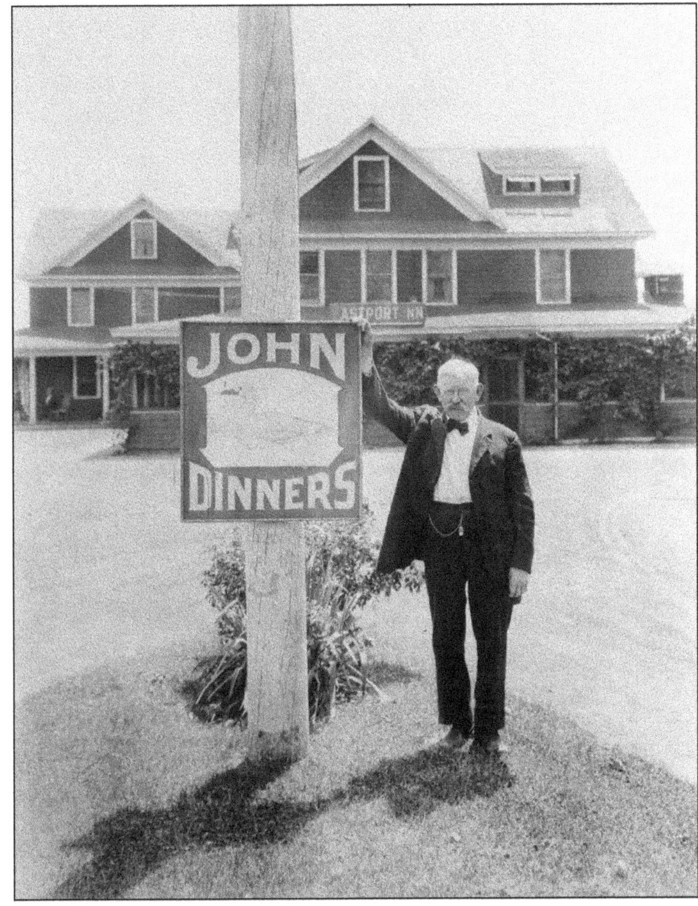

John Westerhoff at the John Duck Restaurant, Eastport Inn, c. 1920s (Right) and Eastport Inn Postcard (Below.) Most white-tablecloth dining establishments have featured "Long Island duckling" on the menu. In 1900, John Westerhoff opened the restaurant John Duck at the Eastport Inn, famous for its "Duck Dinners" and its signature dish of duck with Bing cherries and coleslaw. His son Ben moved it to Southampton under the name John Duck Jr. in 1936. Through the years, it hosted celebrities such as Woody Allen, Elizabeth Taylor and Richard Burton, and countless locals. Failing to bow to the trendy tastes of summer crowds, it closed its doors in 2008. (Right, courtesy National Archives, No. 17-P-16-131; below, courtesy Collection of Eric Woodward.)

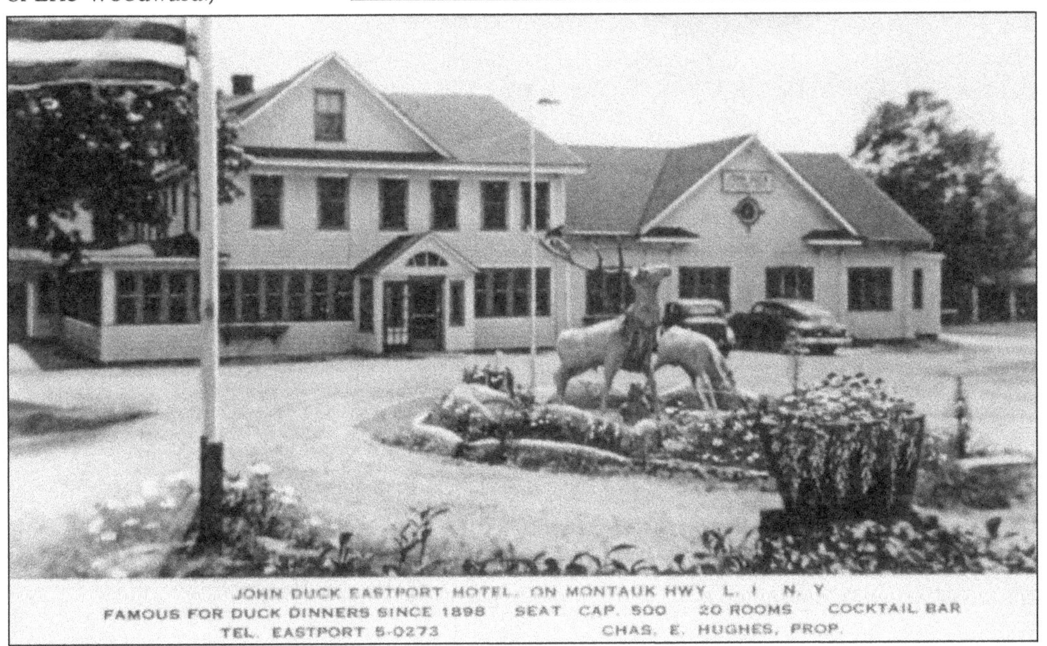

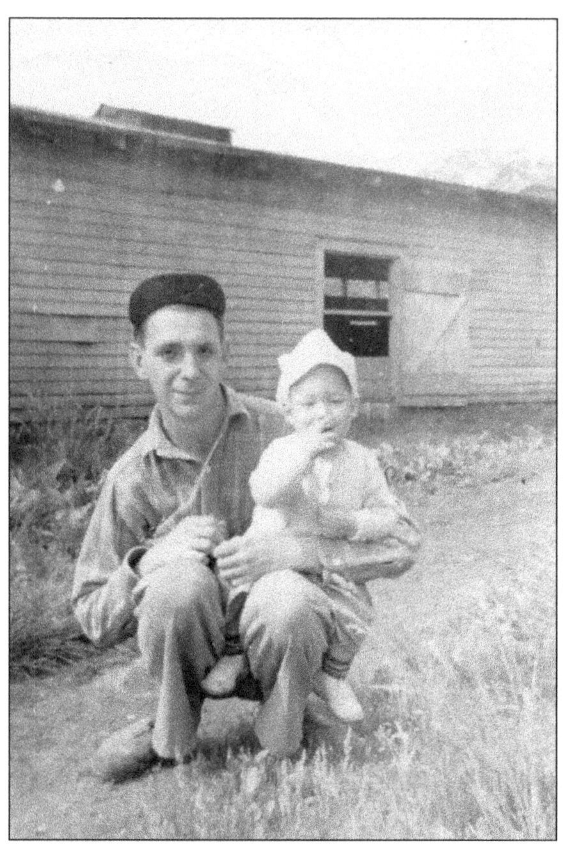

Joseph MacGregor Titmus and Son Mac Titmus at Swift Stream Farms, Moriches, c. 1947. Joseph's father, Joseph Allen Titmus, and Josiah Smith Robert founded Swift Stream in 1918. Josiah thought it would be a good way to make a living. The property was located on 34 acres between Forge River and Herkimer Street in Mastic. (Courtesy family of Joseph Titmus.)

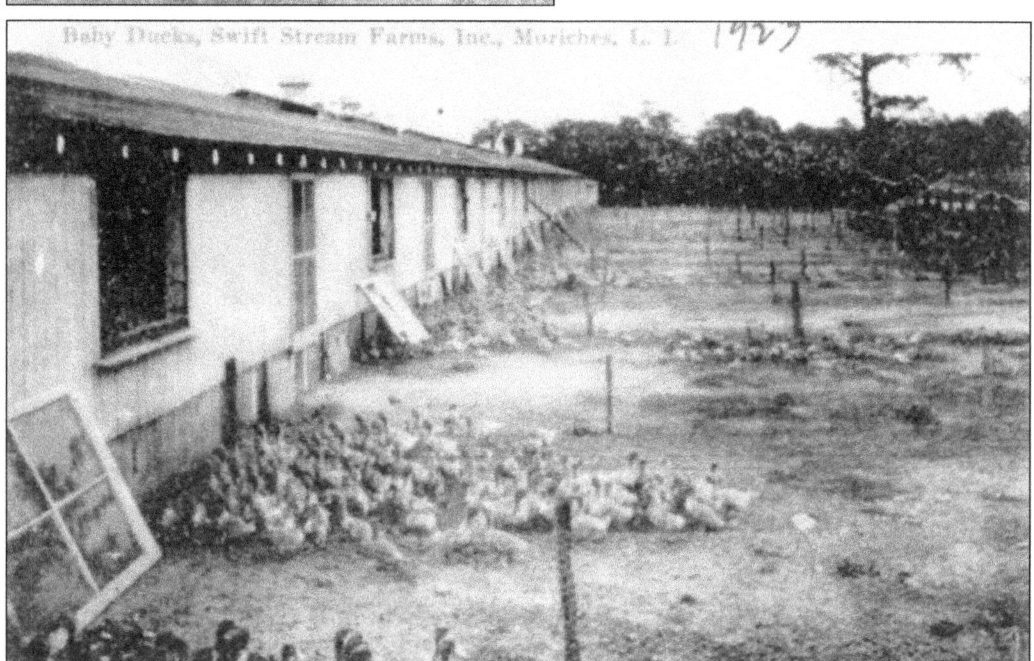

Baby Ducks, Swift Stream Farms, Moriches, 1923. Four-week-old ducks travel through the wall openings on the side of the brooder house to feed. (Courtesy family of Joseph Titmus.)

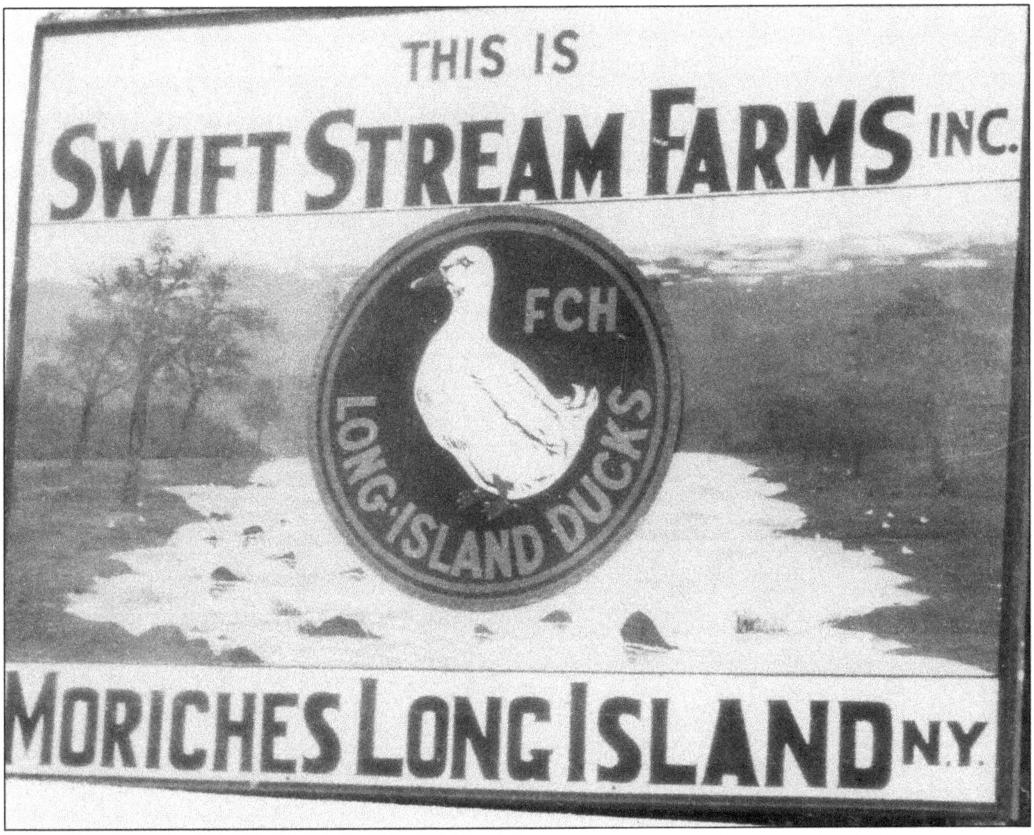

Sign, Swift Stream Farms, Moriches, c. 1947. The signs read, "This is Swift Stream Farms, Inc., Moriches, Long Island N.Y." with the Farmer's Commission House (FCH) logo in the center. FCH was a duck cooperative formed in 1915 and trademarked in 1921 by a group of duck farmers to market the ducks to New York City butchers. The FCH logo became associated with a high standard of quality by poultry buyers. (Courtesy family of Joseph Titmus.)

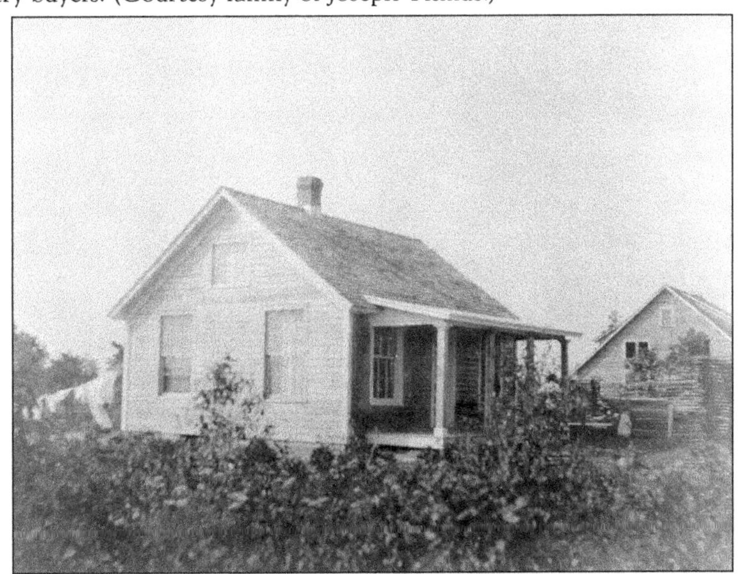

Little House, Swift Stream Farms, c. 1947. Because the work was so demanding, Joe and Josiah had workers live on the farm property. On the east side of Mastic Road, they built homes for some of the workers; this little house was built from lumber from Camp Upton for John Rose Sr. and his wife, Lavisa. John was in charge of the incubators. (Courtesy family of Joseph Titmus.)

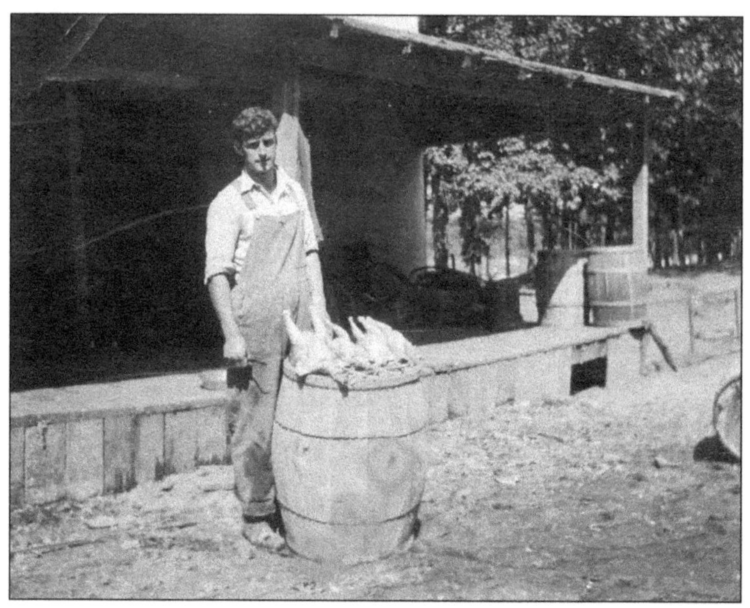

AUGUSTUS "GUS" WILSON IN FRONT OF DUCKS READY FOR PACKING, SWIFT STREAM FARMS, C. 1947. Everything was done by hand, including clearing the land, building, feeding, mixing the feed, breeding ducks, hatching the eggs (before the electric incubators), slaughtering, plucking feathers, and packing them in ice to be taken to market in New York City. (Courtesy family of Joseph Titmus.)

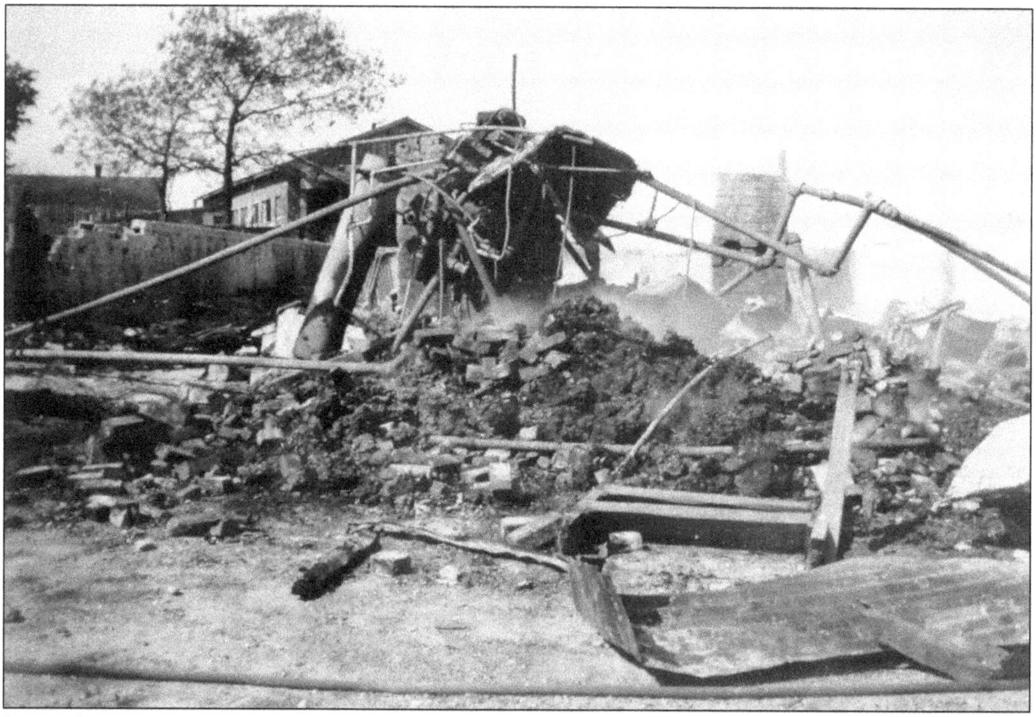

SWIFT STREAM FARMS, MORICHES, LONG ISLAND, 1944. A fire occurred in May 1944 at Swift Stream Farm that destroyed the building used for plucking feathers. Fires were common in duck farms, due to the combustible combination of dry bedding and heaters. (Courtesy family of Joseph Titmus.)

Two

Modernization and the Height of Duck Farming on Long Island

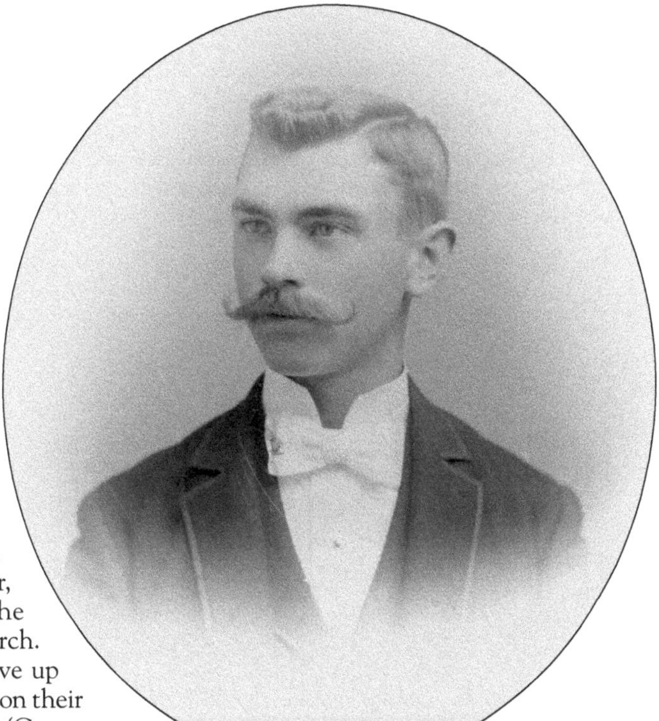

Henry Frank "H.F." Corwin, Founder of Crescent Duck Farm, Aquebogue, c. 1900s. The Corwin family settled on land on the East End of Long Island as early as 1640 and farmed the land. H.F. Corwin worked as a carpenter, laboring on projects such as the Riverhead Congregationalist Church. When his wife became ill, he gave up carpentry and began to raise ducks on their land near Meeting House Creek. (Courtesy Douglas Corwin, Crescent Duck Farm.)

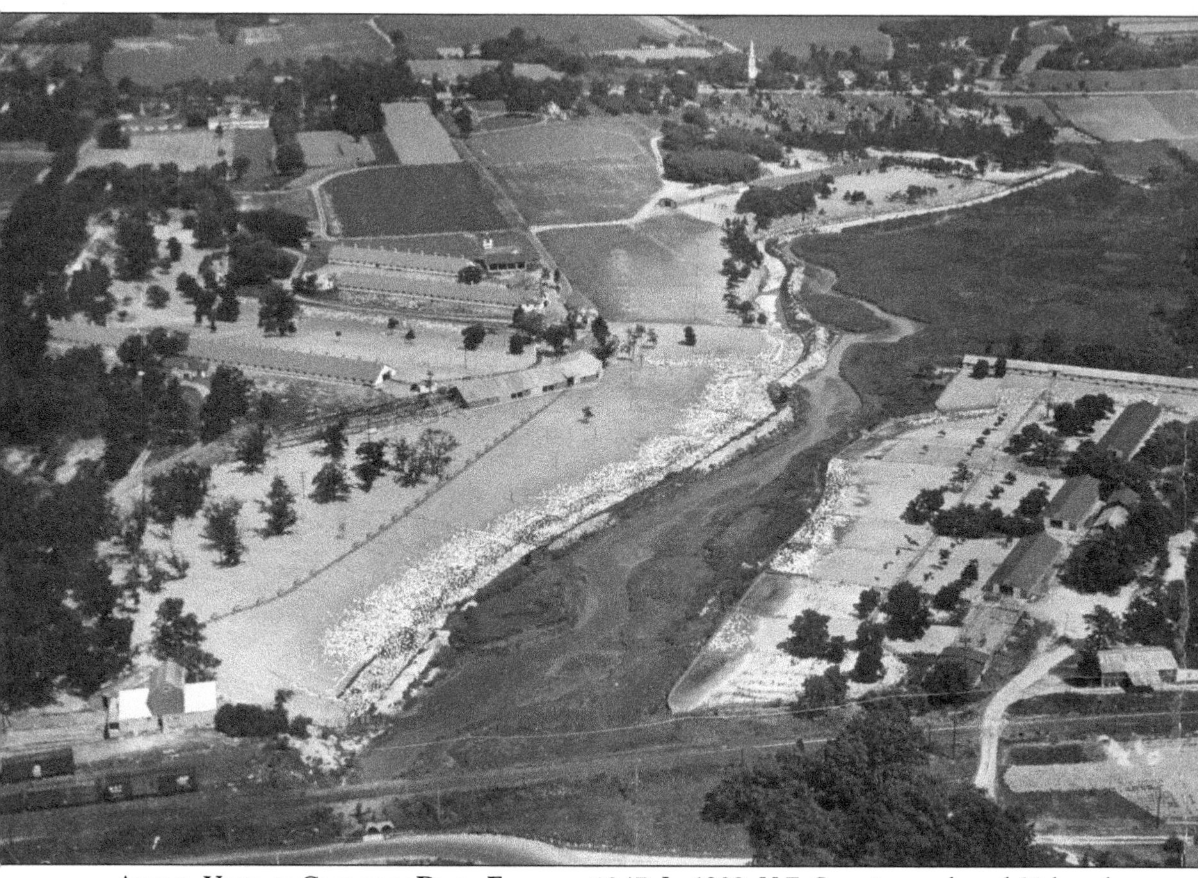

AERIAL VIEW OF CRESCENT DUCK FARM, C. 1947. In 1908, H.F. Corwin purchased 30 breeders and decided to become a farmer full time. Since the creek was in the shape of a crescent, Henry's wife named the farm Crescent Duck Farm. The Old Steeple Community Church on Route 25 is near the top, and the Long Island Railroad tracks run along the bottom of the photograph. (Courtesy Douglas Corwin, Crescent Duck Farm.)

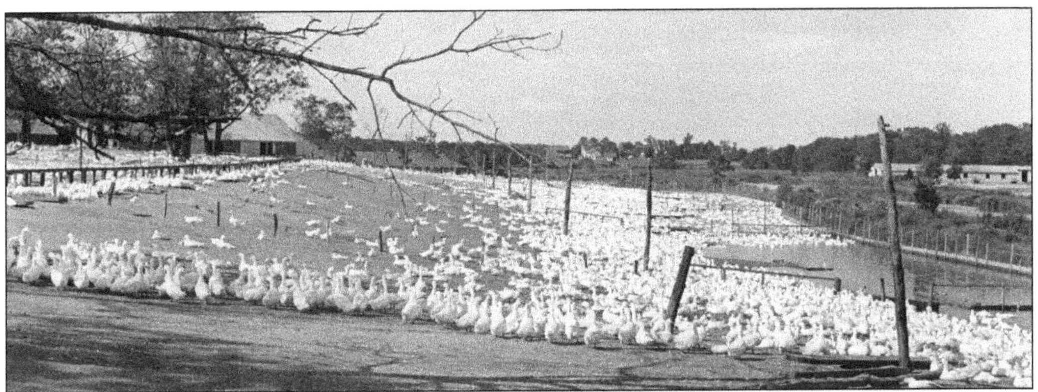

Seven-to-Twelve-Week-Old Ducks on the Shore, Crescent Duck Farm, Aquebogue, c. 1950s. Corwin started with 25 acres and raised 4,000 ducks a year. The farm is still in operation in 2018, the only surviving major duck farm on Long Island—expanding to 142 acres and producing upwards of one million ducks per year. (Courtesy Douglas Corwin, Crescent Duck Farm.)

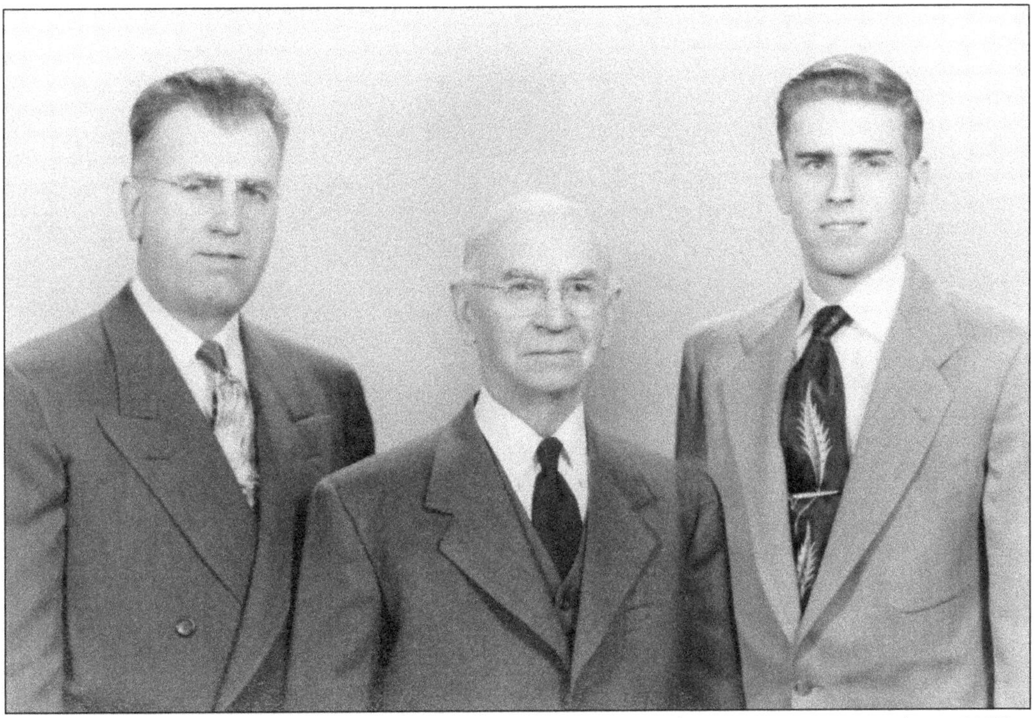

Lloyd Corwin Sr., H.F. Corwin, and Lloyd Corwin Jr. (from left to right), c. 1950s. For over 100 years, Crescent Duck Farm has been family-run. In the 1920s, Lloyd Corwin Sr., H.F.'s son, joined the business. In the 1950s, his son, Lloyd Jr., and his daughter Janet joined after returning home from college. Lloyd Jr.'s son, Douglas, started around 1980 and is currently the president, and his brother Jeffrey and sister Cindy also share ownership and maintain active roles at the farm. Currently, Douglas's sons Blake and Pierce, and Jeffrey's son Jeffrey Jr. also work at the farm, representing the fifth generation of Corwins at Crescent Duck Farm. (Courtesy Douglas Corwin, Crescent Duck Farm.)

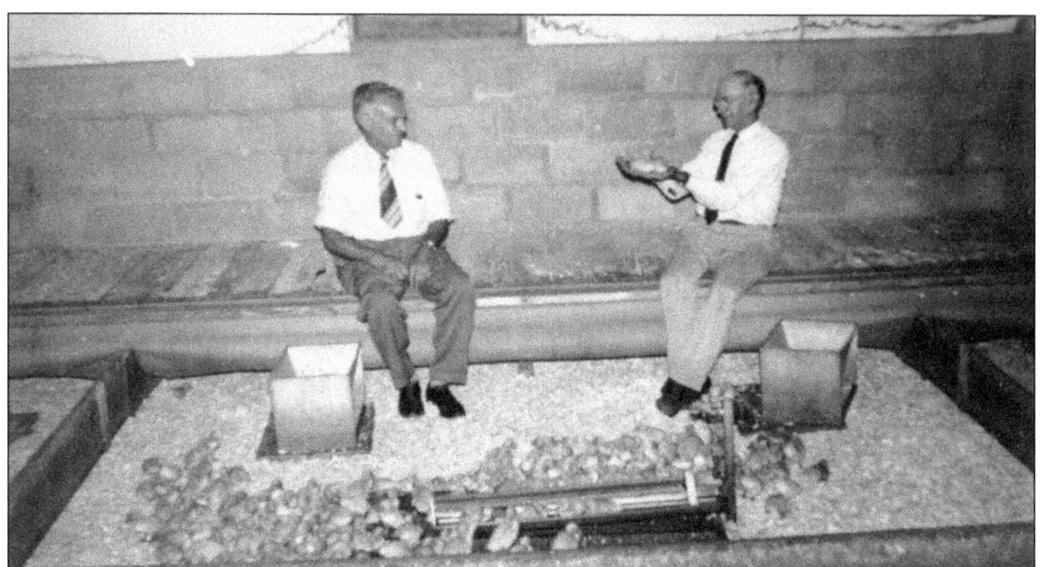

ANDREW HALSEY AND H.F. CORWIN WITH THE BABY DUCKLINGS, C. 1940S. Corwin (right) was always eager to optimize nutrition for the ducklings, expand farm buildings, and update his facilities with the latest technologies. (Courtesy Douglas Corwin, Crescent Duck Farm.)

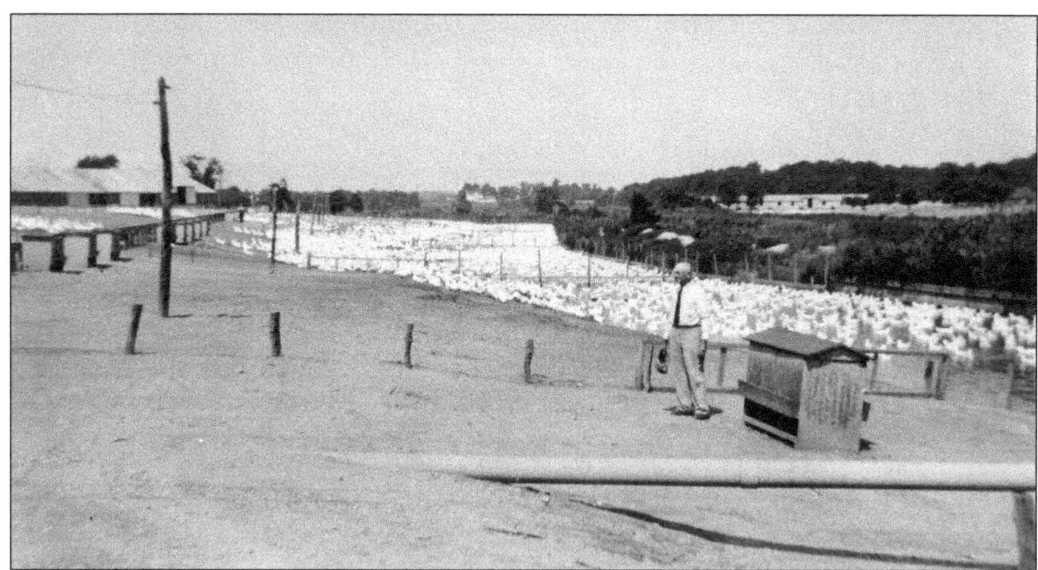

H.F. CORWIN TOURING THE SHOREFRONT OF MEETING HOUSE CREEK, AQUEBOGUE, C. 1940S. Corwin once said, "We've got to sleep with one eye open, so to speak, for if a rain comes up, we've got to get out and see that the ducks get under shelter, or we'd lose a lot of them. They'll put on more weight per pound of feed than any other fowl and they're a lot of fun to raise. If I didn't enjoy it, I wouldn't have turned my hobby into a business!" (Courtesy Douglas Corwin, Crescent Duck Farm.)

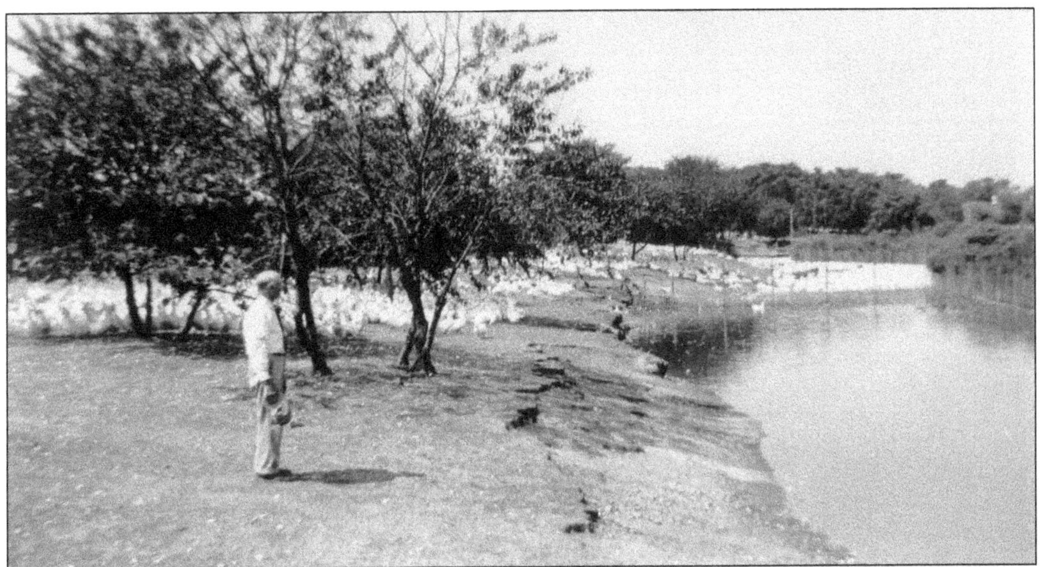

DUCKS ON THE SHORELINE NEAR MEETING HOUSE CREEK, C. 1950S. Crescent Duck Farm was fully equipped with electricity early on. The Corwins used two pumps at the head of the creek when water levels were low to ensure that their ducks had fresh water to drink. (Courtesy Douglas Corwin, Crescent Duck Farm.)

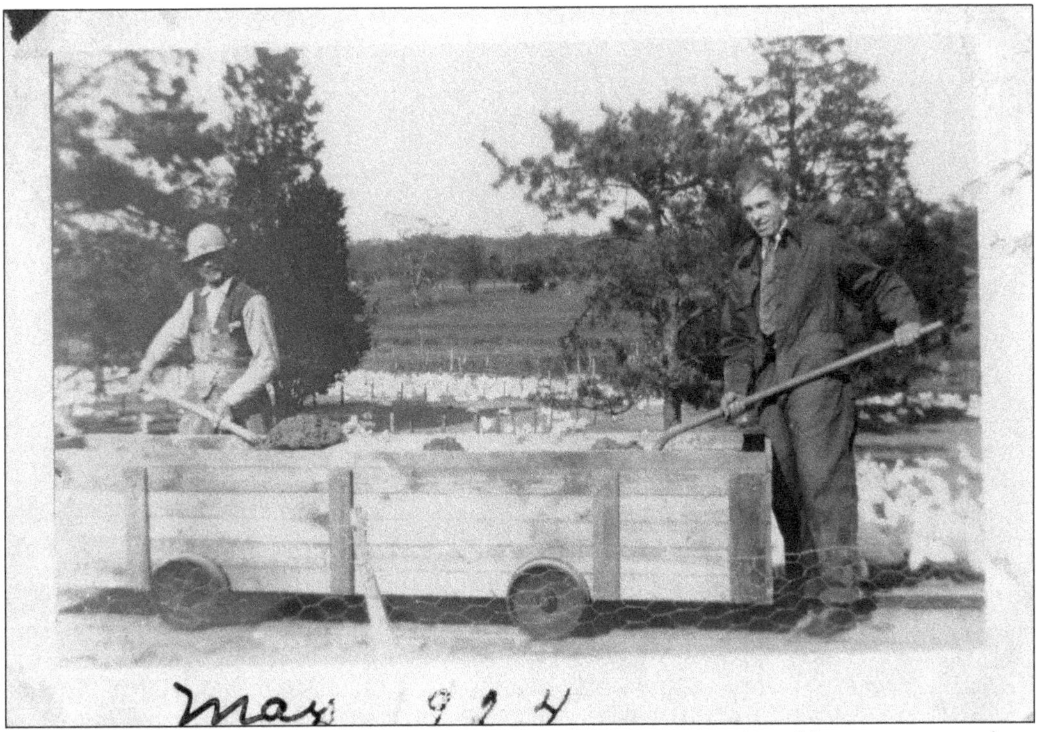

LLOYD JR. SHOVELS FEED TO THE YARD DUCKS, AQUEBOGUE, C. 1940S. Always one to pitch in and work hard, Lloyd Jr. is wearing a suit and tie under his coveralls as he shovels feed to the ducklings. (Courtesy Douglas Corwin, Crescent Duck Farm.)

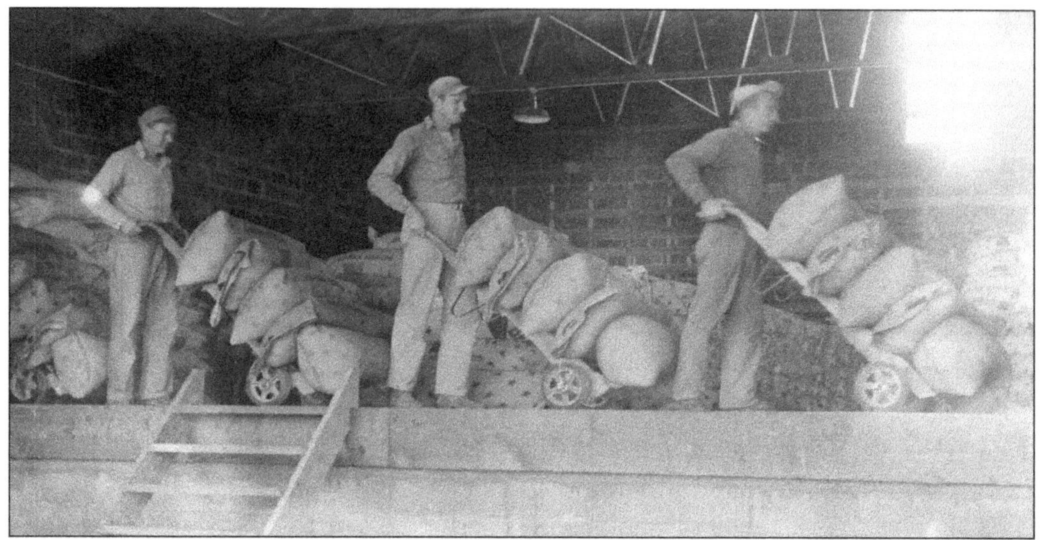

THREE WORKERS WHEEL FEED, CRESCENT DUCK FARM, AQUEBOGUE, C. 1940S. Feeding the large amount of ducks took a lot of manpower. Here, three workers wheel five bags of feed from Beacon Feeds, a feed mill in Eastport, stacked on their hand trucks. (Courtesy Douglas Corwin, Crescent Duck Farm.)

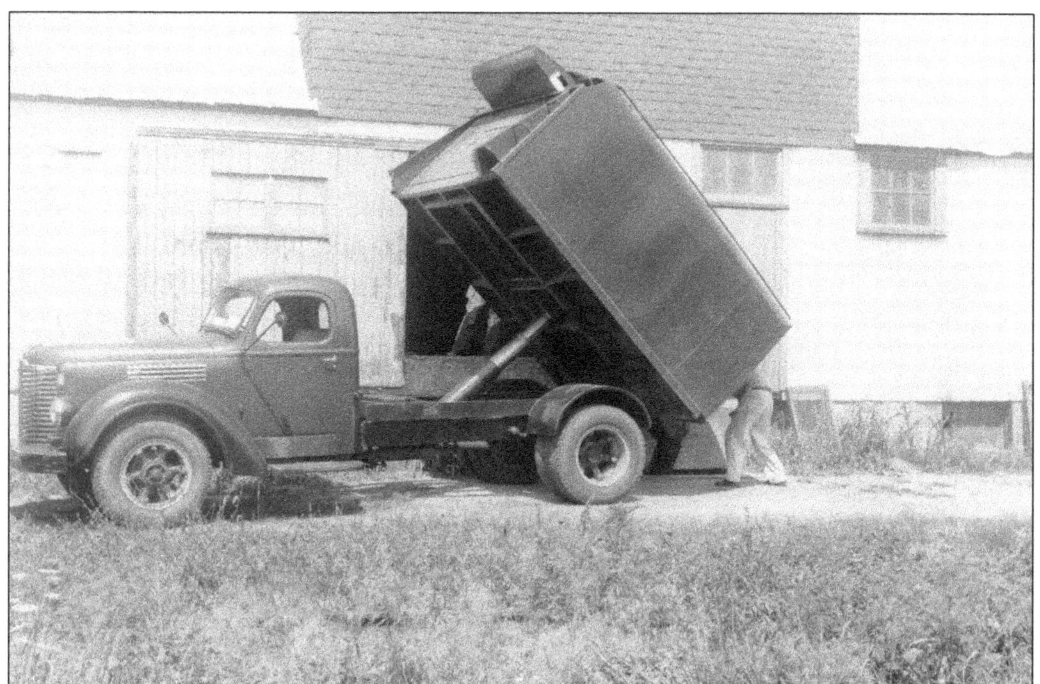

TRUCK CARTING FEED PELLETS FROM THE FEED MILL, AQUEBOGUE, C. 1940S. In the early 1920s, duck farmers on Long Island started to purchase commercially made feed pellets from several farm coops such as Grange League Federation Exchange (GLF) or Agway instead of making hand-mixed feed. Eventually, Crescent Duck Farm built its own feed mill with electric-powered mixers and grinders that produced 10 tons of feed per day. (Courtesy Douglas Corwin, Crescent Duck Farm.)

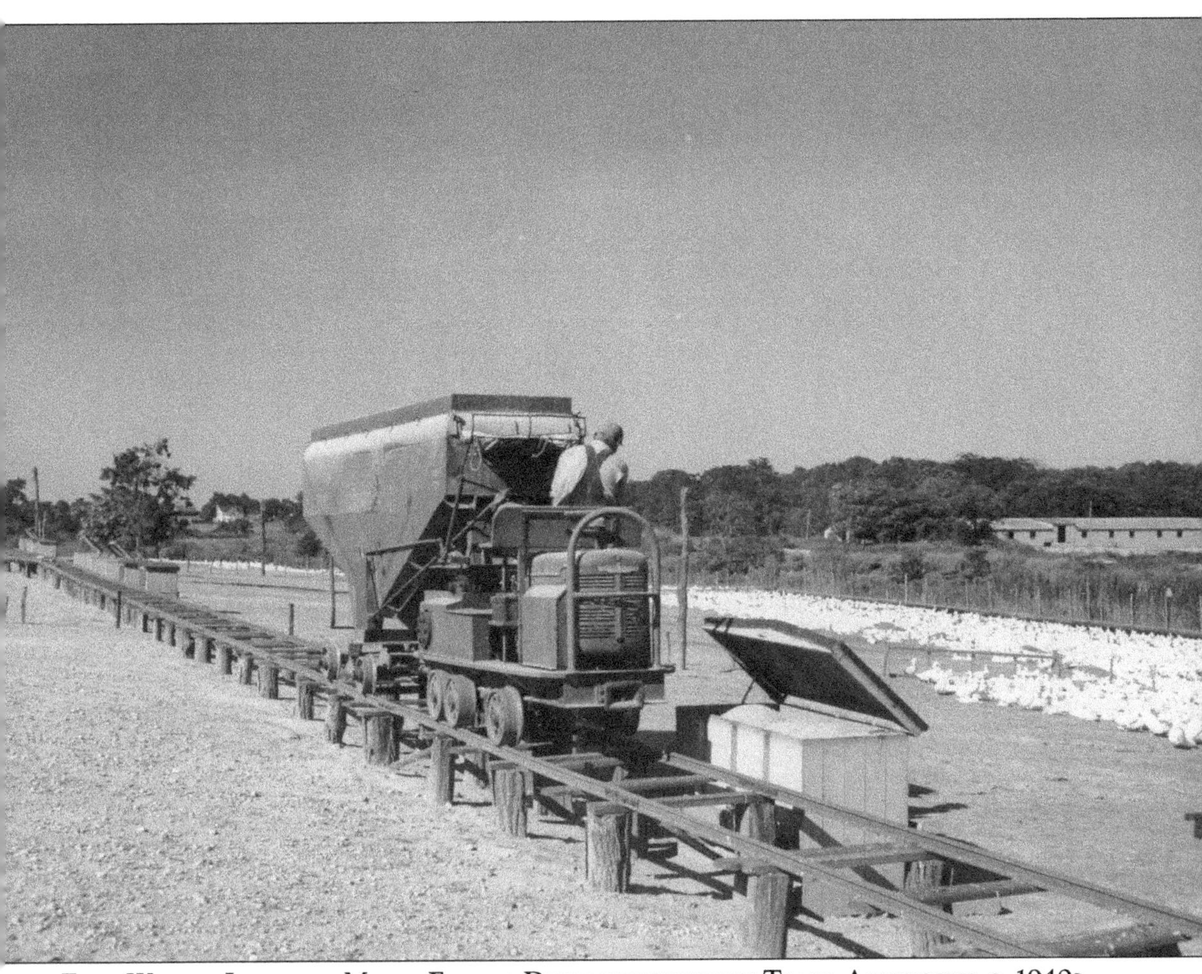

FARM WORKER LAWRENCE MILLER FEEDING DUCKLINGS WITH THE TRAIN, AQUEBOGUE, C. 1940S. Like other farms, the Corwins used a track for feed. However, their track was over a mile long and relied on a battery-operated "dinky" train that could handle three tons of pellets and was powered by an international truck unit battery. (Courtesy Douglas Corwin, Crescent Duck Farm.)

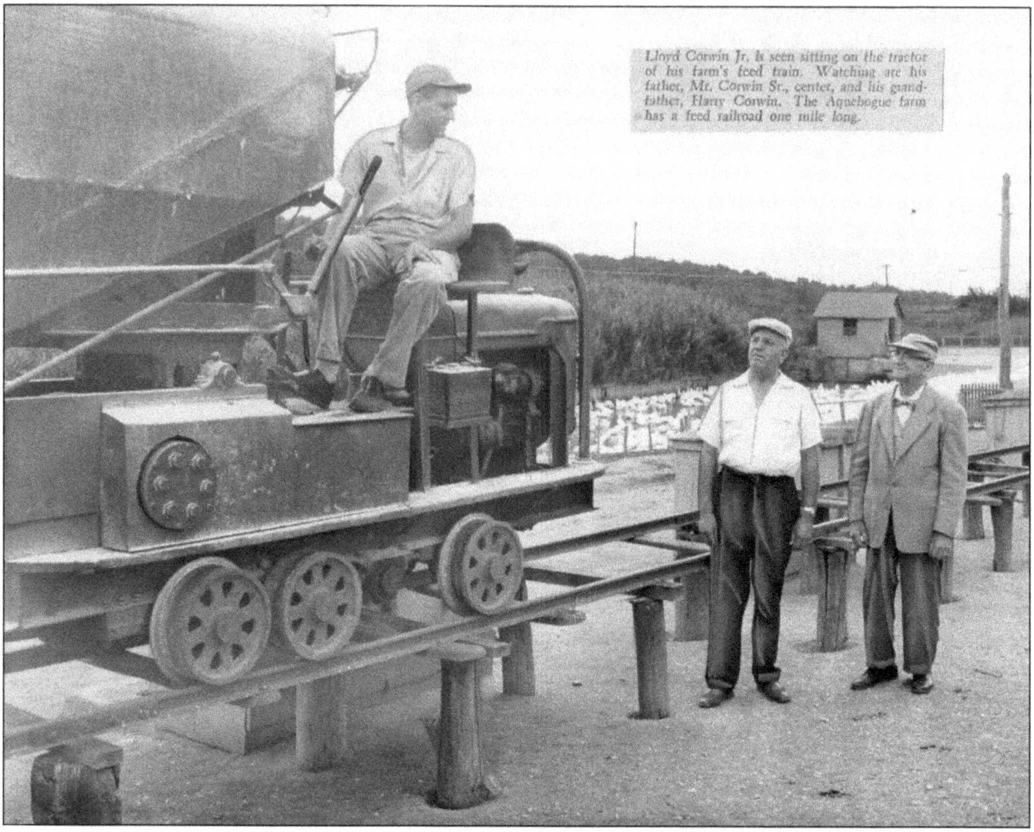

Lloyd Sr. and H.F. Look on as Lloyd Jr. Drives the Feed Train, Aquebogue, c. 1940s. Lloyd Sr. died in 1976 leaving Lloyd Jr. to see the farm through on his own. His son Douglas remarked "My dad had a lot of struggling years when me and my brother were off at college and he was trying to carry this thing alone. If it wasn't for him, we wouldn't be here. He worked pretty hard up until the last few years." Lloyd Jr. passed away in 2017 at the age of 83. (Courtesy Douglas Corwin, Crescent Duck Farm.)

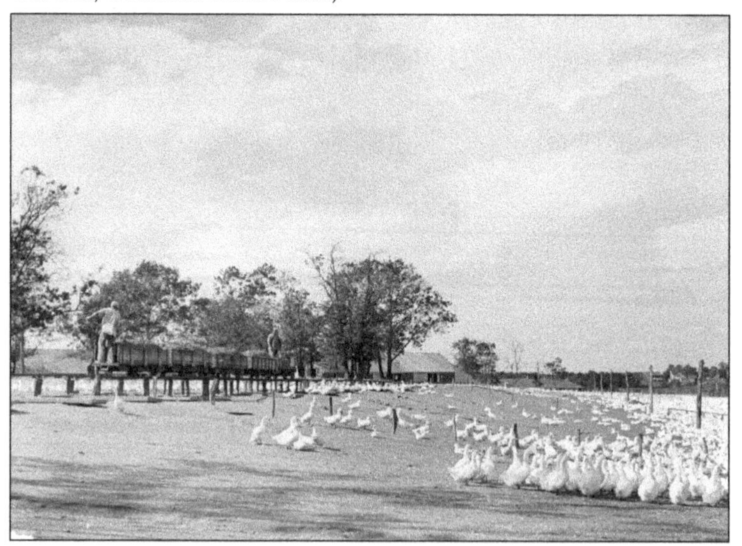

Two Workers Shovel Feed to the Ducklings, Aquebogue, c. 1940s. Here, two workers shovel four cartloads of freshly prepared mash to the ducks. The mini railroad required only two men, replacing the usual six to eight men previously needed for feeding. (Courtesy Douglas Corwin, Crescent Duck Farm.)

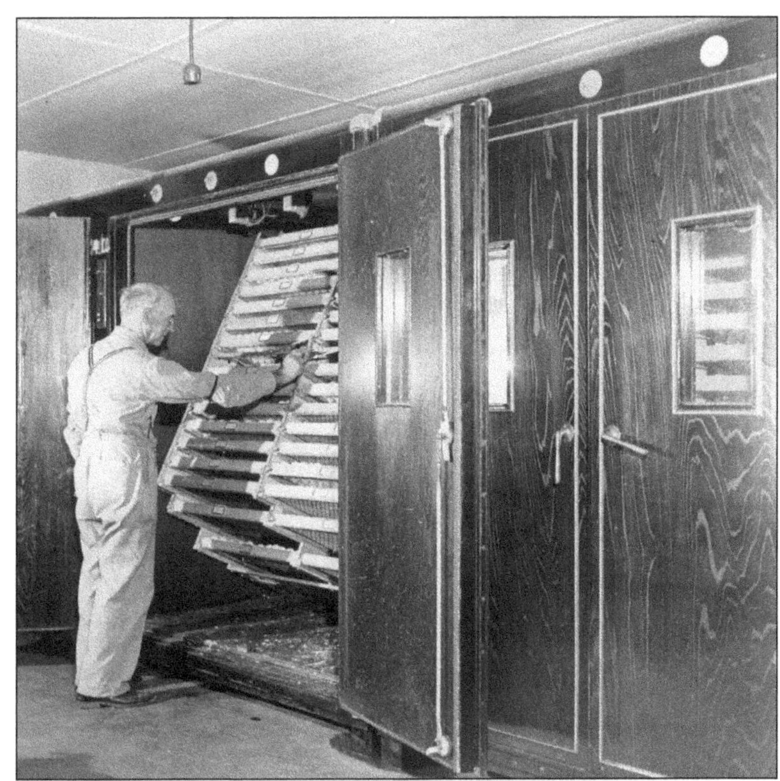

H.F. CORWIN CHECKS ON EGGS IN NEW INCUBATOR, CRESCENT DUCK FARM, AQUEBOGUE, C. 1938. Initially, Corwin would use chicken hens to hatch the duck eggs until he bought a modern incubator. In 1938, Corwin built a state-of-the-art incubation building outfitted with air-conditioning, fluorescent lights, and germicidal lamps preventing the spread of airborne bacteria. He bought three incubator units with a 54,000-egg capacity. (Courtesy Douglas Corwin, Crescent Duck Farm.)

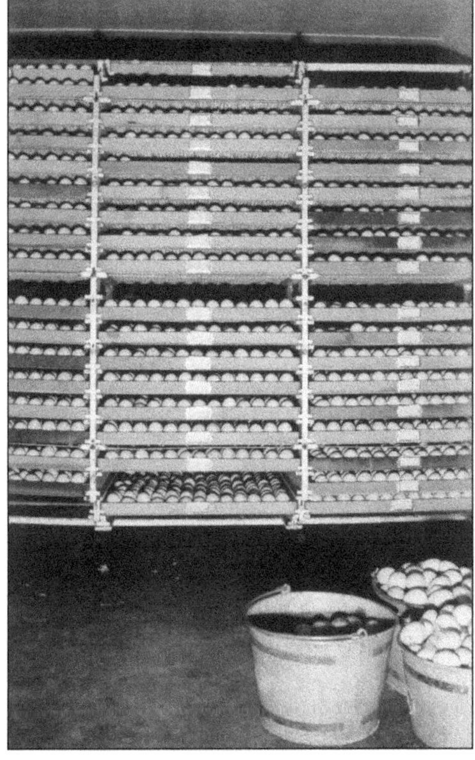

RACKS OF EGGS IN NEW INCUBATOR, CRESCENT DUCK FARM, AQUEBOGUE, C. 1938. Electric controls maintained a steady temperature of 99.5 degrees for the 24-day incubation period. Eggs would be turned automatically every three hours. (Courtesy Douglas Corwin, Crescent Duck Farm.)

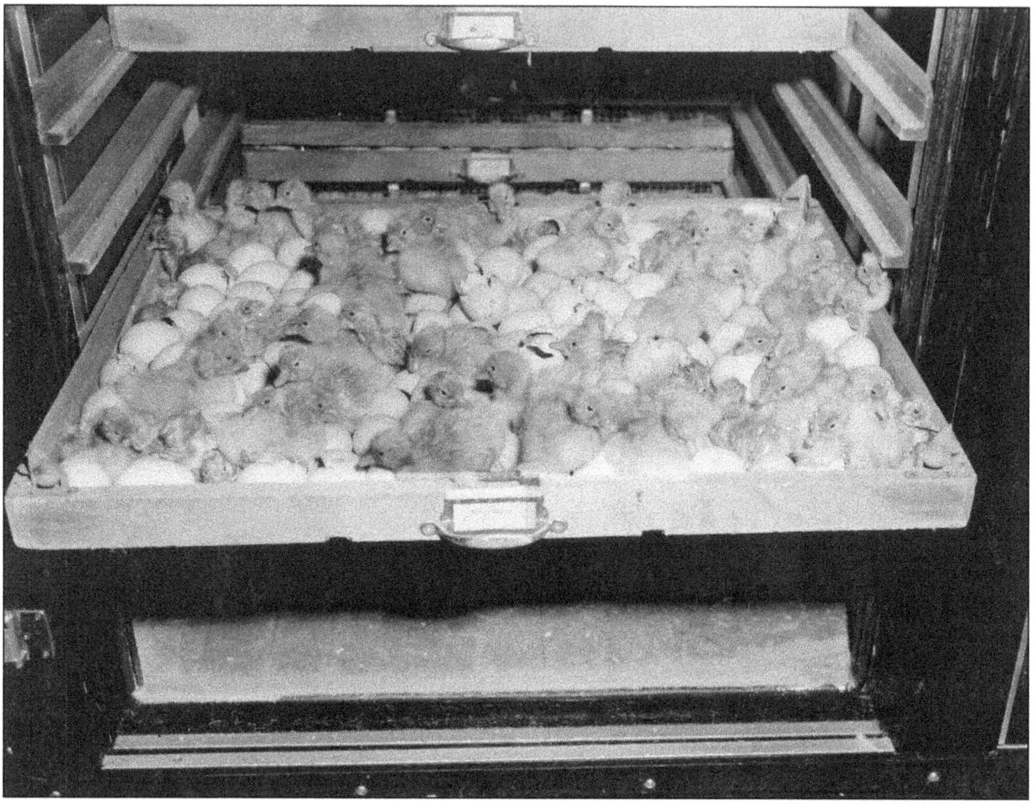

HATCHING CHICKS, CRESCENT DUCK FARM, AQUEBOGUE, C. 1938. Once hatched in the hatching unit that held 6,000 to 8,000 eggs, all the eggshells would fall down into a chute and land on a conveyor belt that transferred the shells out of a building and into a truck for disposal. (Courtesy Douglas Corwin, Crescent Duck Farm.)

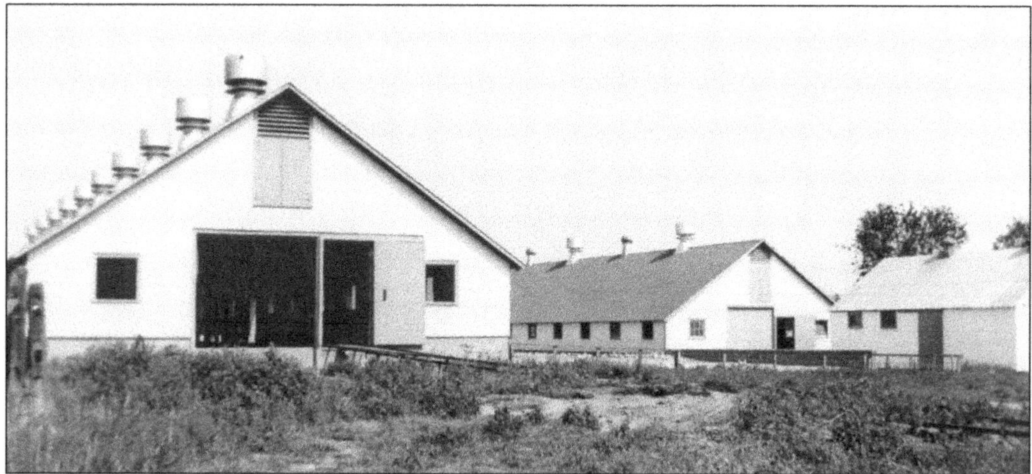

NEW HEATED DUCK BUILDINGS, CRESCENT DUCK FARM, AQUEBOGUE, C. 1938. Eight pumps maintained the temperatures in the hot brooder, warm brooder, and incubation buildings. Once hatched, ducks would stay in the hot brooder for five days, then move to the warm brooder. Electric pumps would supply freshwater in the concrete troughs surrounding the buildings to the newly hatched ducklings. (Courtesy Douglas Corwin, Crescent Duck Farm.)

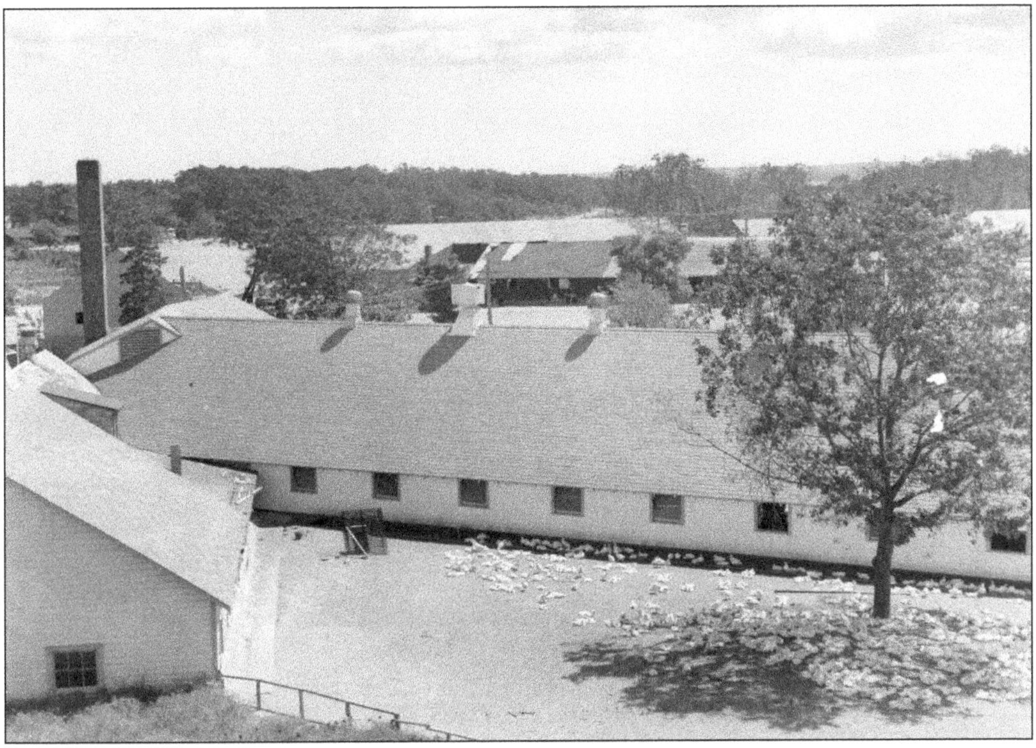

Upgraded Brooder Barns in Front of Smaller, Older Structures, Crescent Duck Farm, Aquebogue, c. 1938. The new barns were much larger and replaced the old tarpaper buildings seen here. The warm brooder barn measured 36 by 250 feet. (Courtesy Douglas Corwin, Crescent Duck Farm.)

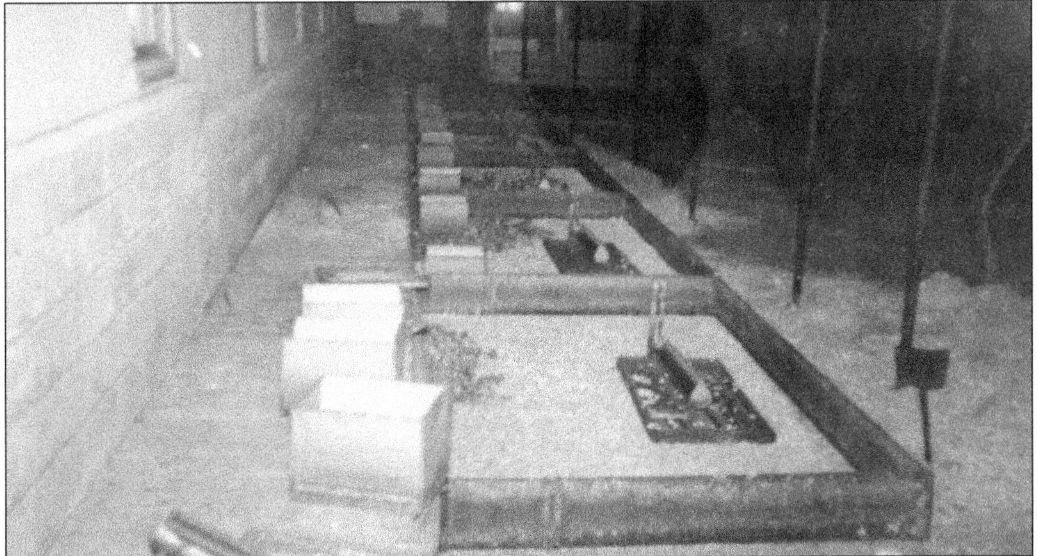

Nursery for Baby Ducklings, Crescent Duck Farm, Aquebogue, c. 1938. Newly hatched ducks were immediately taken to the hot brooder building, where they were separated into pens and given their first feed and water. Powerful pumps provided the thousands of gallons of water needed for the task. (Courtesy Douglas Corwin, Crescent Duck Farm.)

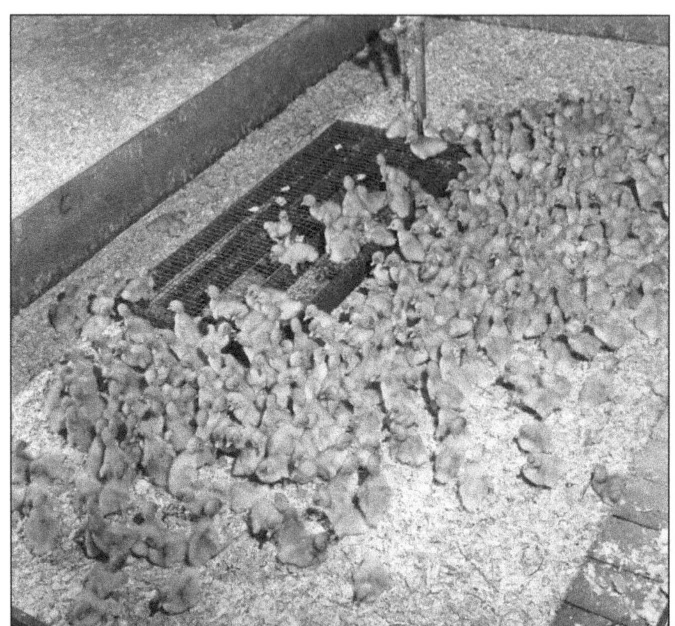

NEWBORN DUCKLINGS IN THEIR PENS, CRESCENT DUCK FARM, AQUEBOGUE, C. 1938. Ducklings stayed in the hot brooder house for five days until they were moved to the warm brooder building. Water grates were specially sized for the ducklings to prevent the wood shavings from getting wet. (Courtesy Douglas Corwin, Crescent Duck Farm.)

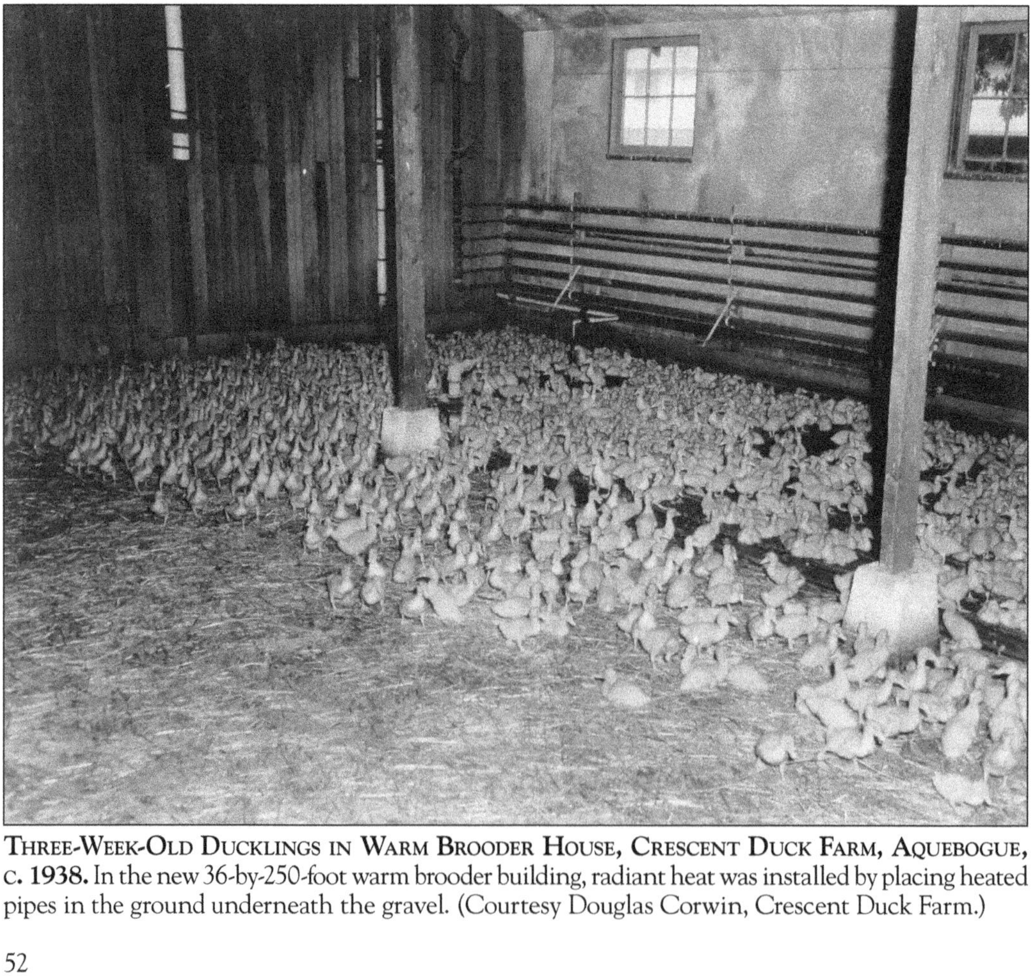

THREE-WEEK-OLD DUCKLINGS IN WARM BROODER HOUSE, CRESCENT DUCK FARM, AQUEBOGUE, C. 1938. In the new 36-by-250-foot warm brooder building, radiant heat was installed by placing heated pipes in the ground underneath the gravel. (Courtesy Douglas Corwin, Crescent Duck Farm.)

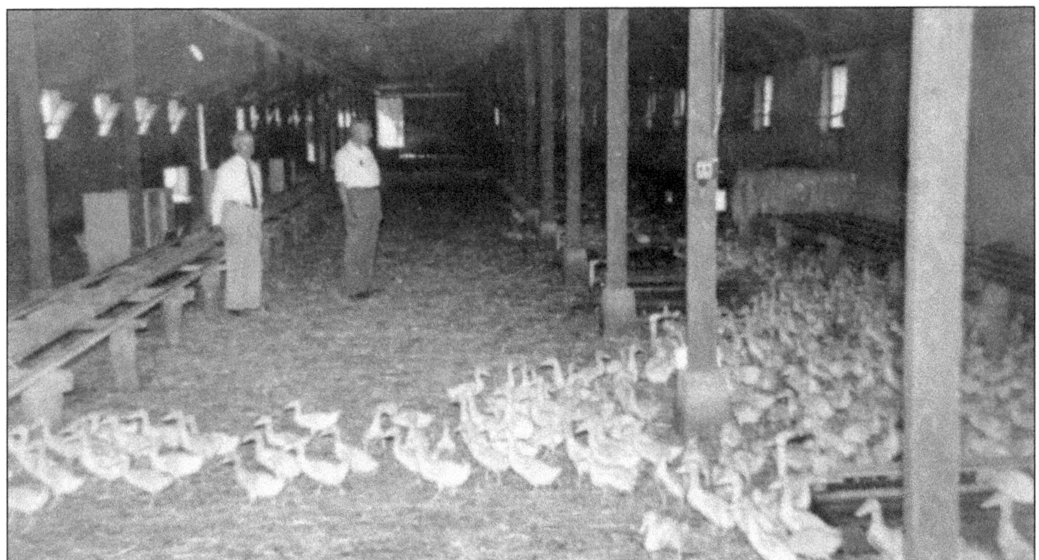

H.F. Corwin and Unidentified Man Tour the Warm Brooder House, Crescent Duck Farm, Aquebogue, c. 1938. Corwin was checking in on the three-week-old ducklings in the warm brooder house. The food tracks were inside for feeding, and the ceiling was outfitted with lights that stayed on all night to prevent stampedes. (Courtesy Douglas Corwin, Crescent Duck Farm.)

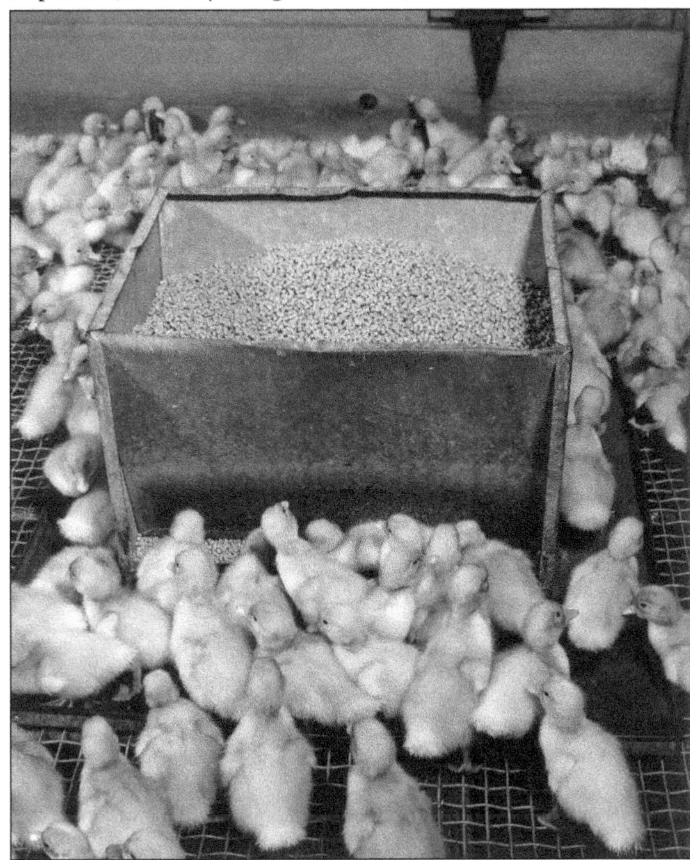

Ducklings, Crescent Duck Farm, Aquebogue, c. 1938. Ducklings enjoyed commercial feed pellets over a wire mesh floor to keep it clean. (Courtesy Douglas Corwin, Crescent Duck Farm.)

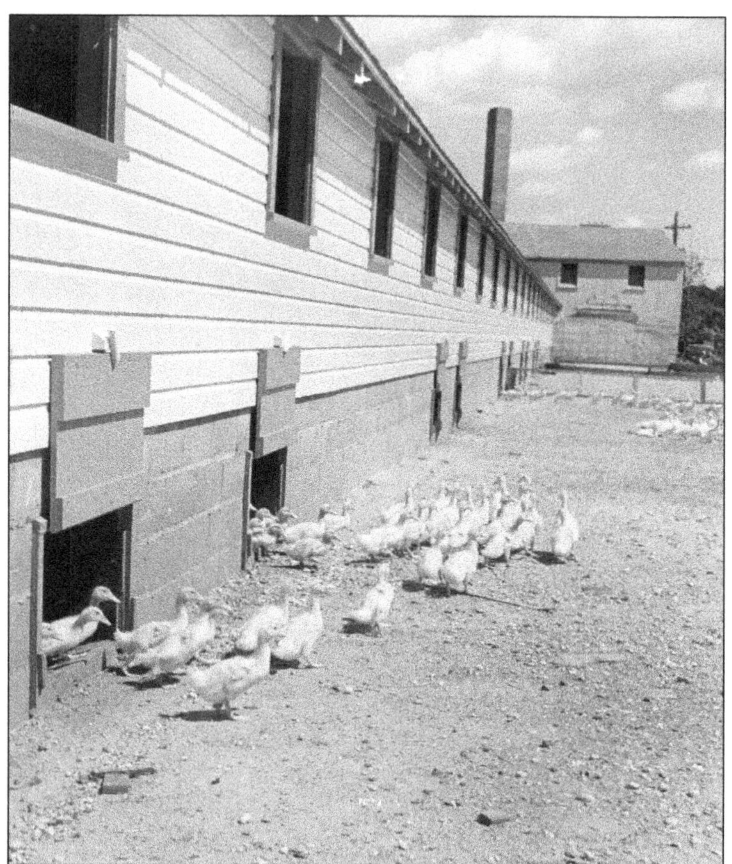

Warm Brooder, Crescent Duck Farm, Aquebogue, c. 1938. Two-week-old ducklings leave the new warm brooder house for fresh air and sun. (Courtesy Douglas Corwin, Crescent Duck Farm.)

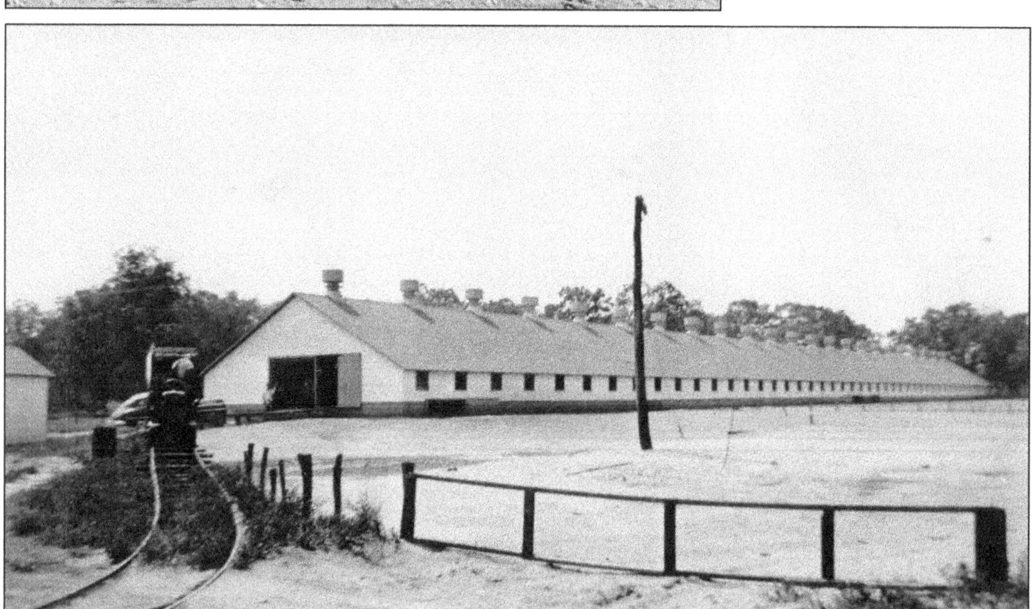

New Cold Brooder Barn, Crescent Duck Farm, Aquebogue, c. 1938. A new cold brooder barn measuring 460 feet long was constructed to house hundreds of ducklings for four to six weeks. (Courtesy Douglas Corwin, Crescent Duck Farm.)

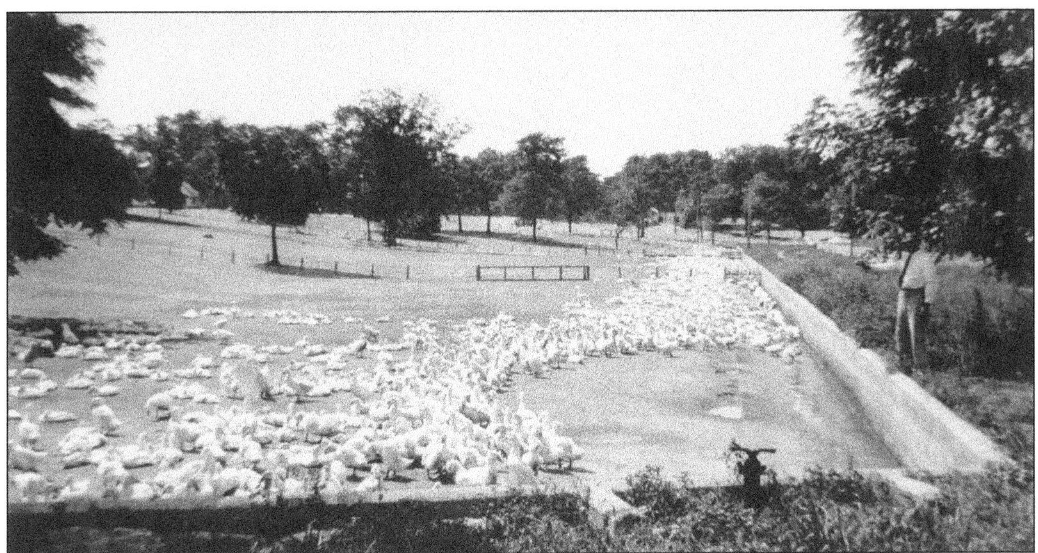

FIVE-WEEK-OLD DUCKLINGS OUTSIDE IN THE YARD, CRESCENT DUCK FARM, AQUEBOGUE, C. 1938. Ducklings were barricaded by cinderblock walls in the yard. (Courtesy Douglas Corwin, Crescent Duck Farm.)

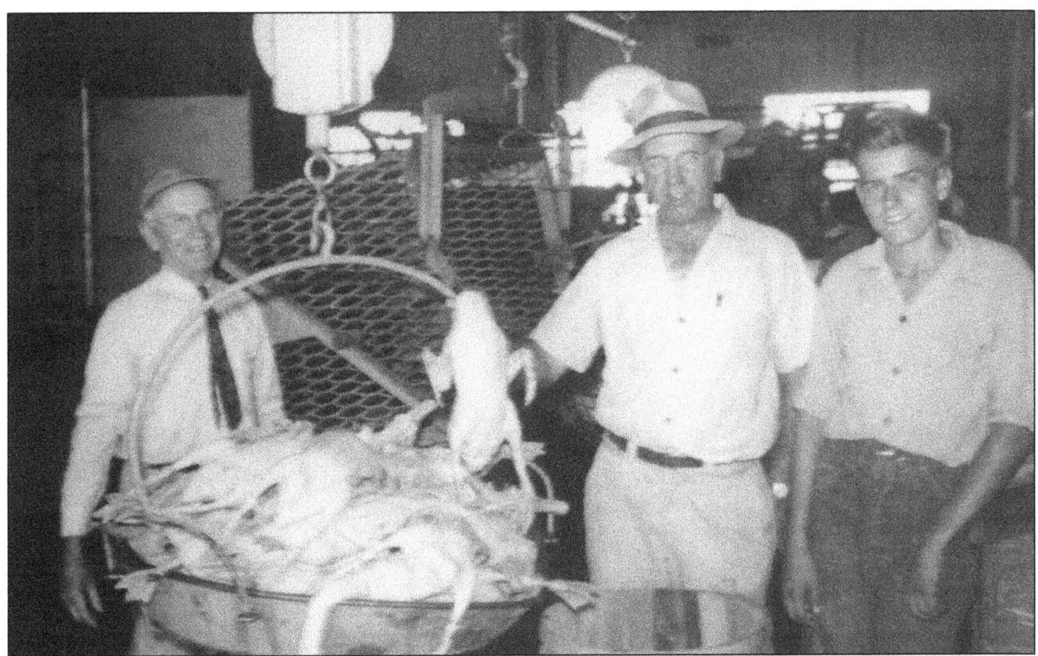

H.F., LLOYD SR., AND LLOYD JR. (FROM LEFT TO RIGHT), PICKING PLANT, CRESCENT DUCK FARM, AQUEBOGUE, 1949. Three generations of Corwins examine the cleanly picked ducks of their new picking plant. Ducks were getting weighed before being packed in vats and shipped to market. (Courtesy Douglas Corwin, Crescent Duck Farm.)

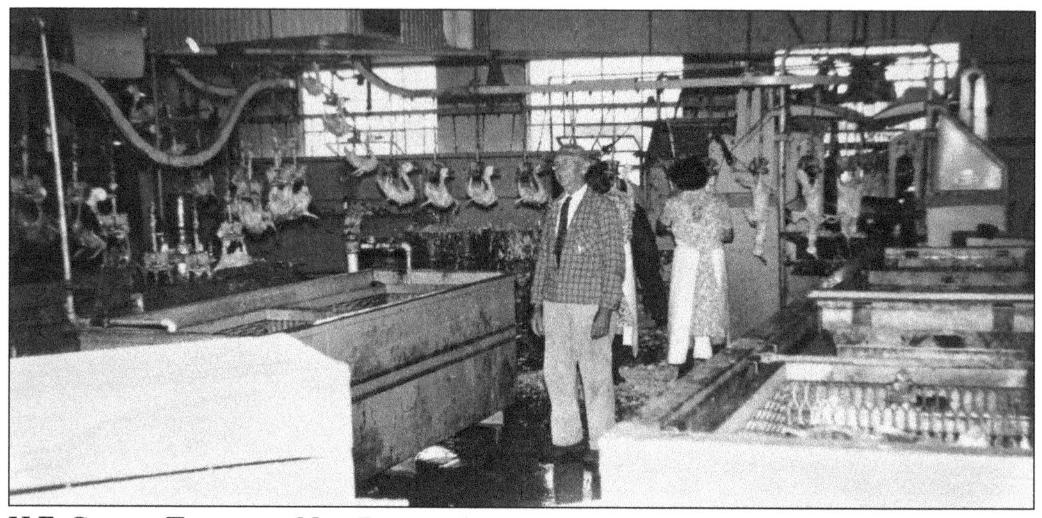

H.F. Corwin Tours the New Picking Plant, Crescent Duck Farm, Aquebogue, 1949. H.F. Corwin explained, "We have what we call 'Long Island dress' . . . the ducks are picked, then quickly chilled, packed 30 to a barrel, packed in ice and sent to the quick-freeze plant, there to be sent on to market." Before 1955, they would be eviscerated in a New York City processing plant until the Corwins built their own. (Courtesy Douglas Corwin, Crescent Duck Farm.)

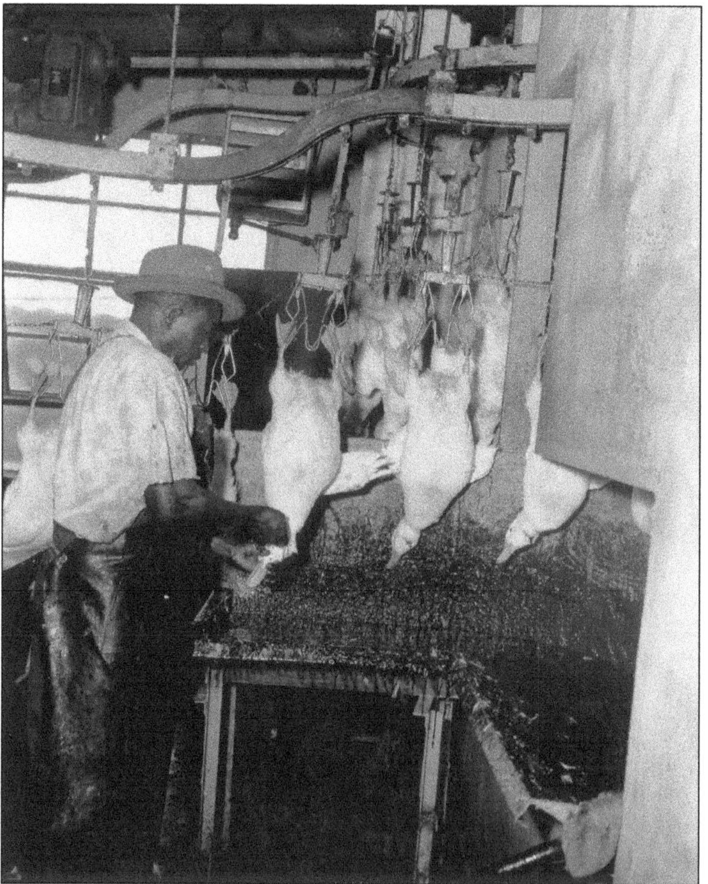

Worker Sticks Ducklings in New Picking Plant, Crescent Duck Farm, Aquebogue, 1949. Despite the modern picking plant, ducks were still hung upside-down while a worker cut a vein in the back of their throats. The ducks bled out into a trough underneath. (Courtesy Douglas Corwin, Crescent Duck Farm.)

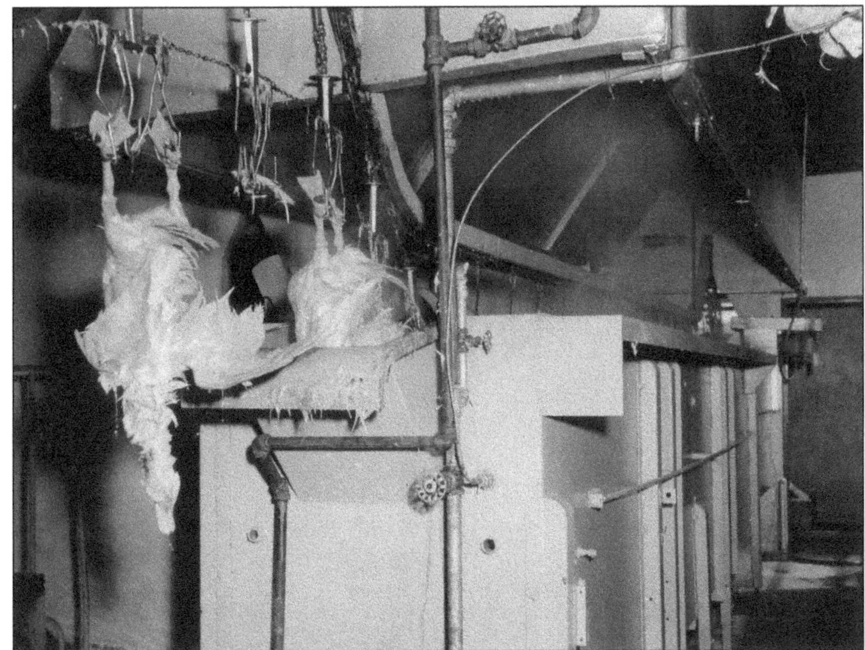

SCALDING DUCKS, CRESCENT DUCK FARM, AQUEBOGUE, 1949. Ducks were dipped into the hot water scalder to loosen their course feathers and to prepare them for the hot wax vats. (Courtesy Douglas Corwin, Crescent Duck Farm.)

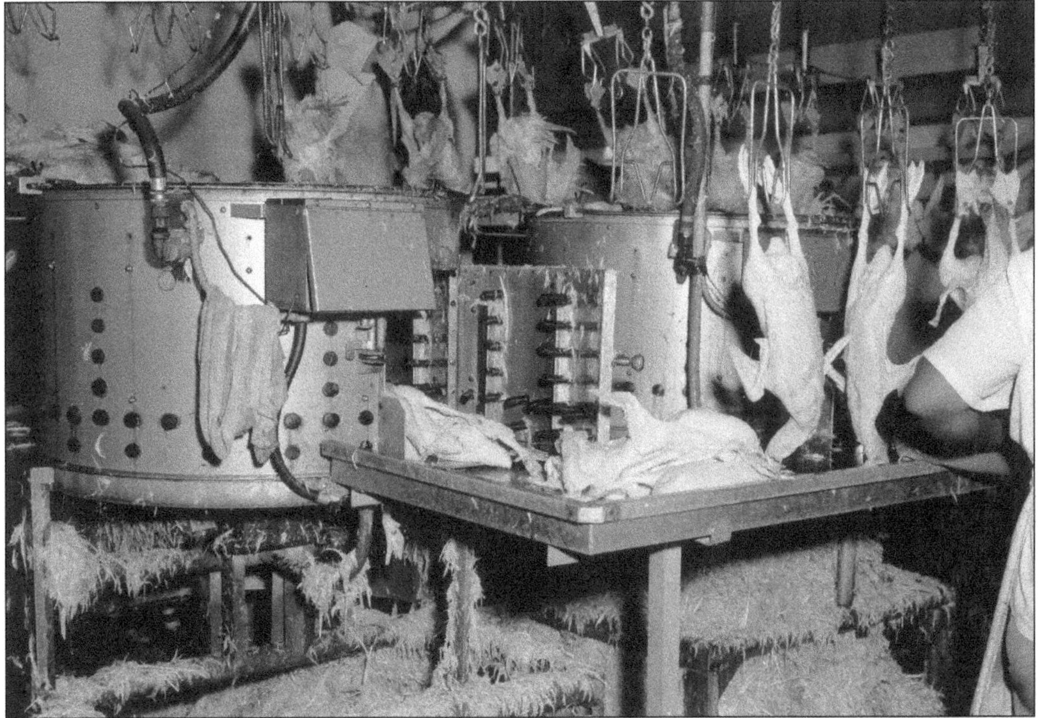

PICKING FEATHERS, CRESCENT DUCK FARM, AQUEBOGUE, 1949. To remove feathers, after scalding, the ducks were inserted into two twin drum pickers to remove feathers. They were dropped into one vat of wax at 160 degrees, then another vat of wax at 145 degrees to add a second layer, then sprayed with cold water to harden the wax. Then the wax was removed by hand. With 10 women on the line, 2,500 ducks a day could be picked. (Courtesy Douglas Corwin, Crescent Duck Farm.)

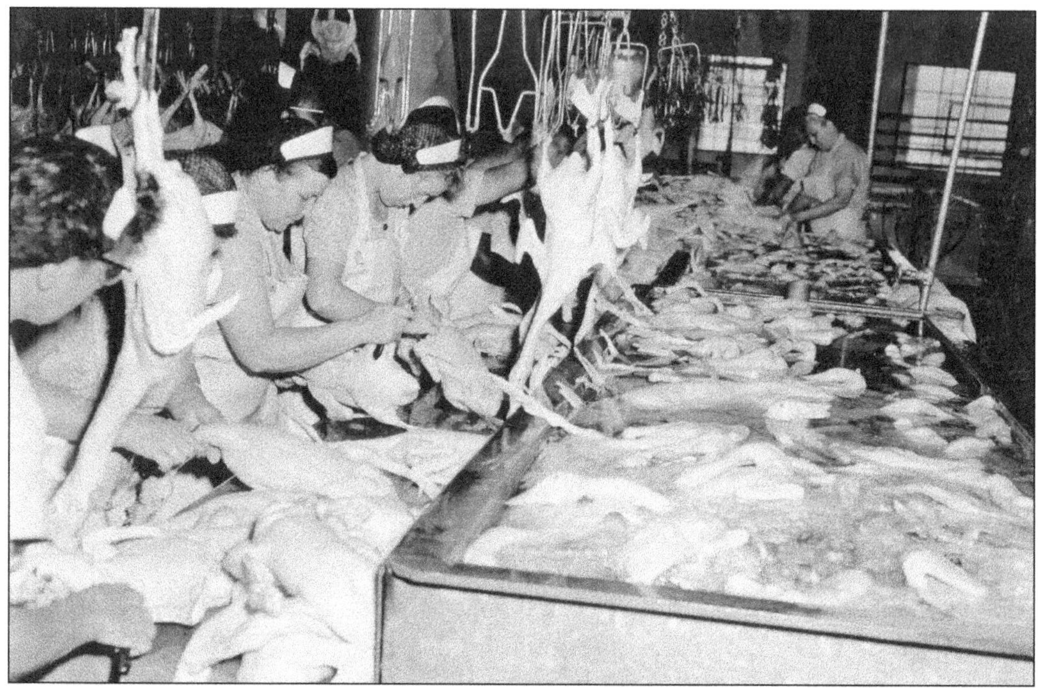

Pinning Ducks, Crescent Duck Farm, Aquebogue, 1949. Female workers removed the hard-to-reach pinfeathers by hand with a pinning knife. (Courtesy Douglas Corwin, Crescent Duck Farm.)

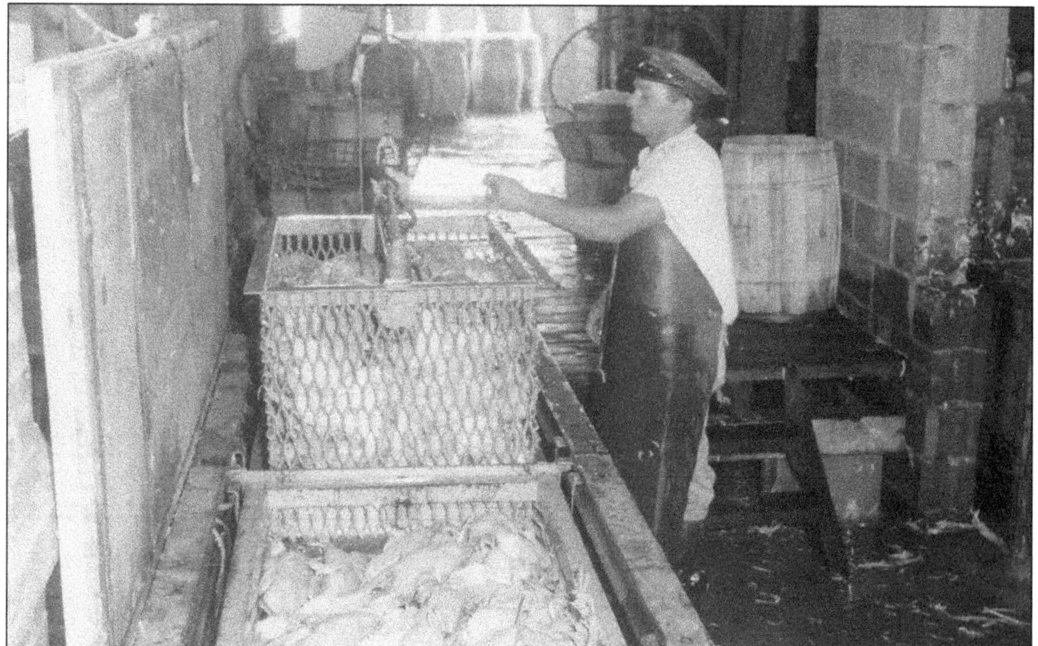

Herman Lewin Removing Ducks from Cooling Tanks, Picking Plant, Crescent Duck Farm, Aquebogue, 1949. Lewin removed the ducks from the cooling baskets and packed 30 to a vat (vats are seen in the background) before they were shipped to market. (Courtesy Douglas Corwin, Crescent Duck Farm.)

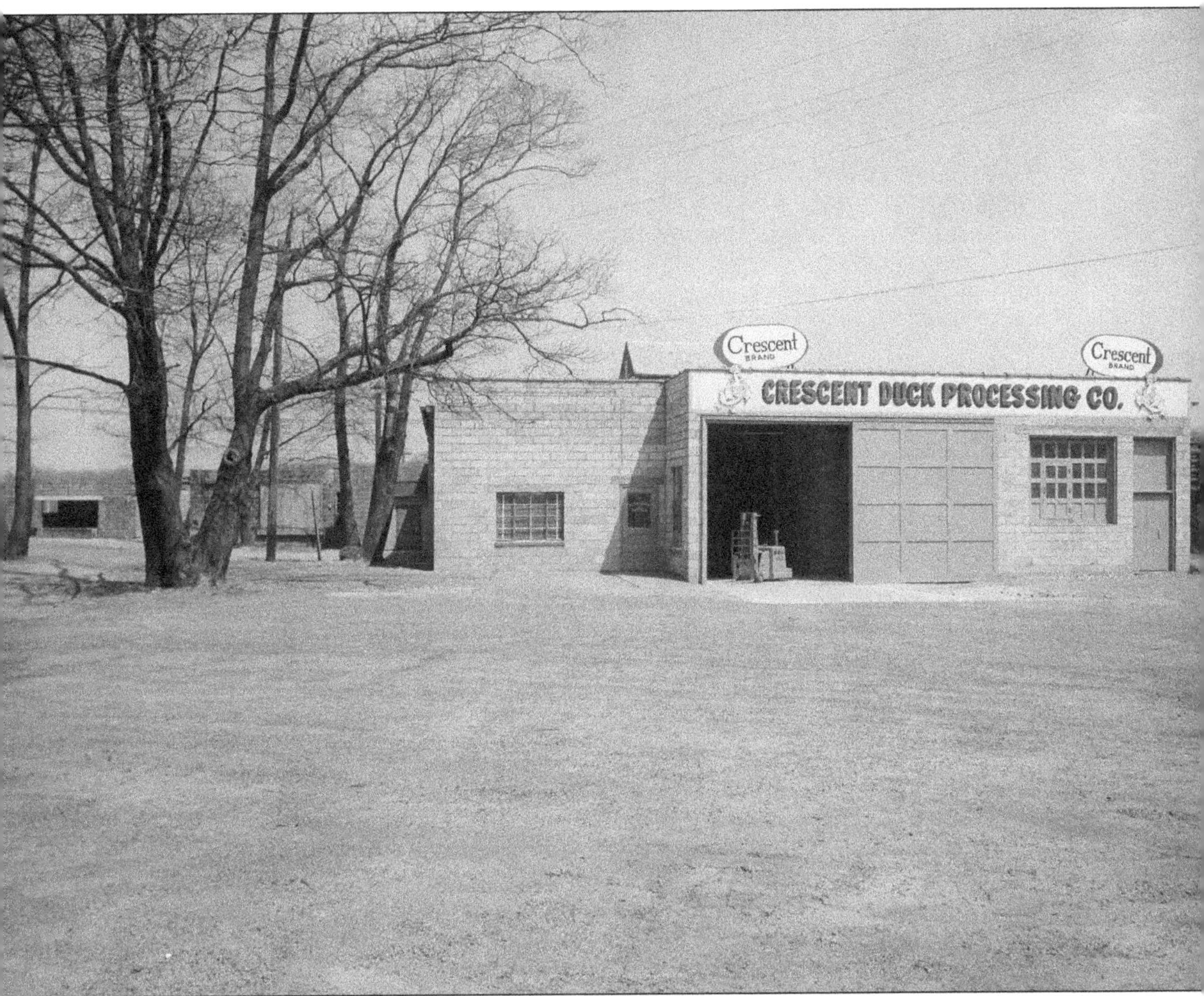

FRONT OF THE NEW EVISCERATING PLANT, CRESCENT DUCK FARM, AQUEBOGUE, 1958. In 1955, the Corwins built a state-of-the-art United States Department of Agriculture (USDA) eviscerating plant for disemboweling and cleaning out the organs. The façade of the building boasted Crescent's logo on either side that also graced its package labels—a cartoon duck wearing a checkered chef's hat and bib standing while sharpening a knife. (Courtesy Douglas Corwin, Crescent Duck Farm.)

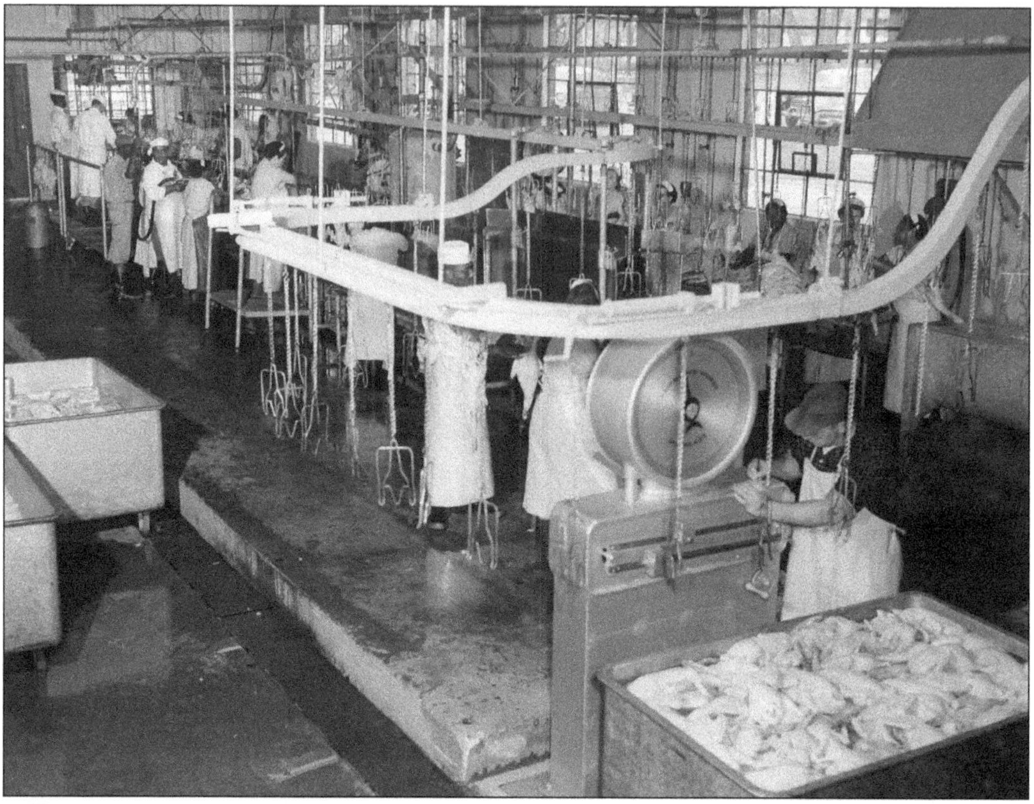

USDA Inspection, Crescent Duck Farm, Aquebogue, 1958. After a USDA inspector (top, second from left) examined the ducks, they were placed into tanks for cooling. A USDA inspector was always on the premises when the factory was operating. (Courtesy Douglas Corwin, Crescent Duck Farm.)

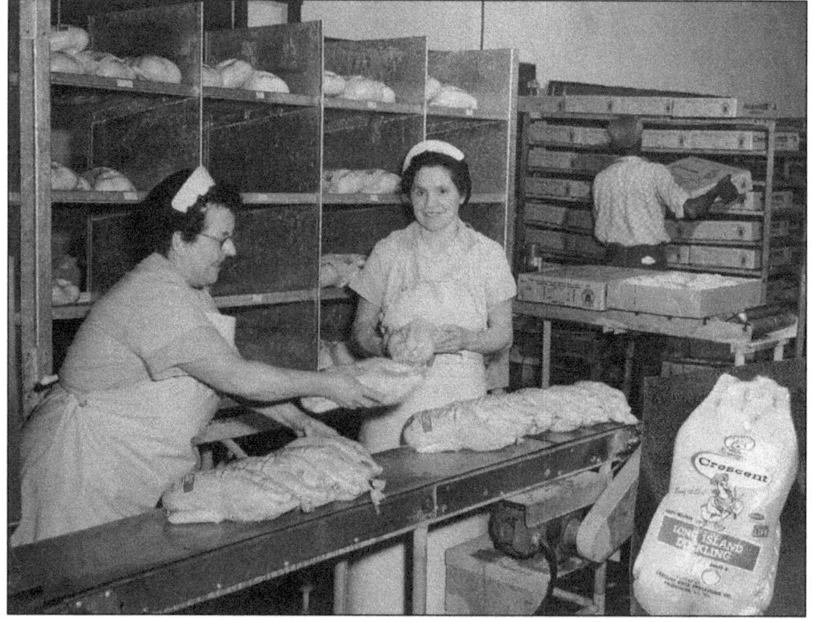

Workers in Eviscerating Plant, Crescent Duck Farm, Aquebogue, 1958. Bagged ducks were sized, boxed, and put into the freezer. They were then shipped to market—first by trains, which were soon replaced by refrigerated trucks. (Courtesy Douglas Corwin, Crescent Duck Farm.)

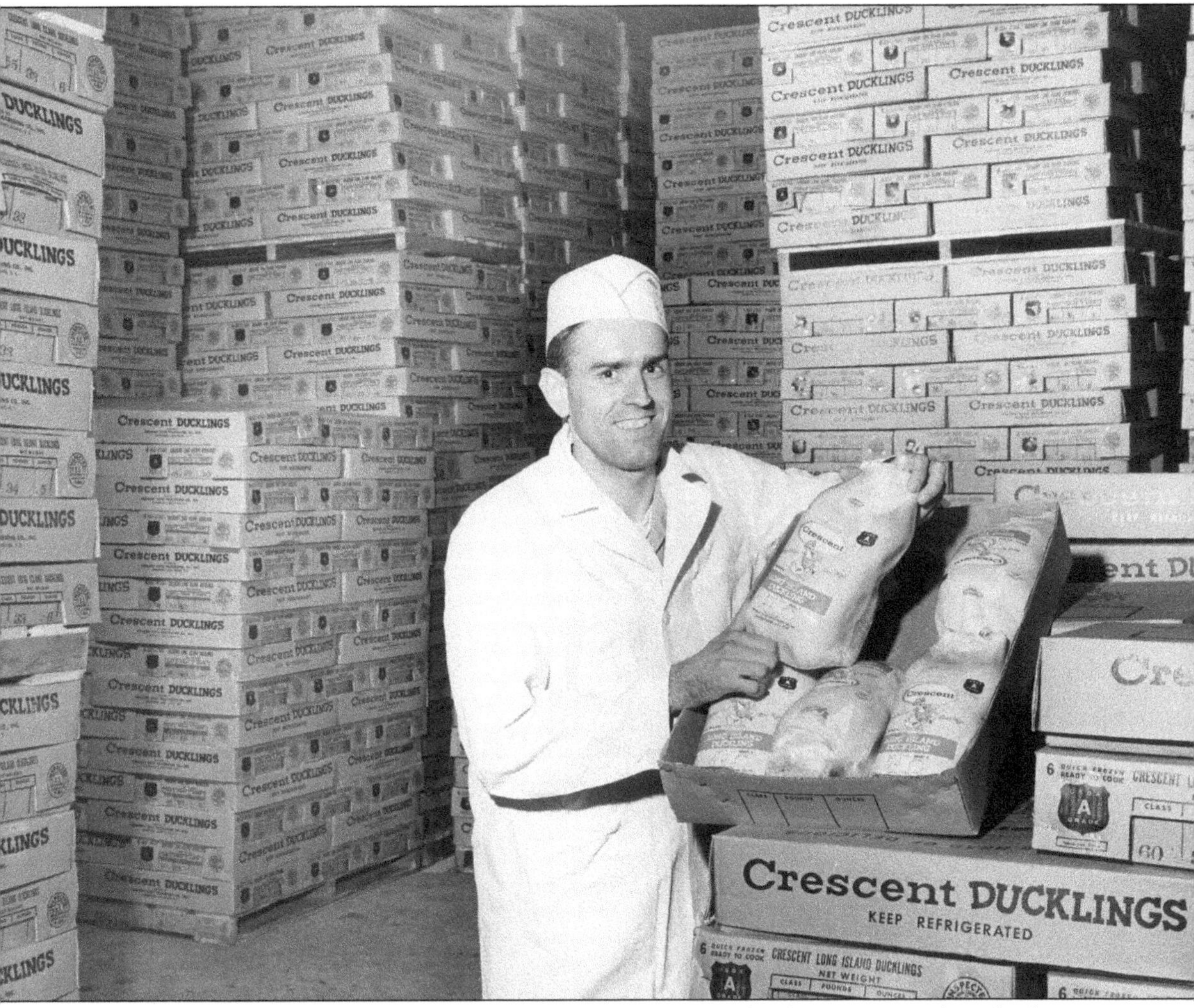

REFRIGERATOR, CRESCENT DUCK FARM, AQUEBOGUE, 1958. Lloyd Jr. is pictured in the large refrigerator with boxes stacked high. The ducks were six to a box with the USDA Grade A seal on the side. (Courtesy Douglas Corwin, Crescent Duck Farm.)

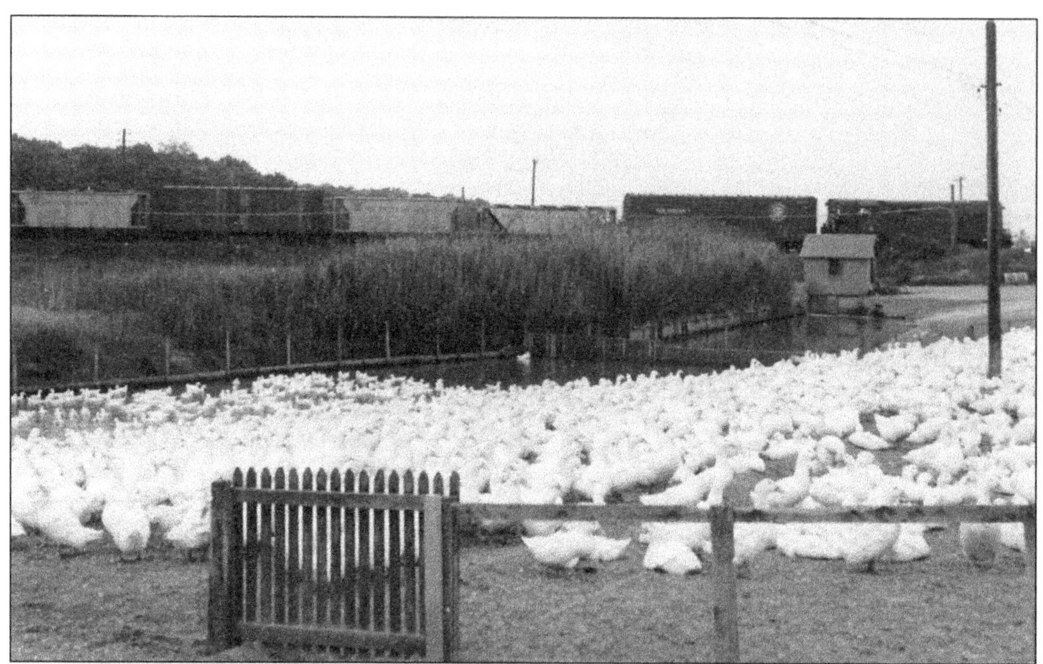

DUCK YARDS IN FRONT OF PASSING TRAIN, CRESCENT DUCK FARM, AQUEBOGUE, C. 1958. Many Long Island Railroad tracks were added to serve the needs of the duck farms to ship ducks, feed, grain, and fertilizer. The Aquebogue train station was constructed in 1892 and was closed in 1967. (Courtesy Douglas Corwin, Crescent Duck Farm.)

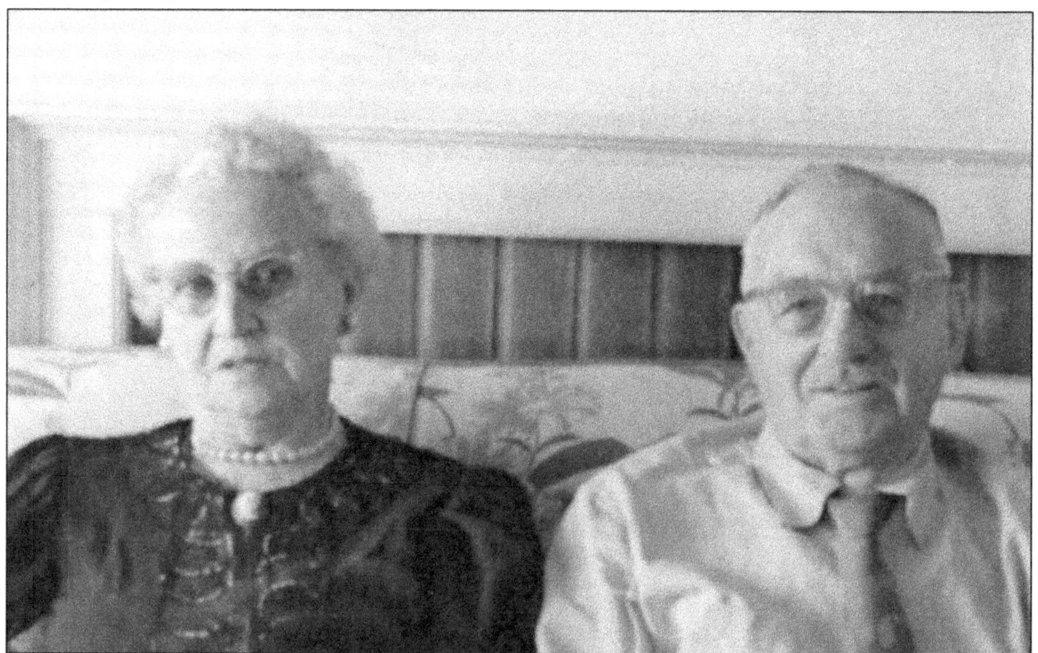

ERNESTINA "TINA" AND CHARLES ROBINSON, C. 1950. Charles Robinson established Robinson Duck Farm (also referred to as Carmans River Duck Farm) in 1922 at South Haven with 1,500 feet of shoreline on Carmans River. They were one of the largest farm operations in South Haven. In the 1960s, they raised about 200,000 ducks per year. (Courtesy Post Morrow Foundation.)

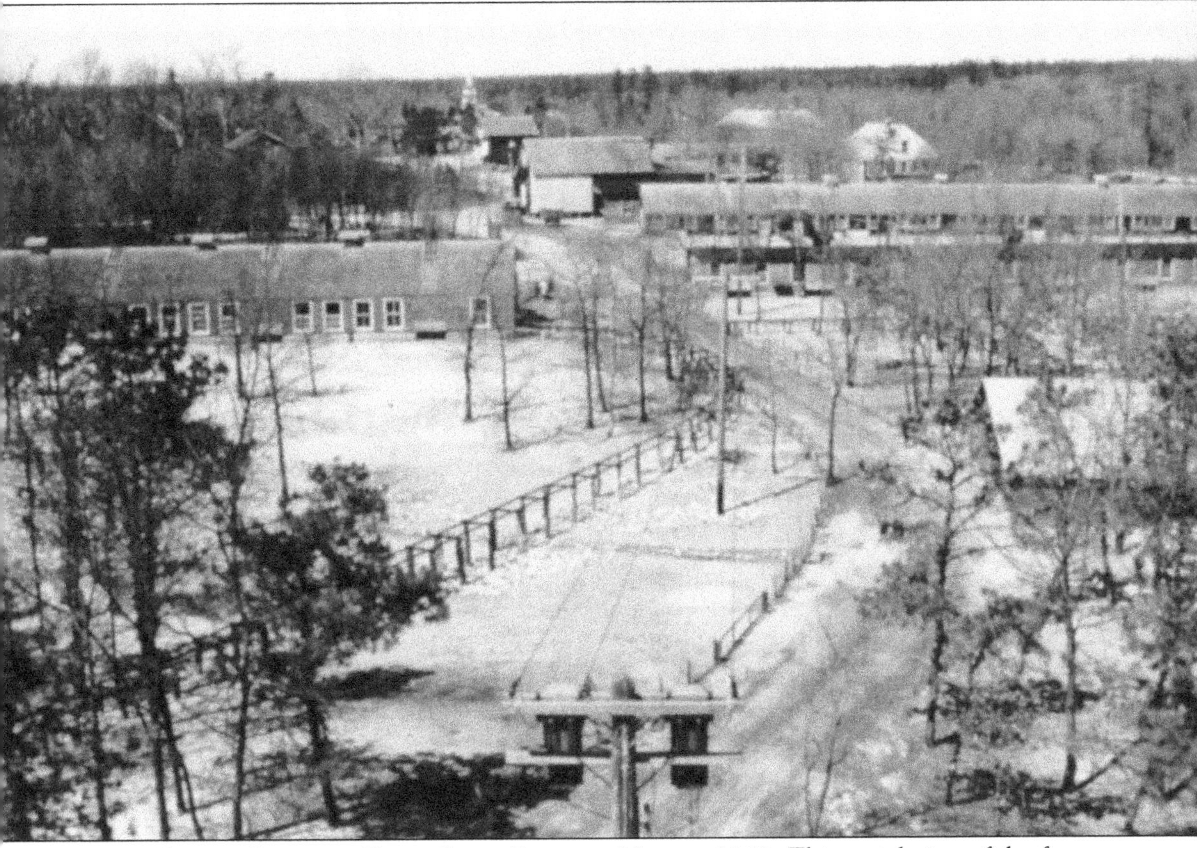

Aerial View of Robinson Duck Farm, Looking North, 1948. This aerial view of the farm looking north shows the brooder barns, power lines, feed track, and the spire of the South Haven Presbyterian Church in the far background. The farm contained an incubation house, hatchery, feed mill, killing house, and processing plant. Richard Beyer, a former worker on the farm, noted that it was so efficient that every part of the duck was sold, "except the quack." (Courtesy Ken Hard, Marty Van Lith, Post Morrow Foundation.)

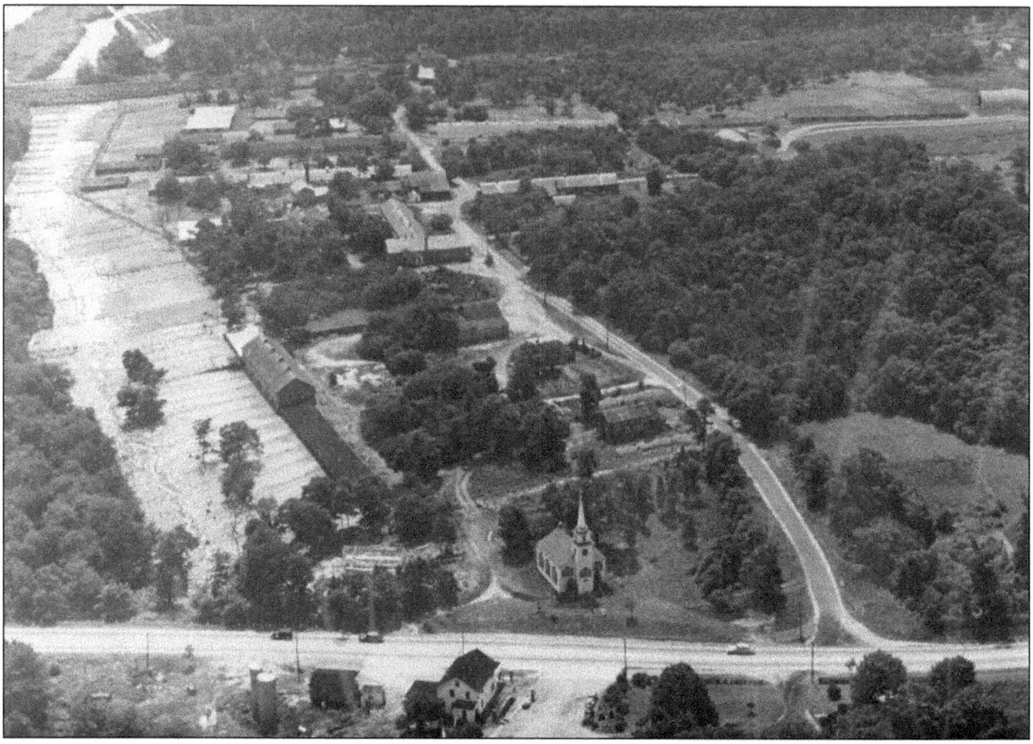

Aerial View of Robinson Duck Farm, Looking South, 1948. This view captures Carmans River in the upper left, the Long Island Railroad crossing the background, South Haven Presbyterian Church in the foreground. The Anson Hard dairy farm was located to the right. It has been said that the smell of the surrounding farms caused congregants at the church to worship at another location. (Courtesy Ron Bush, Post Morrow Foundation.)

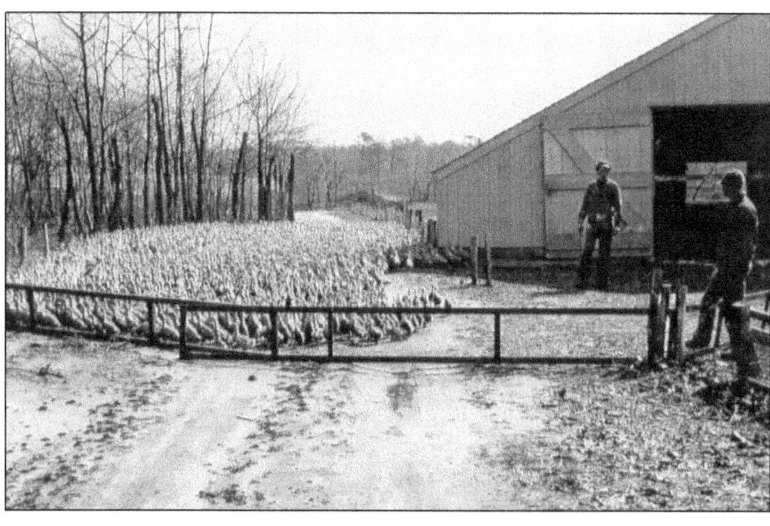

Unidentified Men Moving Ducks, Robinson Duck Farm, South Haven, 1940s. These two men were moving ducks from one brooder to another. (Courtesy Ken Hard, Marty Van Lith, Post Morrow Foundation.)

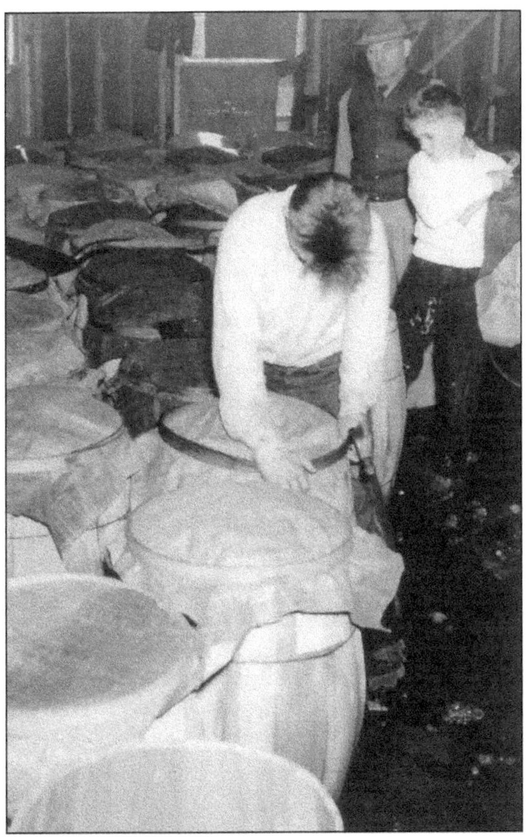

Lloyd Robinson and Charles Robinson Packing Ducks in Vats, Robinson Duck Farm, South Haven, 1940s. Charles's son Lloyd packed ducks in vats and covered them with a fabric cover while Charles looked on. (Courtesy Post Morrow Foundation.)

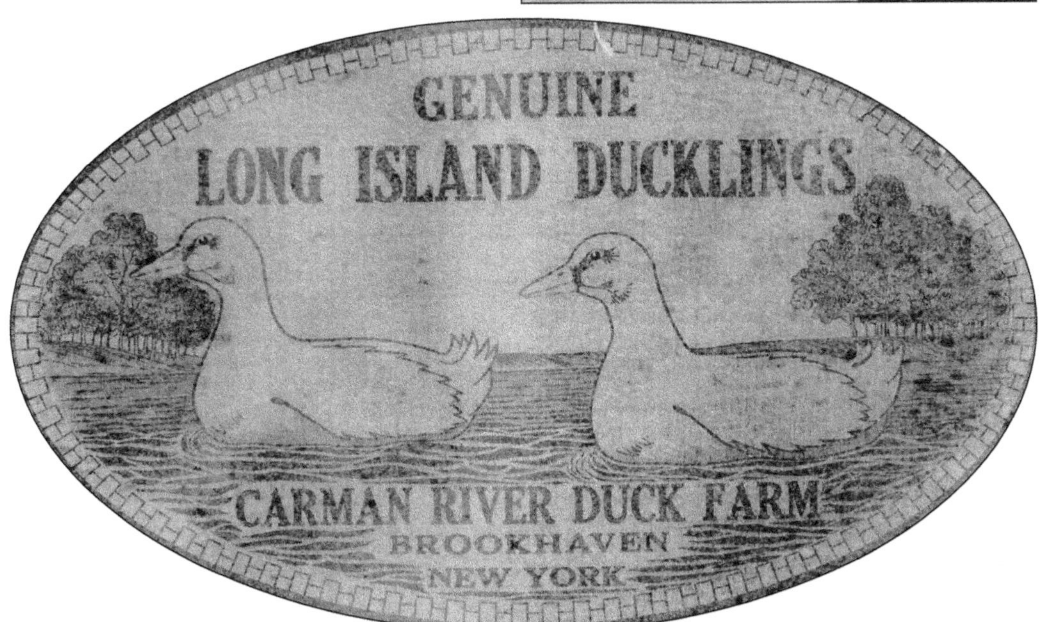

Carman River Duck Farm Decal. This decal was used to adorn the crates used to transport ducks at Carman River Duck Farm. It shows two ducks from side profile views swimming in the Carman River. (Courtesy Ronald Bush.)

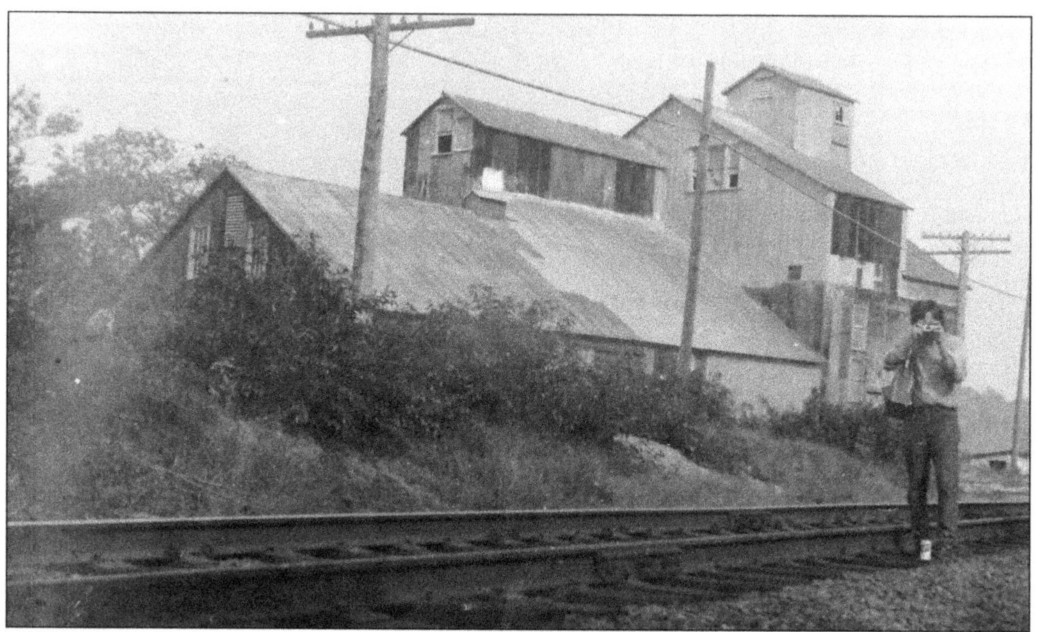

Long Island Railroad Siding and Shed, Robinson Duck Farm, South Haven, 1974. On the southern portion of the farm, the railroad siding and shed received bulk shipments of corn, wheat, fish, alfalfa, and other types of feed. By the early 1980s, the farm had fallen into disrepair. In 1991, the land was acquired by Suffolk County, and portions of it have been repurposed as county parks (see chapter four). (Courtesy Marty Van Lith, Post Morrow Foundation.)

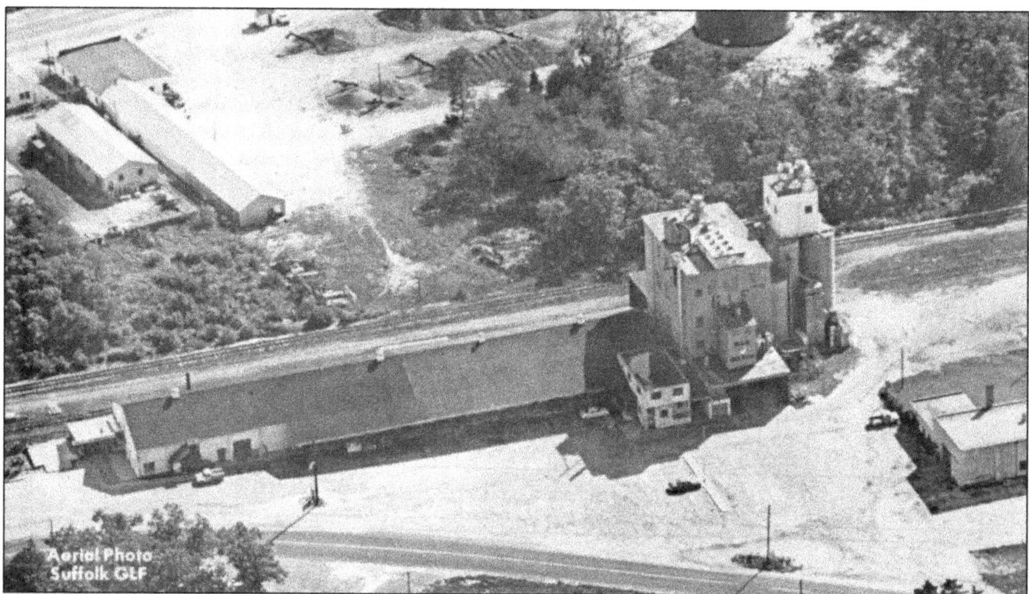

Grange League Federation Exchange Feed Mill Aerial View, Riverhead, 1947. In 1920, the New York Grange League Federation Exchange (GLF) Cooperation was formed. A duck farmer could purchase feed and farm machinery from the GLF. In 1947, the GLF built a seven-story grain elevator and feed mill in Riverhead to serve the duck industry. The feed mill produced 75 percent of the feed for the five million ducks produced on Long Island annually. In 1964, GLF and Long Island Produce merged and were bought by Agway. (Courtesy Douglas Corwin, Crescent Duck Farm.)

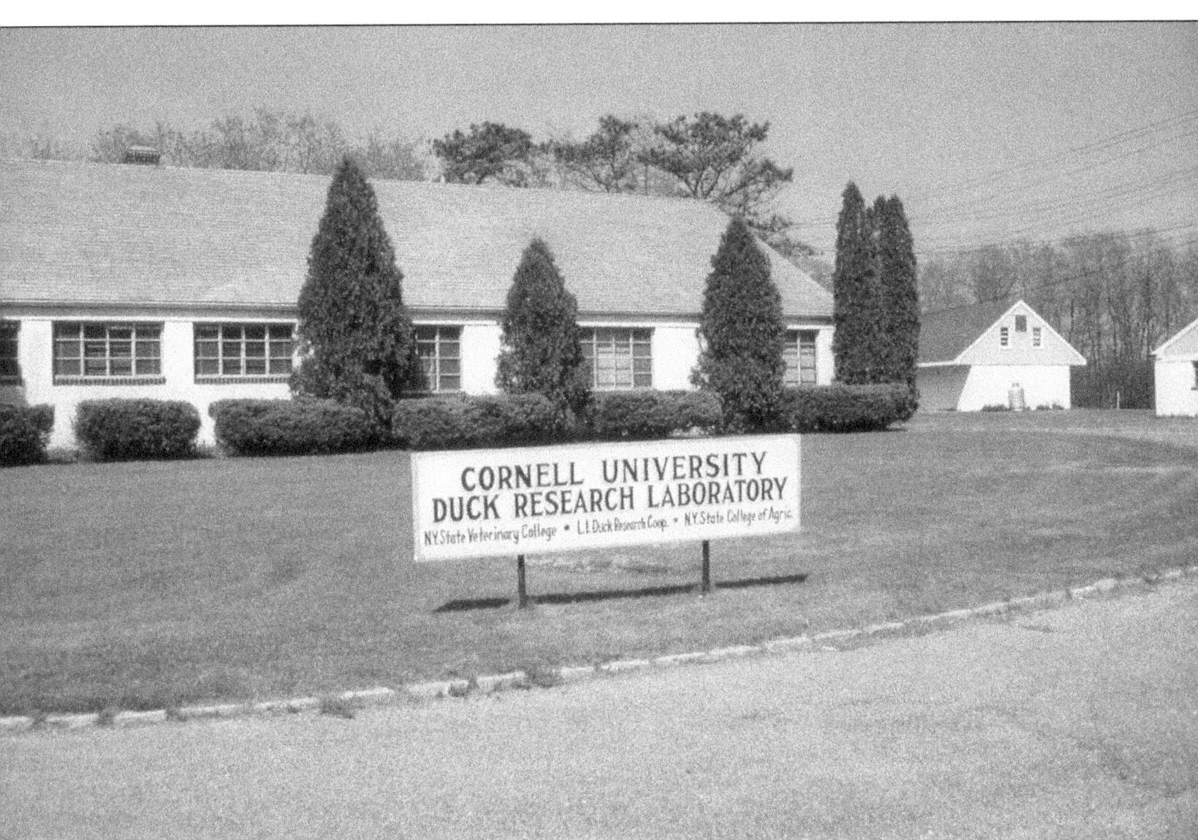

Cornell University Duck Research Laboratory, Eastport, c. 1949. The height of duck farming on Long Island occurred immediately after World War II; in 1948, 50 percent of the national duck production came from Long Island duck farms. The Duck Laboratory and the Long Island Duck Research Cooperative was formed in 1949 by Cornell University in cooperation with Long Island Duck growers in an effort to fill the research void on ducks and the diseases that afflicted them at that time. (Courtesy Dr. William F. Dean.)

Program

FOURTH ANNUAL
LONG ISLAND
DUCK FESTIVAL

SETH A. HUBBARD
Master of Ceremonies

3:00 P. M. Dinner Is Served

4:00 P. M. Beauty Pageant
Rudolph Kammerer Chairman of Judges' Committee

5:00 P. M. Welcome
John B. Fleischman, Sr
Exalted Ruler
Riverhead Lodge, No. 2044, B. P. O. E.

William J. Leonard
Supervisor of the Town of Riverhead

H. Lee Dennison
Suffolk County Executive

Otis G. Pike
Congressman, First Congressional District

6:00 P. M. Crowning of the Long Island Duck Queen by Janet Boring, 1961 Duck Queen

Menu

Long Island Duckling
Long Island Potatoes
Local Sweet Corn
Tomatoes
Coleslaw
Rolls and Butter
Beer and Soda
Coffee

Souvenir Program

WELCOME TO THE

Fifth Annual

Long Island Duck Festival

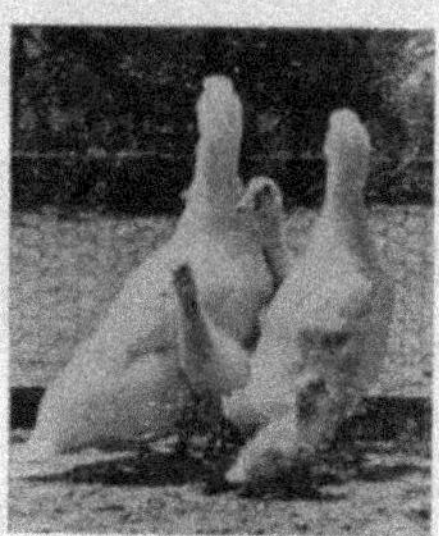

Saturday, July 28, 1962

3 P. M. - 8 P. M.

B. P. O. ELKS GROUNDS
RIVERHEAD, L. I., N. Y.

PRICE 25 CENTS

ANNUAL DUCK FESTIVAL PAMPHLET AND PROGRAM, 1962. Other marketing strategies for Long Island Duck included the Annual Duck Festival, started in 1957, featuring a beauty pageant that crowned a "Duck Queen," after which guests enjoyed a dinner of Long Island duckling, local corn, Long Island potatoes, and watermelon. (Courtesy Vic Prusinowski, Suffolk County Parks Collection.)

PORCELAIN SIGN WITH FCH LOGO. This 60-inch double-sided porcelain sign bears the FCH logo, or Farmer's Commission House, that was trademarked in 1921. Member farms received a sign to advertise on their roadsides. The sign now hangs inside the Big Duck gift shop behind the counter. (Author's collection.)

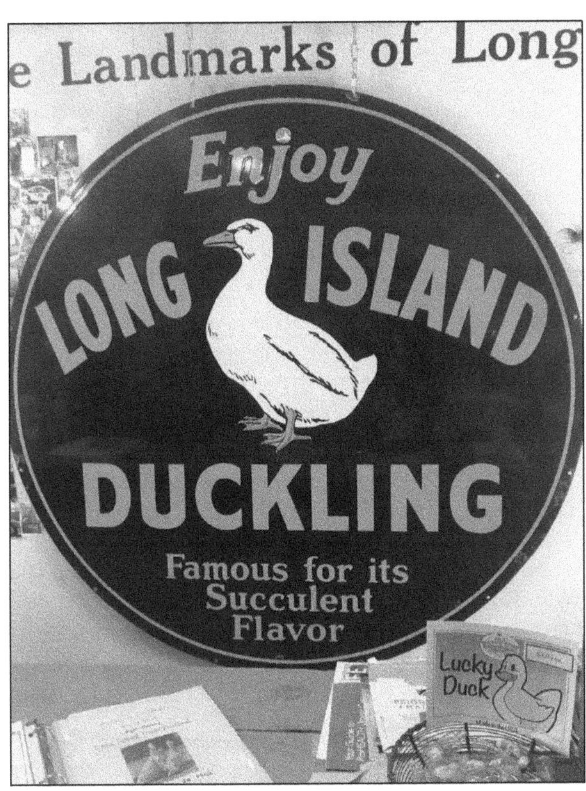

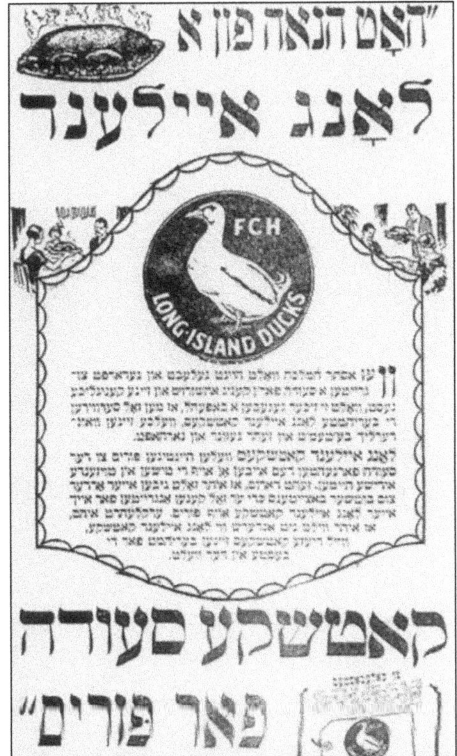

PURIM FCH LONG ISLAND DUCKLING ADVERTISEMENT IN YIDDISH *FORVERTS*, MARCH 5, 1925. This advertisement illustrates how FCH marketed toward certain ethnic groups in New York, such as Chinese and Yiddish consumers. This particular text suggests that Yiddish housewives prepare duck for their Purim celebration and that if a modern Queen Esther were to throw a Purim party for her husband, King Achashverosh, she would do well to prepare Long Island *katshkes*, which is Yiddish for ducks. (Courtesy *Forward* Archive.)

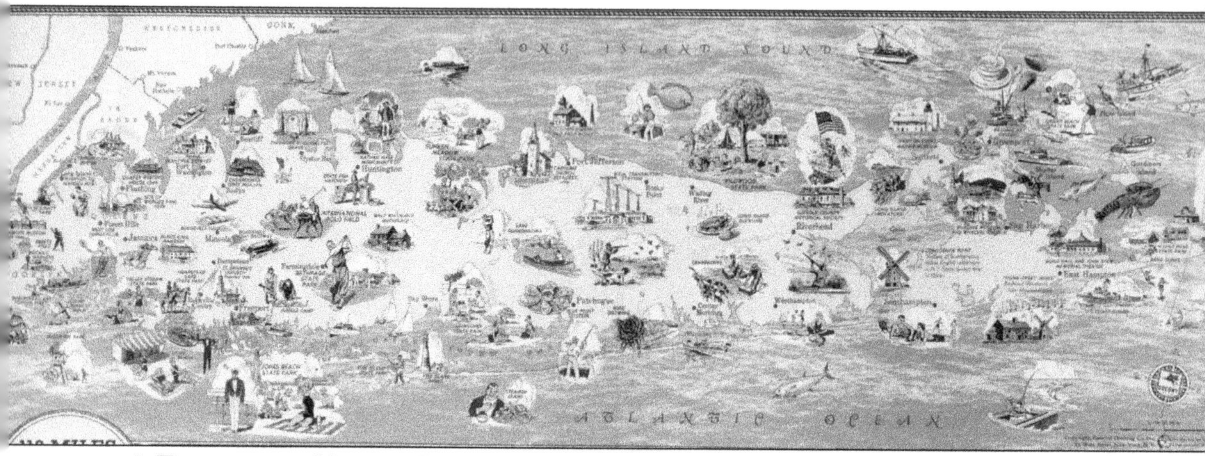

A Total of 118 Miles of Recreation and Romance, Standard Oil Company Map, 1938. This map published by Standard Oil Company was used to promote automobile travel on Long Island. The map is illustrated throughout with small pictures showing various types of recreation found in specific towns on Long Island such as golf, tennis, flying, and beaches. Cuisine is also included and placed in a location associated with it—a steaming plate of "Long Island Duckling" is inserted north of the Peconic River, just west of Riverhead. (Courtesy PJ Mode Collection of Persuasive Cartography, Cornell University.)

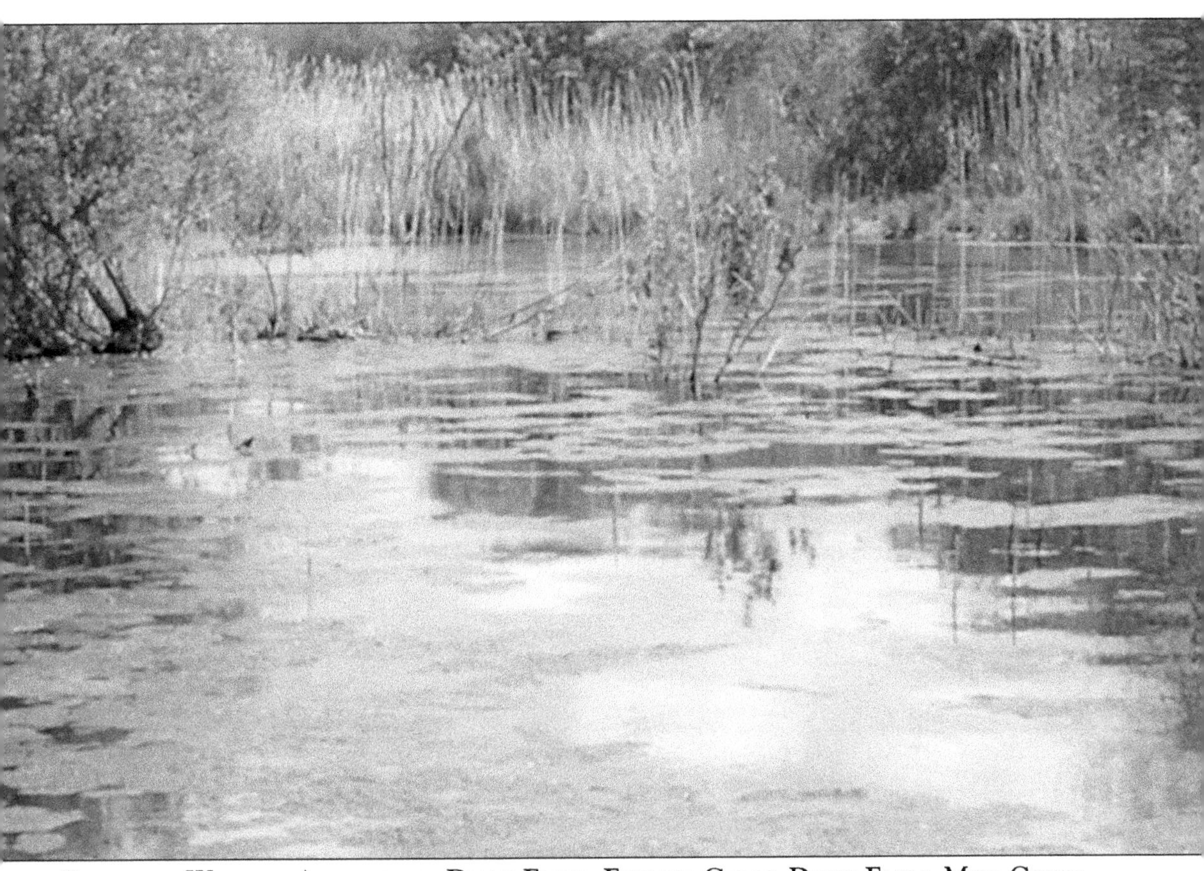

Polluted Waters, Abandoned Duck Farm, Former Gallo Duck Farm, Mud Creek, Brookhaven, 2009. Ducks farms slowly became "public enemy number one," owing to their noxious odors and heavy burden on the environment. H. Lee Dennison, the first Suffolk County executive, who served from 1960 to 1972, vowed to make Suffolk County "a duckless county." The county and state introduced a number of regulations that negatively impacted the duck farmers in addition to the Federal Clean Water Act of 1972. Many duck farmers were fined repeatedly for failing to comply with the new requirements. Faced with millions of dollars of upgrades and increasing property taxes and grain costs, most duck farmers chose to sell their valuable land and close their farms or move their farms to Pennsylvania or the Midwest, where costs were lower and environmental restrictions less onerous or nonexistent. (Courtesy Suffolk County Department of Planning.)

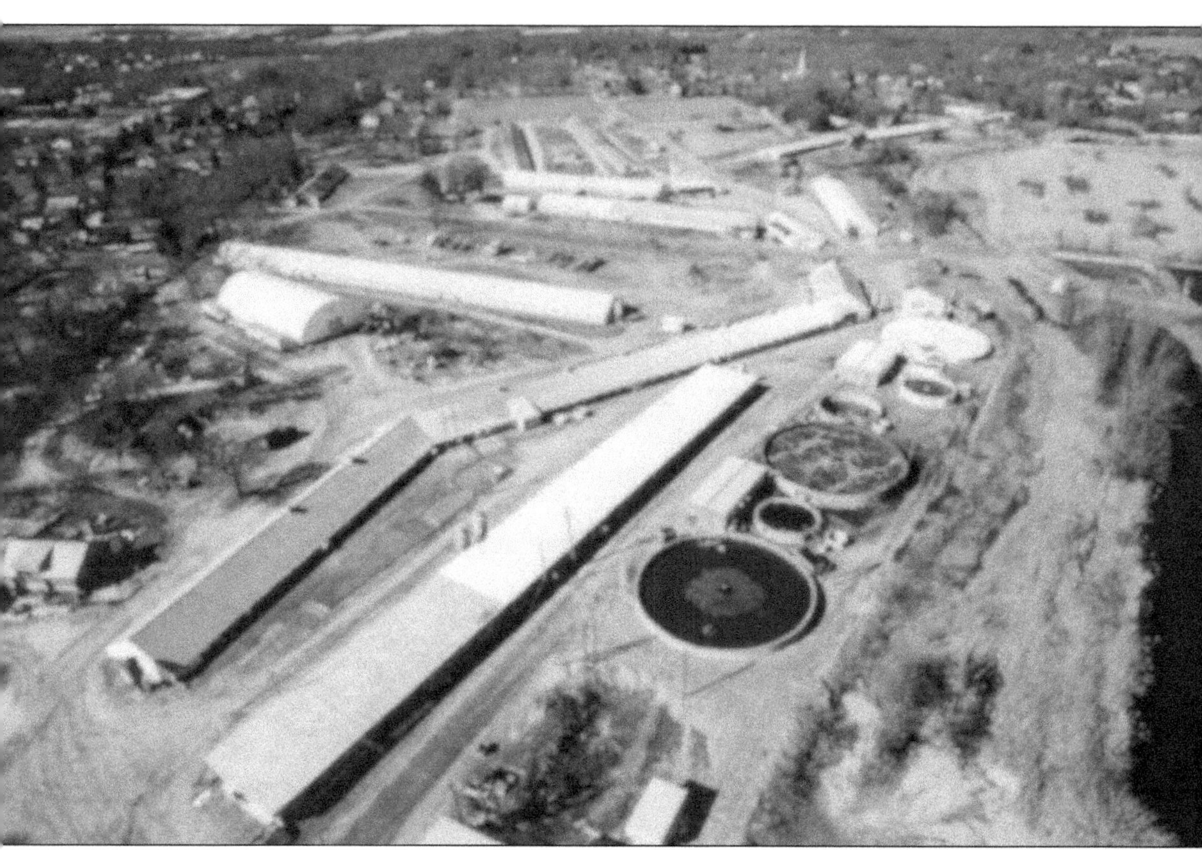

AERIAL VIEW OF CRESCENT DUCK FARM WITH UPGRADED WASTEWATER TREATMENT PLANT, AQUEBOGUE, 2015. In 1940, there were 90 duck farms on Long Island. Due to stricter environmental regulations and rising costs, the number of farms decreased to 48 in 1963. By 2009, it decreased to three. The penultimate holdout, Chester Massey & Sons, closed in 2015, making Crescent the last duck farm left on Long Island. Douglas Corwin credits Crescent's longevity with their ability to constantly evolve and their willingness to follow new regulations proposed by legislators. For instance, since 1967, the ducks at Crescent were raised inside to prevent water pollution. In the early 2000s, they added a wastewater treatment facility, and in 2015, they invested $5.25 million to upgrade it. (Courtesy Douglas Corwin, Crescent Duck Farm.)

Three

THE BIG DUCK

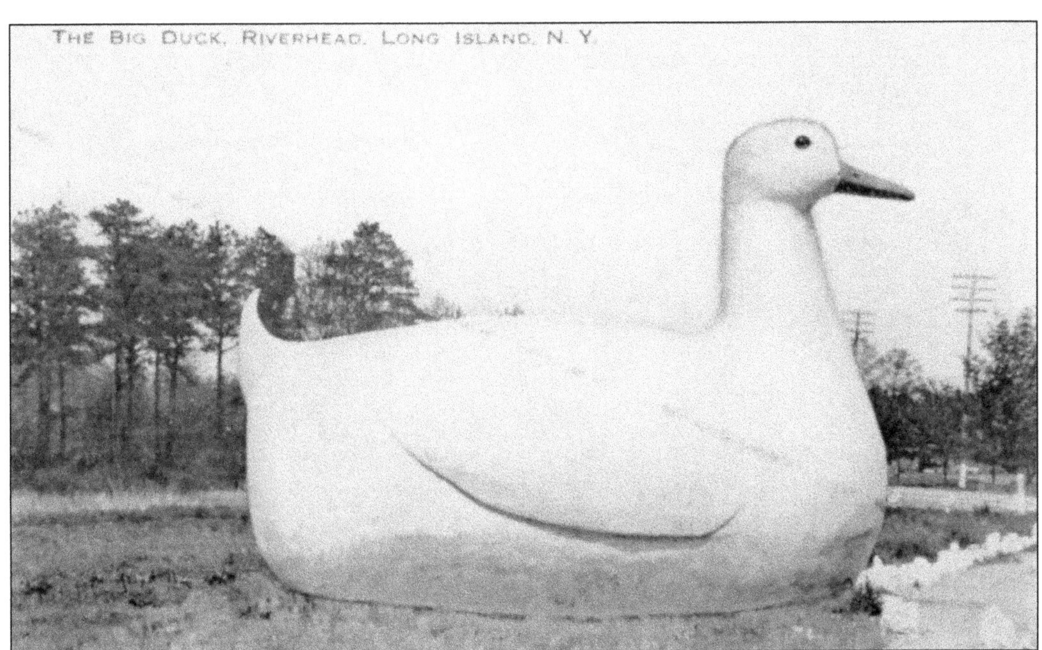

THE BIG DUCK, RIVERHEAD. The Big Duck was first erected by duck farmer Martin Maurer on the former land of the Pugsley farm in Upper Mills, Riverhead, in 1931. The farm had the reputation of producing the heaviest ducks, due to the careful selection of breeders and the fact that the ducks were not as crowded as on the other farms and enjoyed ample water and shade. (Courtesy Collection of Eric Woodward.)

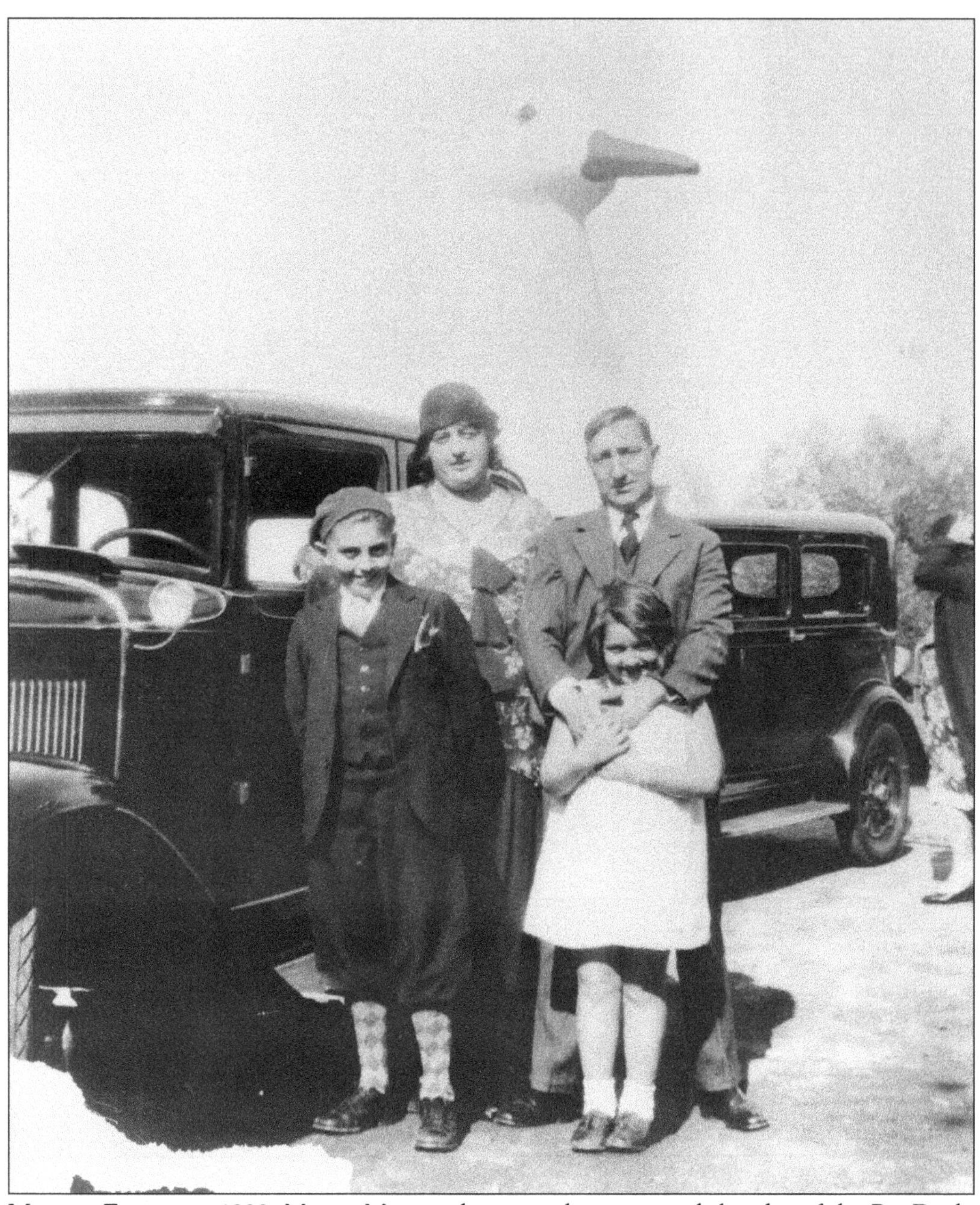

Maurer Family, c. 1932. Martin Maurer, the man who conceived the idea of the Big Duck, was born in 1883 in New Jersey to German immigrants. By 1929, Maurer married his second wife, Jeule, who was 13 years younger, and they rented a house in Riverhead where they lived with Jeule's 14-year-old son from a previous marriage, Pelham Molloy. Maurer worked as a feed salesman. He eventually became the manager and half-owner of a duck farm with P.W. Meyer. In 1931, in the throes of the Great Depression, Maurer and Jeule went on a cross-country trip to Los Angeles, and after visiting a coffee shop in the shape of a coffee percolator, he had the idea to erect a building in the shape of a duck to sell duck broilers and duck eggs. Pictured from left to right are (first row) Pelham Molloy and an unidentified female; (second row) Julia "Jeule" Maurer and Martin Maurer. (Courtesy Suffolk County Parks.)

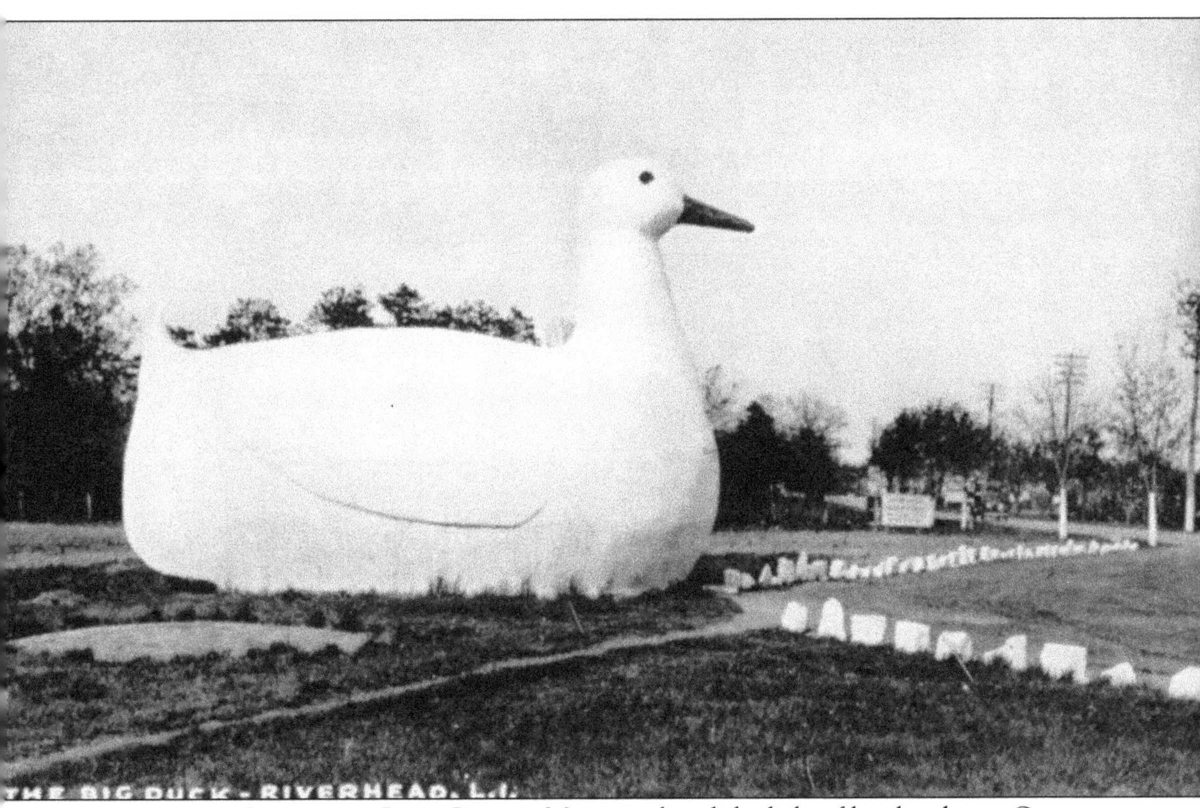

THE BIG DUCK, RIVERHEAD, LONG ISLAND. Maurer enlisted the help of local architect George Reeve of Calverton to design the duck. Reeve asked his wife, Ella, to cook a chicken so that he could study the skeleton of the animal in order to create the plans. Reeve also hired Broadway theater set designer William Collins and his brother Samuel, of Manorville, to construct the wooden framework. They tied a duck to a balcony to study its form. They built a wooden frame on a concrete block foundation and covered it with wire mesh. Then, Smith & Yeager of Riverhead did the masonry. The Big Duck measures 20 feet tall by 30 feet long by 15 feet wide. The interior space measures 165 square feet. It is believed to have cost around $3,800 to build. (Courtesy Collection of Eric Woodward.)

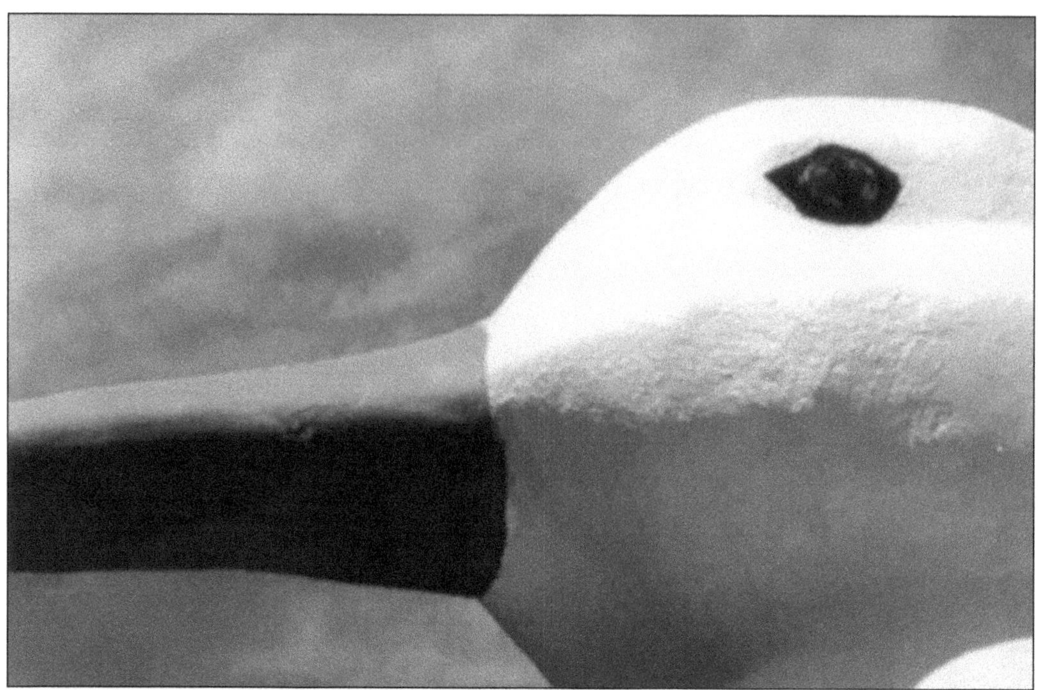

Big Duck's Eyes, Flanders, 2018. When the head was finished, Ford Model T taillights that glowed red were employed for the duck's eyes. It is under debate whose idea it was, but many believe it was the work of former Broadway set designer William Collins. The Ford Model T was produced from 1908 to 1927 and one of the first cars whose assembly line production lowered costs made it affordable to many. By the construction date of the Big Duck, in 1931, the Model T had already been replaced by the improved Ford Model A. (Author's collection.)

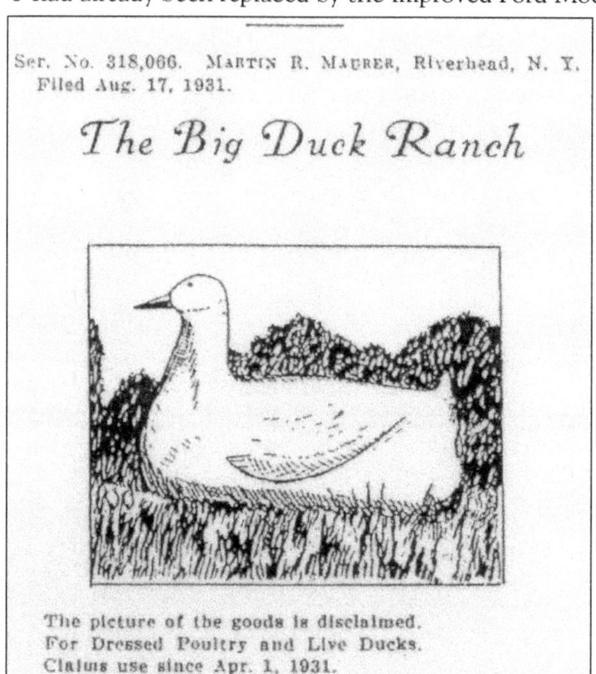

Ser. No. 318,066. Martin R. Maurer, Riverhead, N. Y. Filed Aug. 17, 1931.

The Big Duck Ranch

The picture of the goods is disclaimed. For Dressed Poultry and Live Ducks. Claims use since Apr. 1, 1931.

Big Duck Trademark, 1931. Fearful that someone would steal his idea of a duck-shaped building, Maurer immediately applied for a trademark for the duck in August 1931. The Big Duck Ranch earned a separate trademark in 1932. (Courtesy Suffolk County Parks.)

A Prize Recipe – Potted Duckling

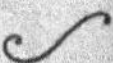

As a change from our roast duckling, try this tempting dish: Singe duck; cut into desired pieces for serving. Wash and dry thoroughly; season with salt and pepper, and roll in flour. Put 1 tablespoon butter in Dutch Oven (or Iron Skillet having a tight cover), and brown carefully. Remove from pot, drain all grease. Replace pieces, sprinkle with 1 tablespoon minced onion and ½ teaspoon thyme. Add 1 cup heavy cream and simmer gently for 1¾ hours, or until tender, with pot tightly covered. Strain gravy and serve hot.

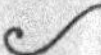

ALL OUR PRODUCTS ARE LABELED WITH OUR TRADE MARK AND SOLD ONLY AT OUR "BIG DUCK"

Allow No One to Claim Them for Sale Elsewhere

THE BIG DUCK

FLANDERS ROAD :: RIVERHEAD, L. I.
Located on Route 24
(State Highway between Riverhead and Hampton Bays)

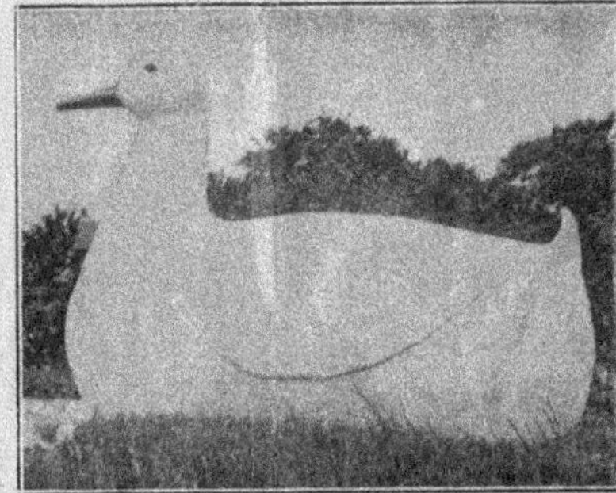

Trade Mark Registered
U. S. Pat. Off.

FRESHLY KILLED DUCKLINGS - BROILERS
FRYERS - YOUNG ROASTERS

Dressed Ready for the Oven — *Our Specialty*

Phone: Riverhead 2831

BIG DUCK BROCHURE, C. 1936. Maurer capitalized on all the attention garnered by the Big Duck and marketed it fiercely. He consistently ran newspaper advertisements announcing its annual opening every March and touting its modern and sanitary facilities and printed brochures with recipes for duck dinners (illustrated here.) It was featured in a 1931 Atlas Cement calendar, in *Popular Mechanics* magazine in 1932, and as a mascot for Drake's Cakes for the World's Fair in Flushing in 1939. (Courtesy Linda Apsey, Suffolk County Parks.)

OUR PRIME DUCKLING

As We Roast It at the BIG DUCK and Our Favorite Dressing

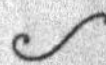

Singe, wash and drain duck thoroughly, standing it on end. Meanwhile take half a loaf of white bread, slice and soak for an instant in water, then squeeze as dry as possible. Put in mixing bowl, adding two beaten eggs. Through food chopper put one small green pepper, five pieces of celery, and giblets. Add to bread, together with two tablespoons finely cut parsley, one teaspoon poultry seasoning, and salt and pepper to taste. Into your frying pan put three tablespoons butter, add an onion cut fine. Brown for a few minutes, then add bread mixture. Cook for about ten minutes, turning occasionally.

Stuff duck, dry and salt outer skin and sprinkle lightly with paprika. Tie legs and wings close to the body and place breast down in open roaster. Put into hot oven, 475 degrees, for one hour. Drain most of the grease and in its place add one cup hot water. Turn duck on its back and continue roasting for one and a half hours longer, lowering temperature to 400 degrees. Baste every twenty minutes during this last period. Remove duck from pan, thicken gravy and serve with apple sauce.

Time for roasting based on 6-pound duck. Heavier duck requires longer roasting period.

NOTE—Ducks require a hot oven and should not be roasted as chicken. They are best when roasted in an uncovered roasting pan.

OUR FAVORITE BROILER RECIPE:

Wash, dry, quarter and fry in heavy skillet with four tablespoons butter until golden brown. Season with salt and pepper and onion salt, then cover and let steam for about forty minutes — according to size. (Do not add water.) Remove pieces from pan, add one-half cup cream or top milk, stirring thoroly. Pour hot over broiler.

TO BROIL:

Cut chicken in half, wash and dry. Spread inside liberally with butter, and put in pan of broiler — not on rack. Set thermostat at 450, brown chicken 15 minutes, keeping two inches from flame. Turn, and after 10 minutes, or when chicken starts to brown, add one-half cup hot water. Baste three times at five-minute intervals, add salt and pepper and remove from oven.

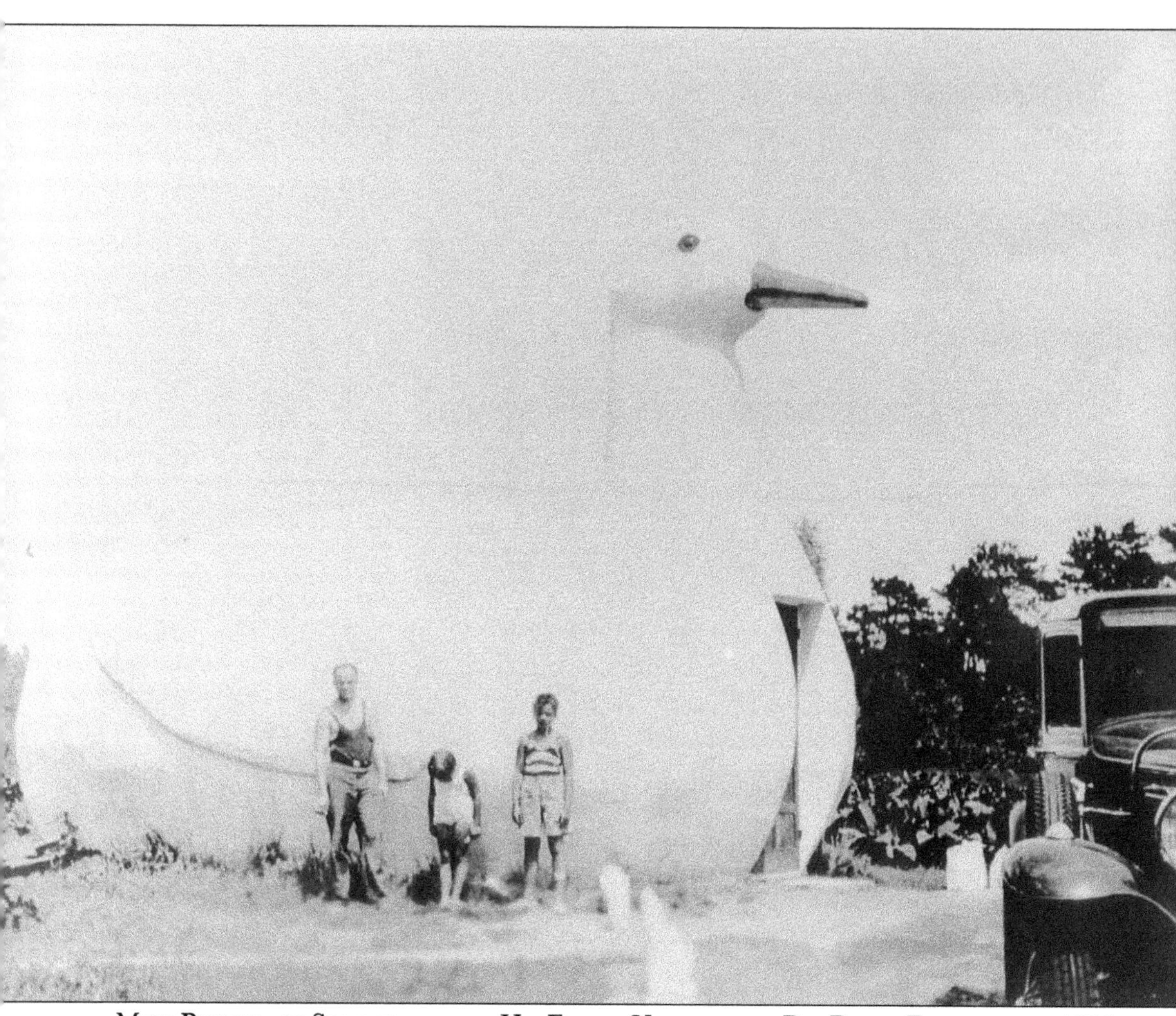

Mike Reuter, of Southold, with His Family Visiting the Big Duck, Flanders, c. 1936. The Big Duck was completed in June 1931, and, unsurprisingly, it did not go unnoticed. The same month, an article in the *Riverhead News* stated, "Motorists passing through Riverhead now have something else quite distinctive to remember us by; it is the big duck on the Maurer ranch in Upper Mills . . . it is the biggest duck ever 'raised' anywhere in the world." Maurer's marketing plan worked, and he grew successful enough that he purchased his own farm on Route 24 in Flanders in 1936 and took the Big Duck with him. Maurer raised ducks there until he retired to Florida in 1952. (Courtesy Mike Reuter, Suffolk County Parks.)

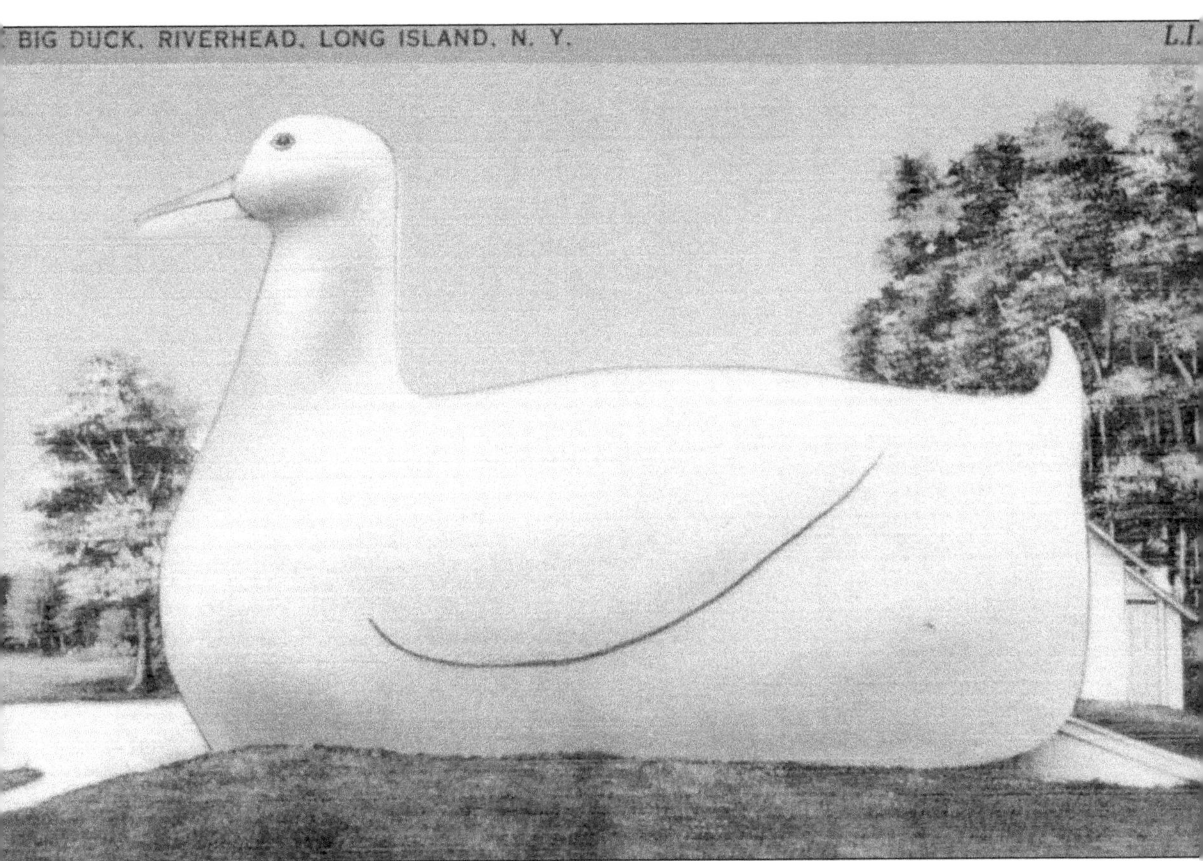

BIG DUCK POSTCARD. Soon after its construction, the Big Duck became a popular postcard subject for those who visited Long Island. Many commented on the large amount of ducks and duck farms seen on the East End. (Courtesy Collection of Eric Woodward.)

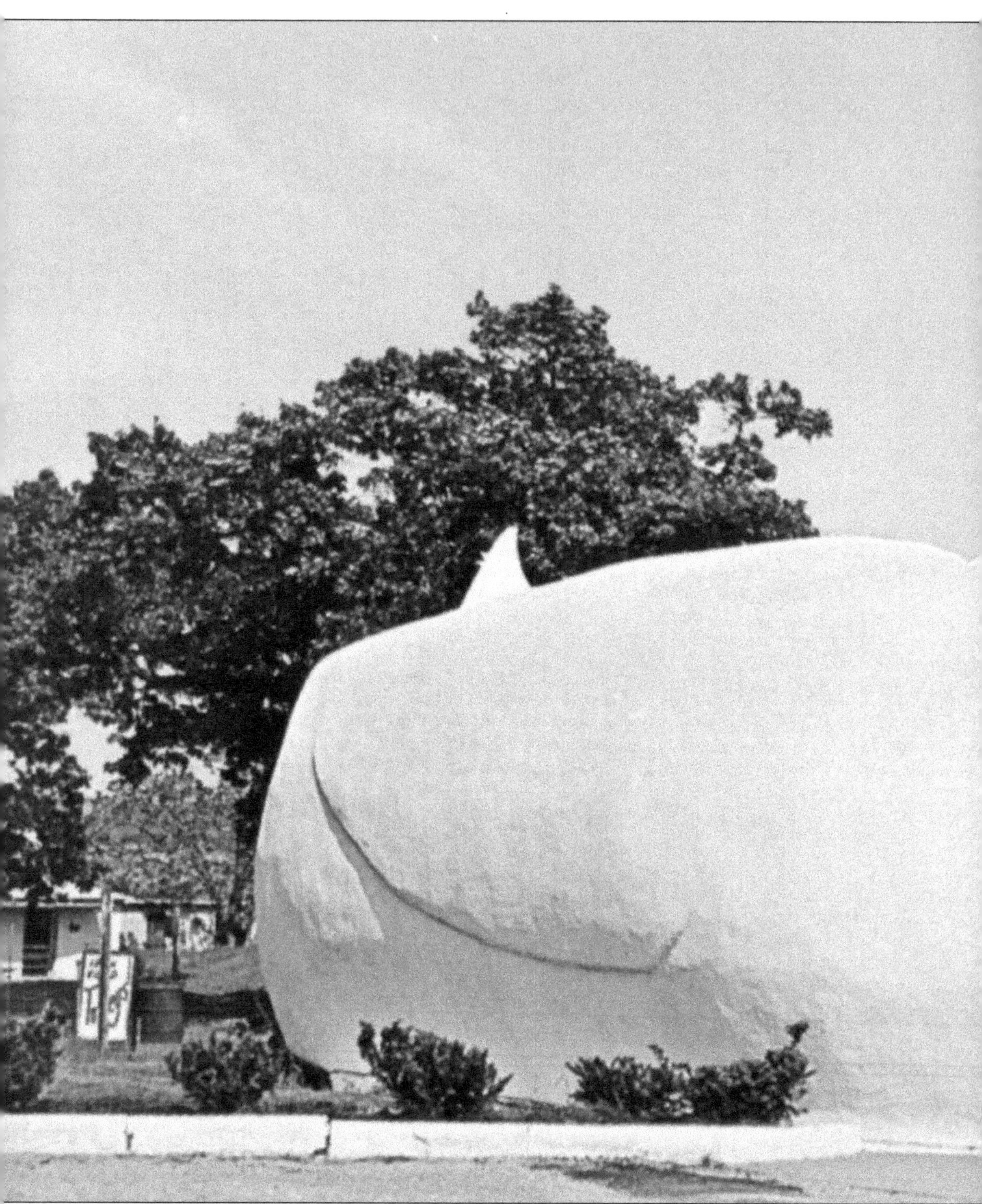

Big Duck Postcard, 1950s. Due to its highly unusual shape and prominence on Route 24 in Flanders (which was once the main thoroughfare out to the Hamptons), the Big Duck also became a landmark from which travelers gauged the arrival time to their destination. Motorists, especially

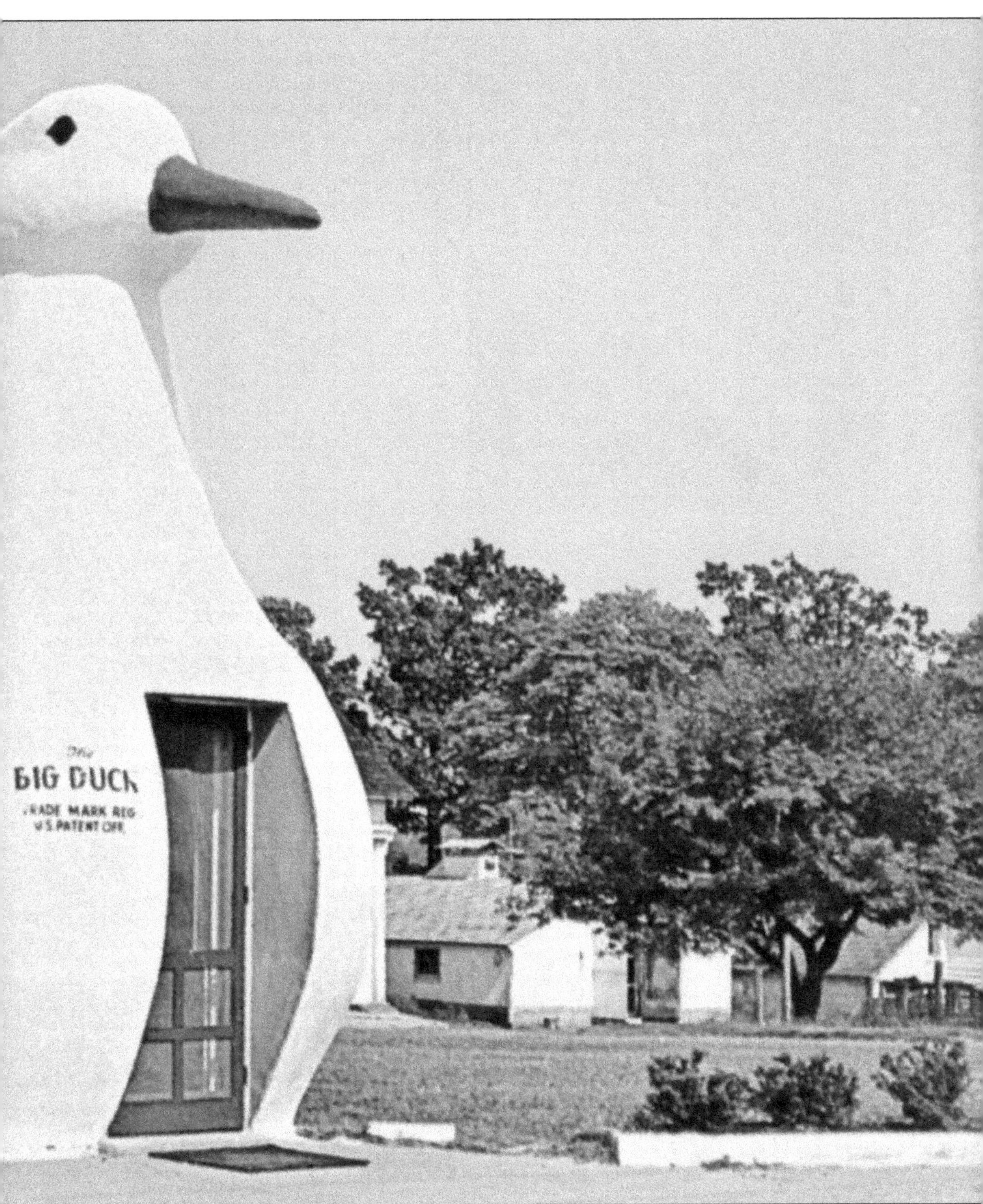

children, would strain to see the Big Duck out of their car windows, as it would help answer the age-old question, "Are we there yet?" (Courtesy Collection of Eric Woodward.)

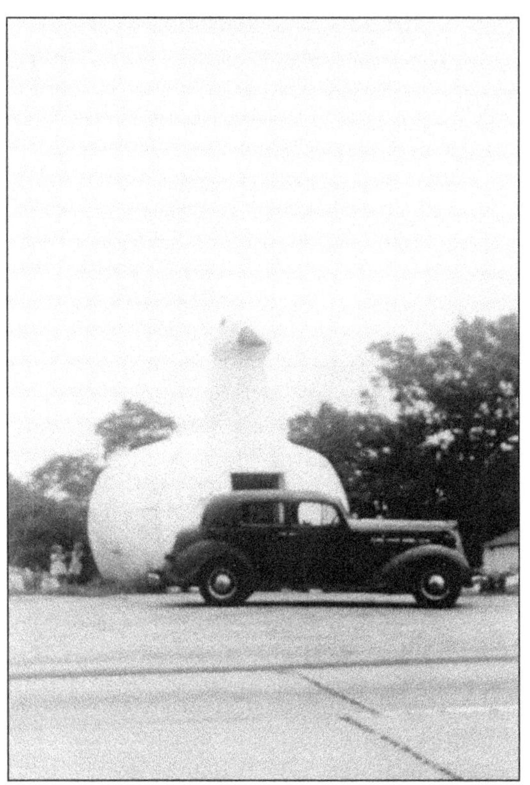

Car in Front of Big Duck, c. 1953. The Desson family bought the farm from Martin Maurer in 1951 and owned it until 1971. Here, they raised mostly chickens, sourcing the ducks that they sold from Crescent Duck Farm in Aquebogue. Customers would drive up directly in front of the door to get their poultry. (Courtesy Leonard Desson.)

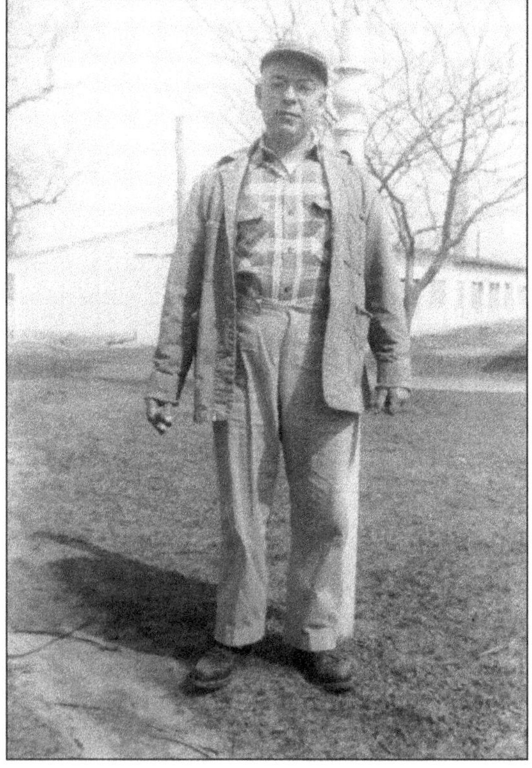

Leonard Desson Sr. Leonard Desson Sr. often had a cigar in his hand. According to his son Leonard Desson Jr., he lived through World War I, the Great Depression, and World War II, so he learned how to be frugal. He was always searching for a way to improve his product, and he never raised prices once during his 20-year tenure at the farm. (Courtesy Leonard Desson.)

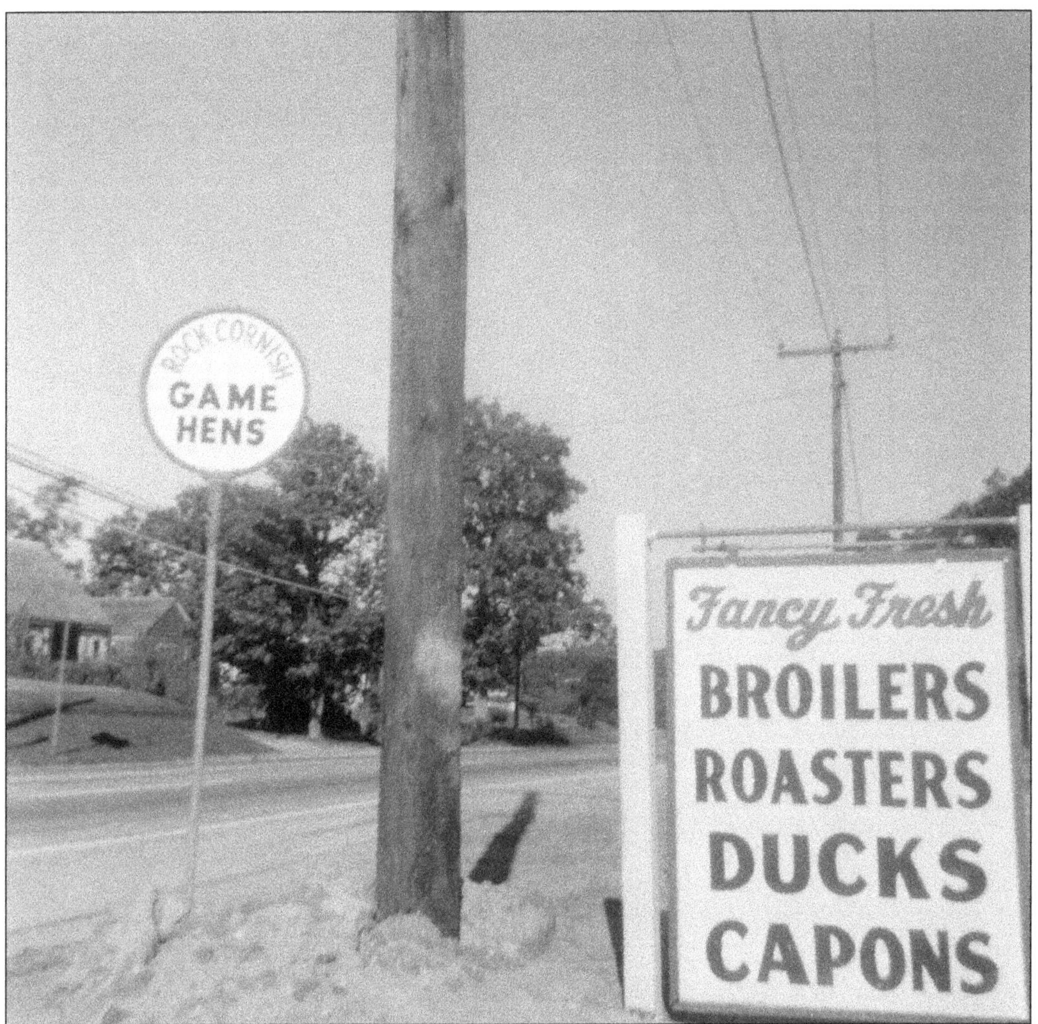

Roadside Signs, Route 24, Flanders, c. 1960s. These were the two signs advertising the shop on the main road on the way to the Hamptons. The Dessons sold broilers, roasters, ducks, capons, and eggs (when they were available). Never one to throw anything out, Leonard Desson Sr. repurposed the "Rock Cornish Game Hens" sign from an old Gulf Oil sign. (Courtesy Leonard Desson.)

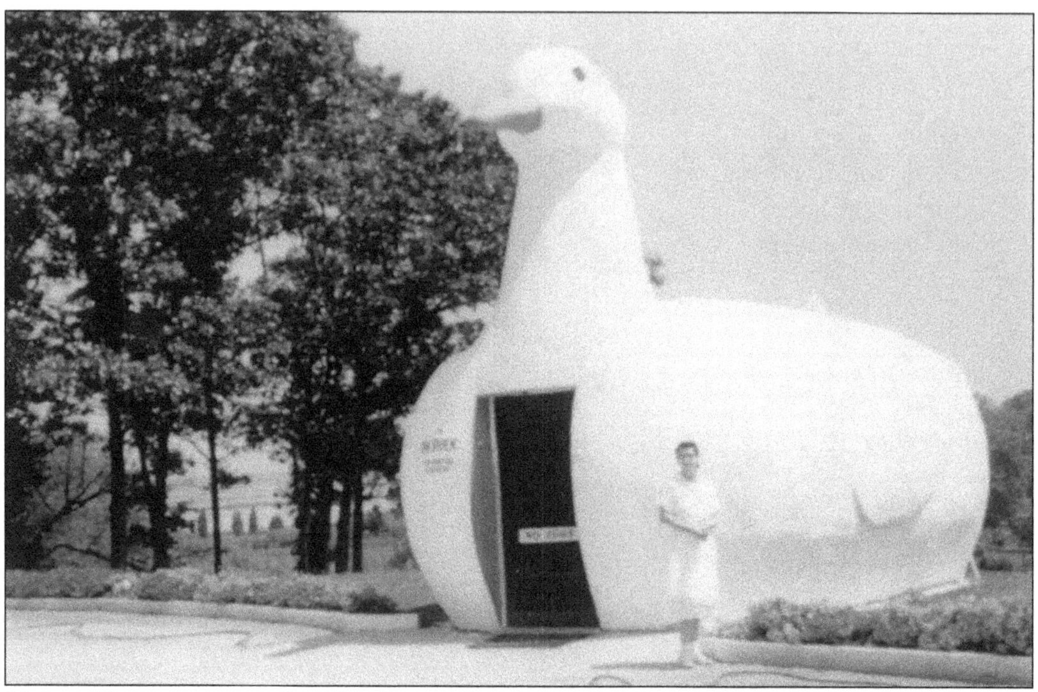

Maude Desson at the Big Duck with Peconic Bay, July 1962. Maude Desson worked from 8:00 a.m. to 8:00 p.m., 84 hours a week, from the third Friday in March to the day before Thanksgiving. The black air hoses in the foreground would buzz in the farmhouse when a car drove over them to alert them that the customers were there. At first, there were white rocks on the border between the grass and drive, but Leonard Desson Sr. eventually replaced it with a white concrete edge. The border was edged with red and white petunias every year. Maude would walk the dirt path to the farmhouse until Leonard Sr. made a concrete path for her as a surprise, but it was too hard on her knees. (Courtesy Leonard Desson.)

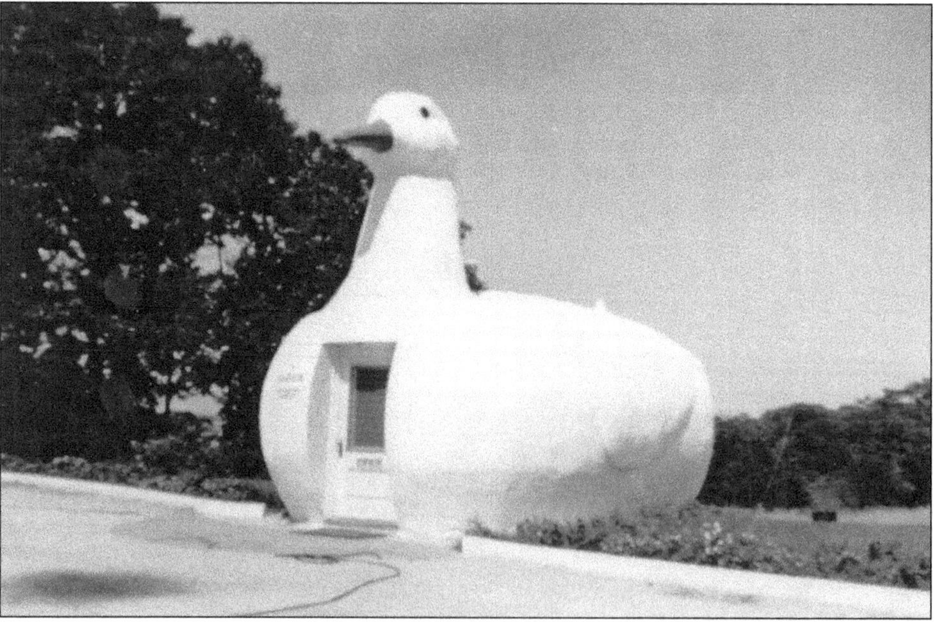

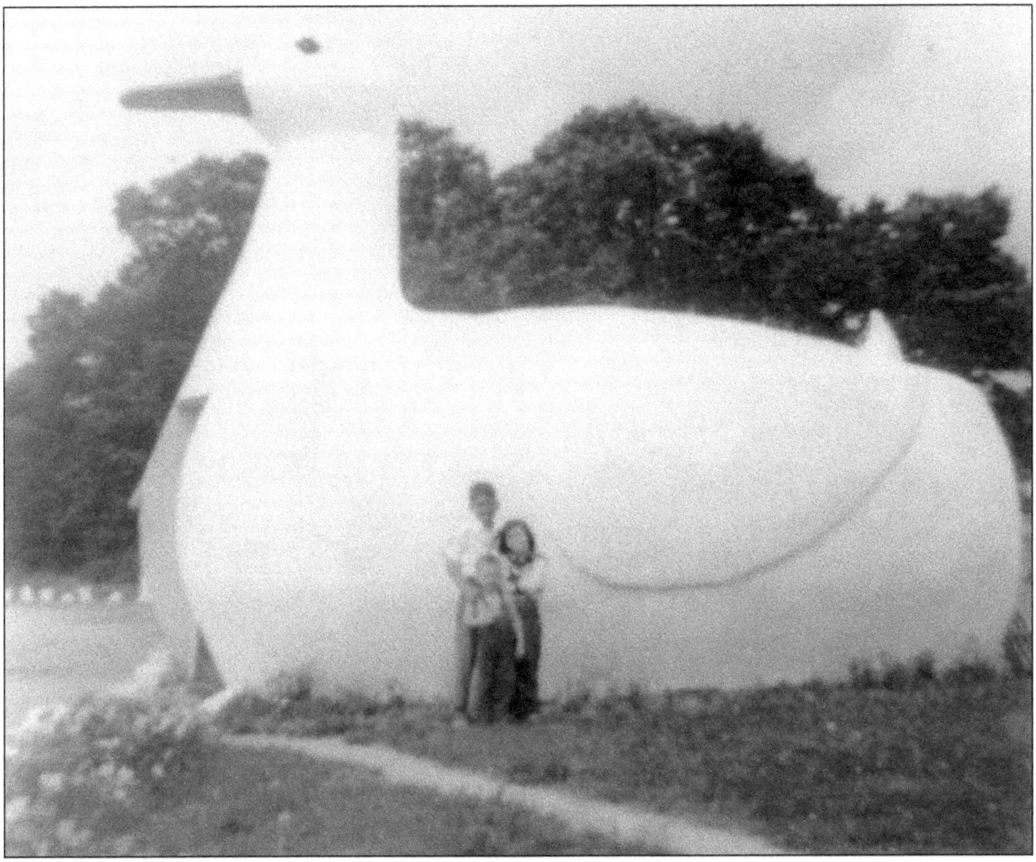

Len and Carolyn Desson with Cousin Lou at the Big Duck, c. 1953. The family often enjoyed posing in front of the shop to take pictures. (Courtesy Leonard Desson.)

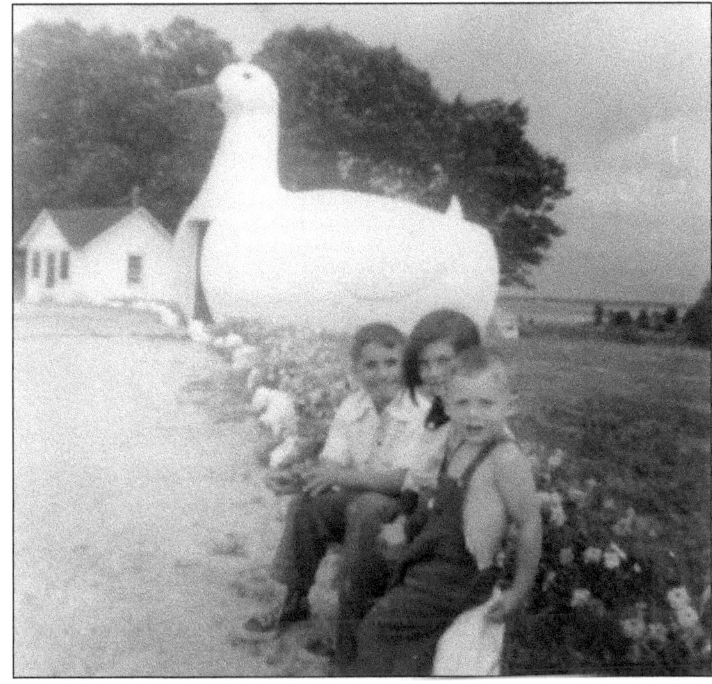

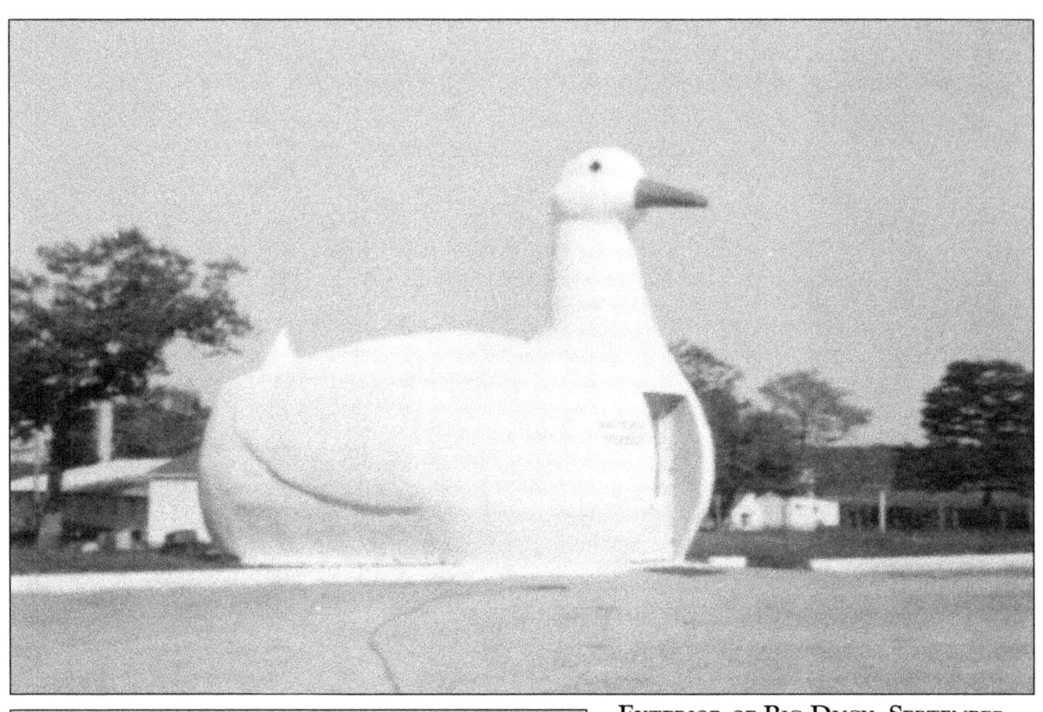

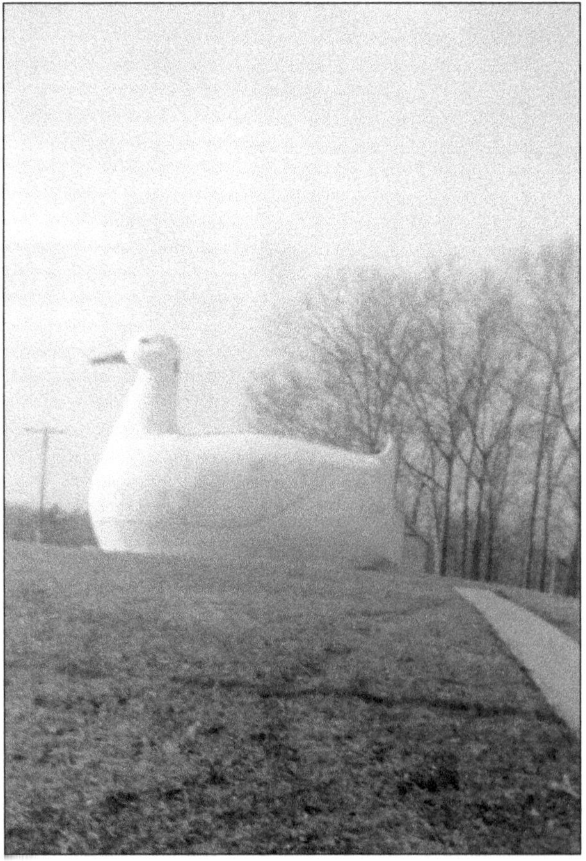

Exterior of Big Duck, September 1958. Under the Dessons' ownership, every five years, the duck was wire brushed by hand and then professionally repainted, except for the orange beak and eyes, which were painted by Leonard Desson Sr. (Courtesy Leonard Desson.)

Back of the Duck, c. 1958. The square opening in the back of the duck's neck provided access to change the lightbulbs for the duck's glowing red eyes. (Courtesy Leonard Desson.)

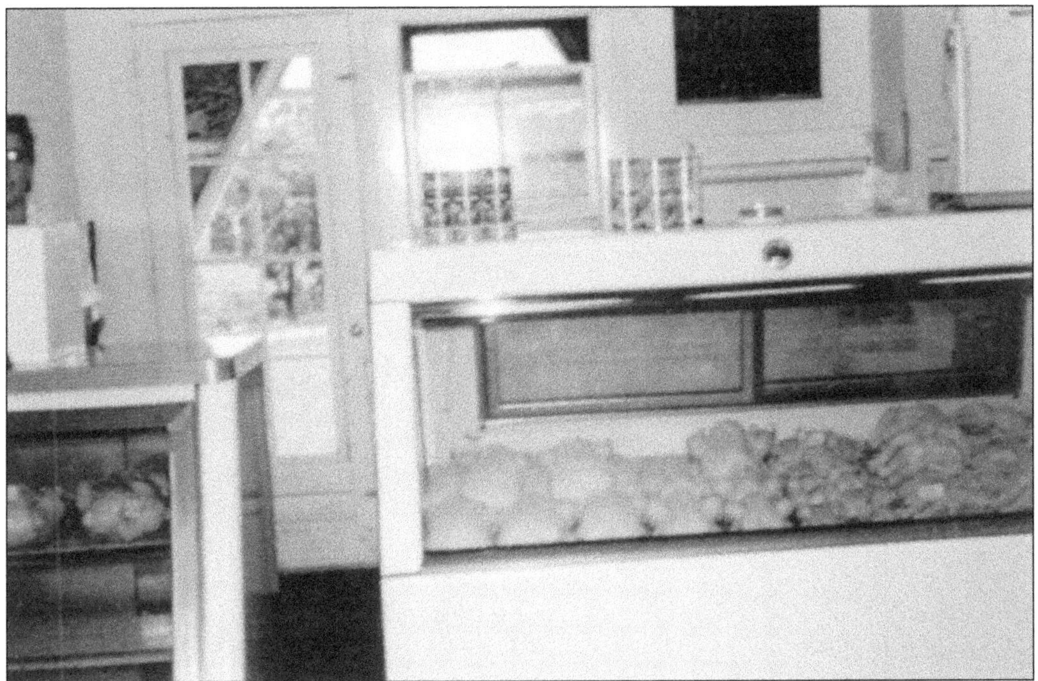

Maude Desson behind the Counter inside the Big Duck, July 1962. Like the Maurers, the Dessons also used the Big Duck as a shop, with Maude as the counter help. The largest refrigerated case held ducks, capons, roasters, Cornish game hens, and broilers. They were pre-weighed and tagged with a scale nearby that was required by law if the customers wanted to see the weight themselves. Then Maude would wrap them up in wax paper (seen behind her) and tie them with string. (Courtesy Leonard Desson.)

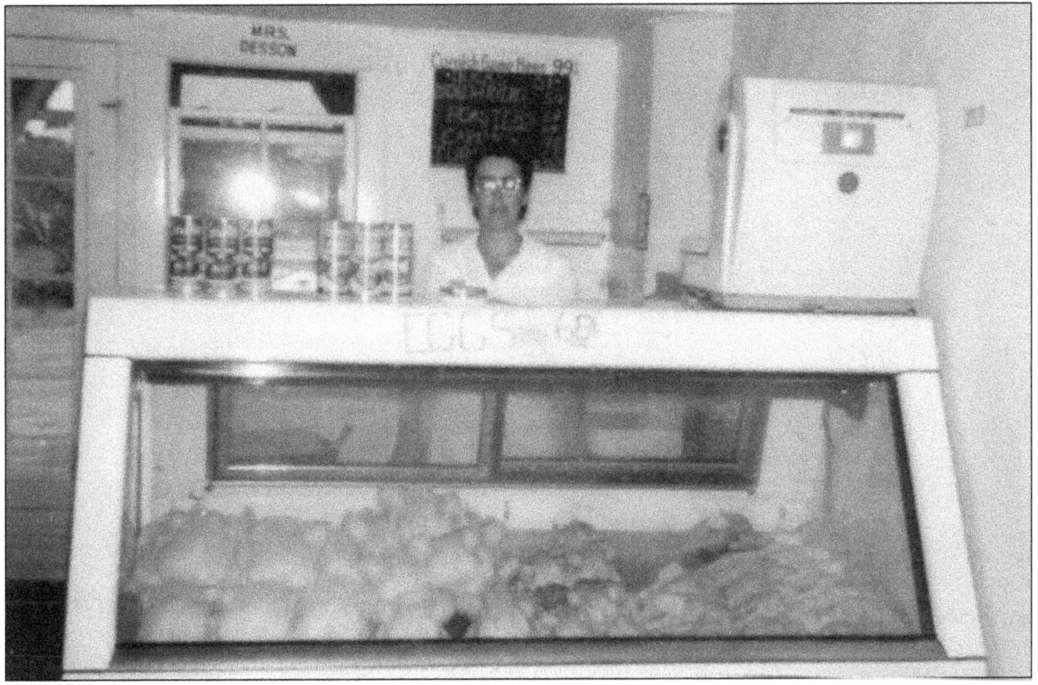

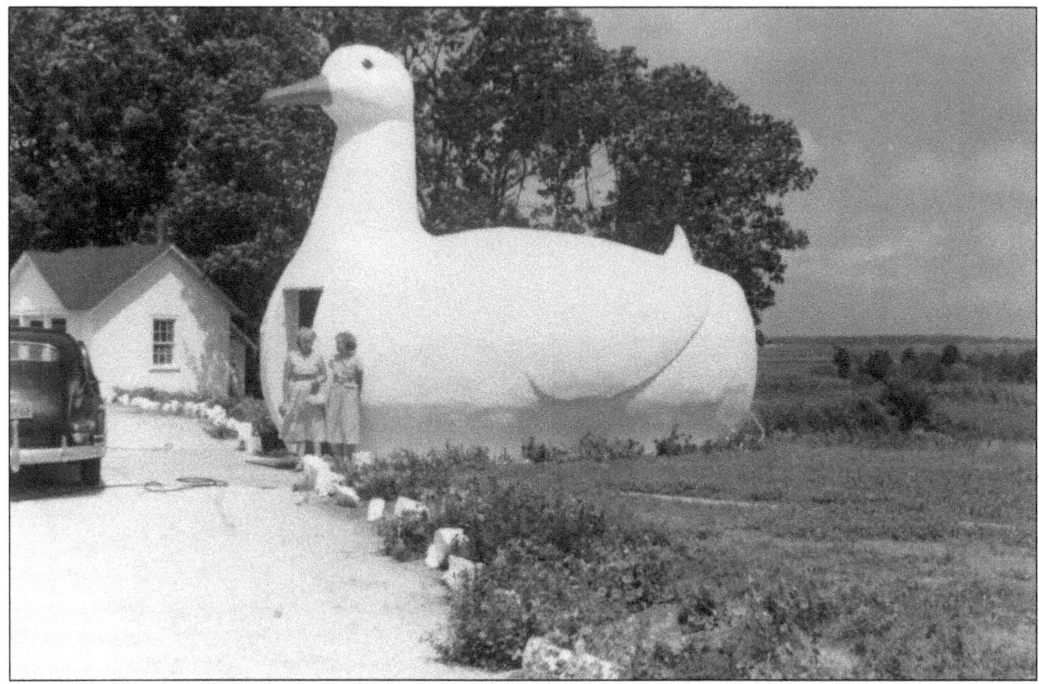

TWO FEMALE SHOPPERS OUTSIDE THE BIG DUCK, C. 1960S. Through the years, Maude Desson waited on Hattie Yastrzemski (Carl Yastrzemski's mother), journalist Alistair Cooke, and *New York Times* food critic Craig Claiborne. (Courtesy Leonard Desson.)

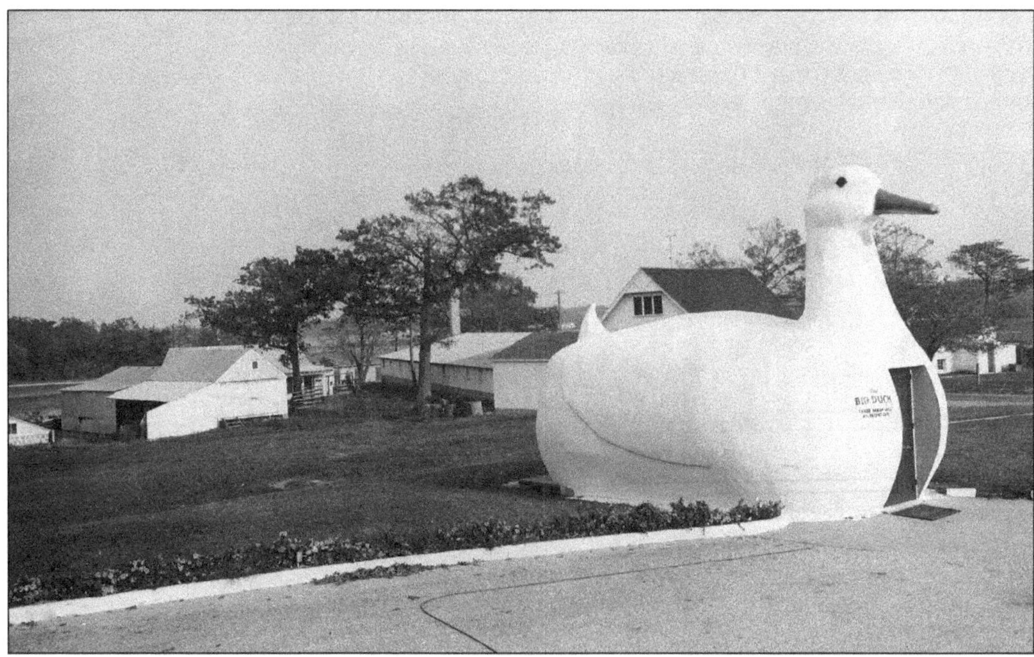

FARM BUILDINGS, BIG DUCK, FLANDERS, C. 1962. Buildings on the property, some of which were numbered, included the farmhouse; the manure house; the toolshed with attached garage; the rooster house; Nos. 1, 2, and 3 for housing the young stock; No. 6 for the broilers; the garden house; the battery house; and the killing room. (Courtesy Leonard Desson.)

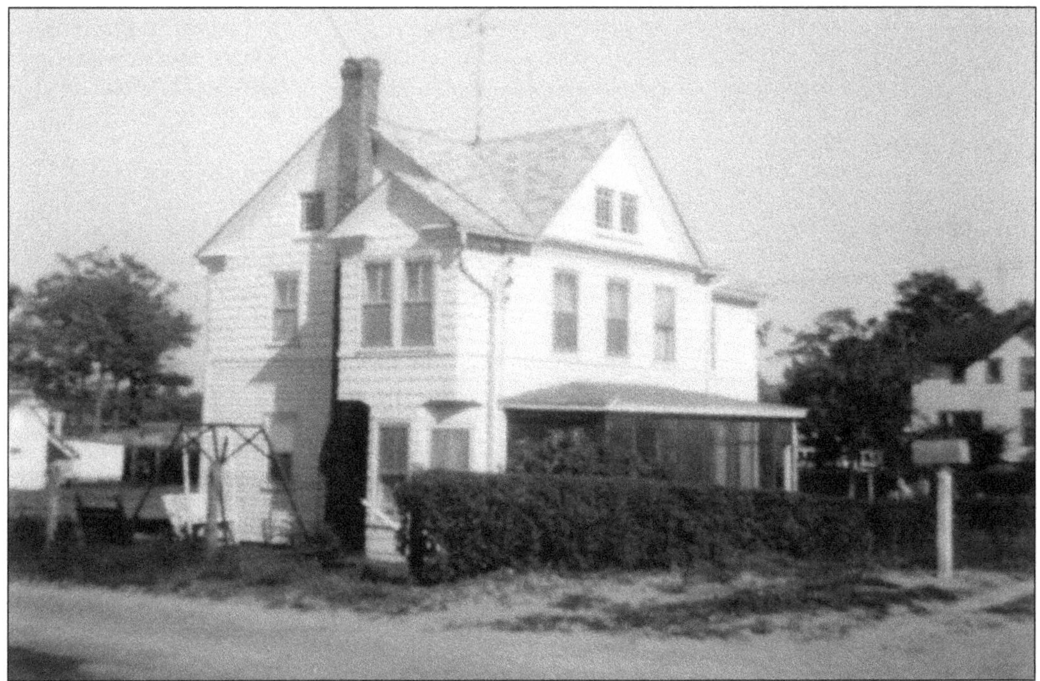

FRONT OF FARMHOUSE, BIG DUCK RANCH, FLANDERS, C. 1963. The farmhouse was surrounded by a glider swing, clothesline, and varieties of fruit trees including apple, peach, pear, and grape. The Dessons took pride in the fancy attic grille windows. (Courtesy Leonard Desson.)

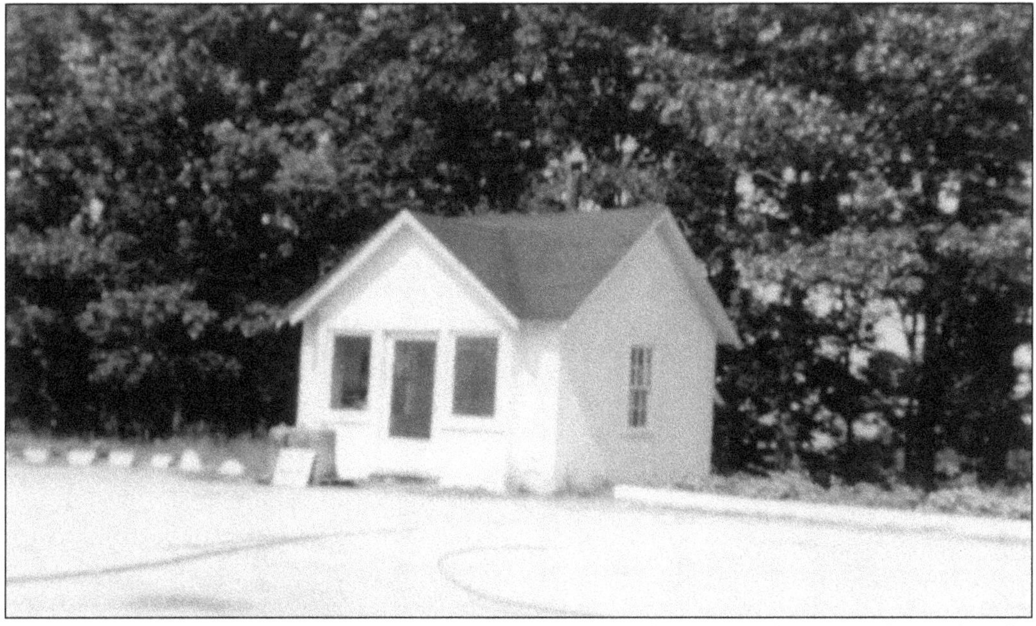

MANURE HOUSE, BIG DUCK RANCH, FLANDERS, C. 1962. The manure house was located to the left of the Big Duck. Before 1957, this building held feedbags and feed trains would deliver the feed throughout the farm from this building. After 1957, at the end of the season, the litter beds would be brushed of feathers and bedding to reveal the manure underneath. They would shovel it into 75-pound bags and sell it for a $1 a bag (see bags to the left). (Courtesy Leonard Desson.)

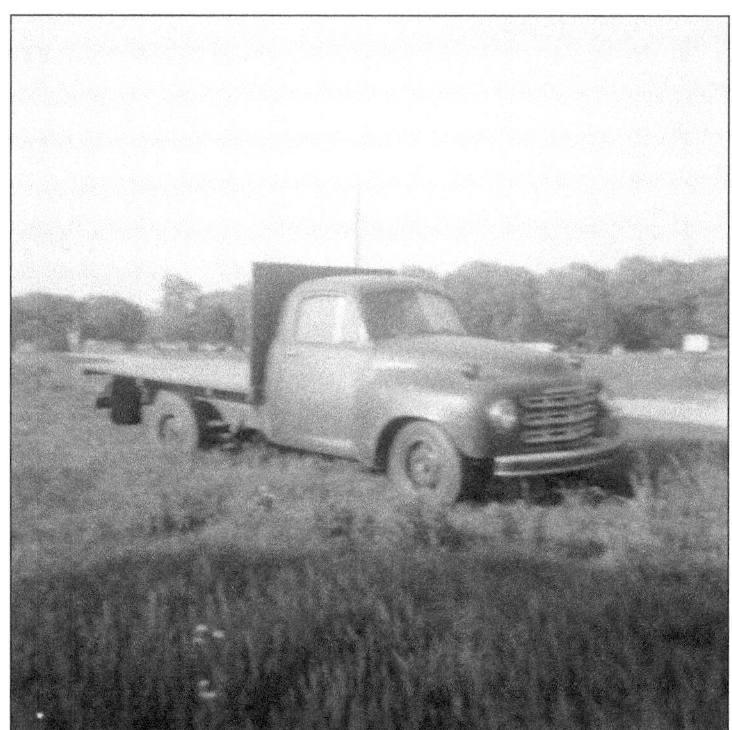

Studebaker Platform Truck from 1949, c. 1960s. The Dessons would use this truck to carry crates of live chickens to the killing room. The road featured here led down to the Flanders Men's Club. (Courtesy Leonard Desson.)

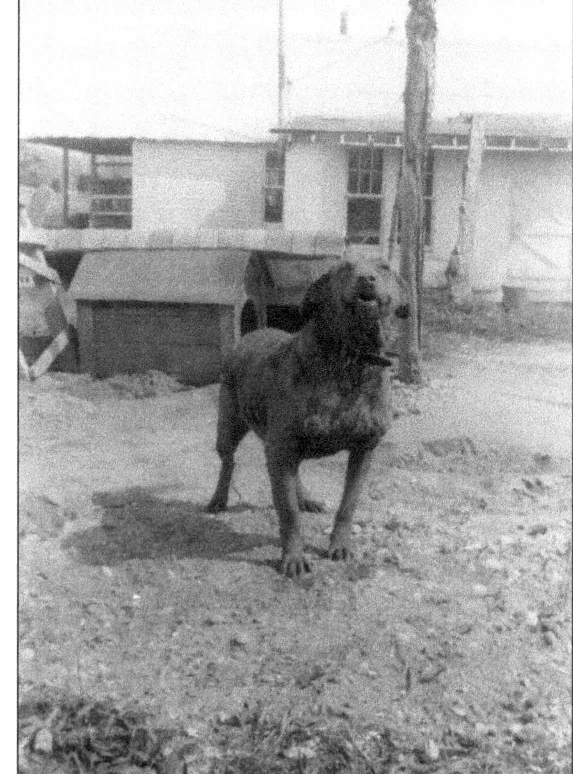

Queenie, the Dessons' Dog. Queenie was a short–curly hair Chesapeake retriever who came with the sale of the farm. Leonard Desson Sr. fashioned the extended roof of the doghouse in the background to give Queenie more shade in the summer. (Courtesy Leonard Desson.)

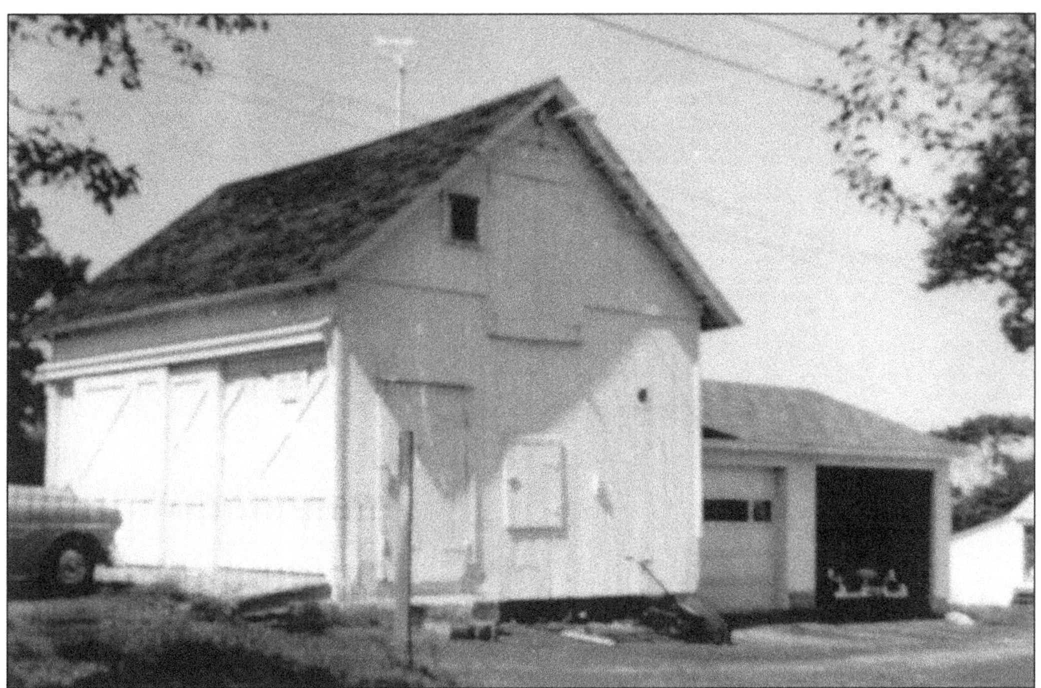

Tool Shed and Garages, Big Duck Ranch, Flanders, 1958. Leonard Desson Sr. relied heavily on the white weather vane on top of the tool shed to adjust the opening and closing of all the building's windows three times a day to regulate the temperature of the rooms for the livestock. (Courtesy Leonard Desson.)

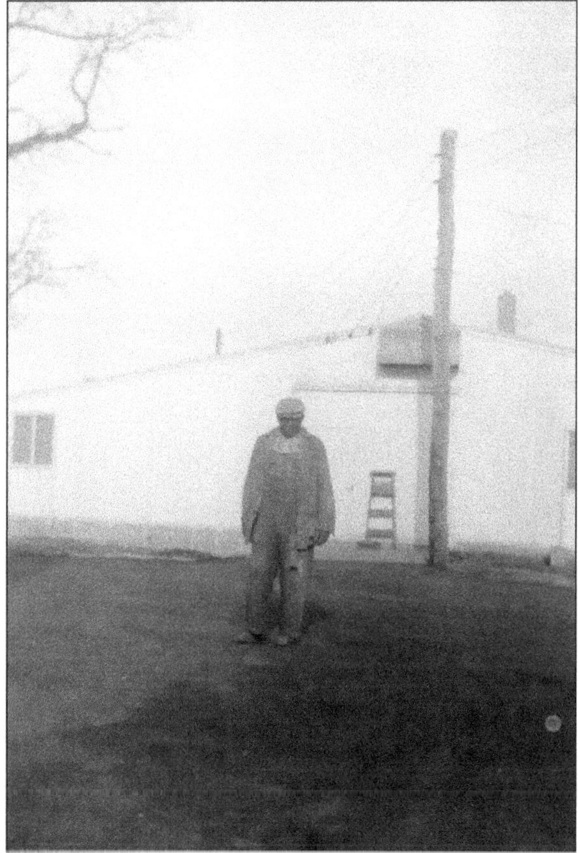

John Booker in Front of Building No. 3, c. 1958. John Booker fed and cleaned the waterers in the buildings. His son Frank also worked at the farm. (Courtesy Leonard Desson.)

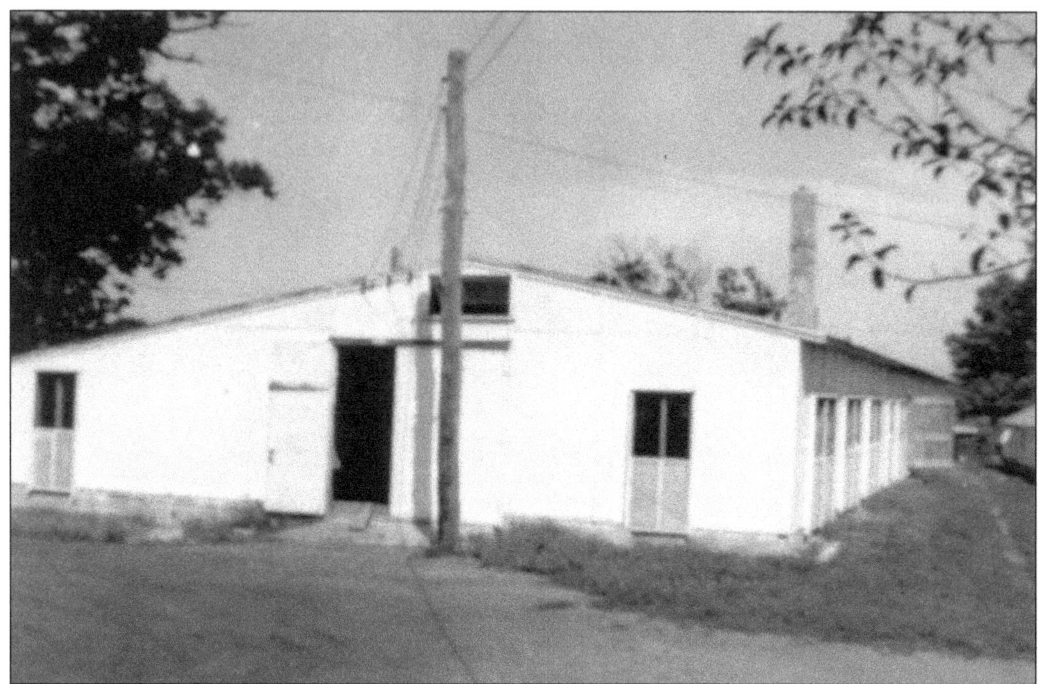

Building No. 3, Big Duck Ranch, Flanders, c. 1962. This was the largest building on the grounds—a three-room structure. Broilers would be kept in here at about seven weeks old, weighing about two to two and a half pounds. (Courtesy Leonard Desson.)

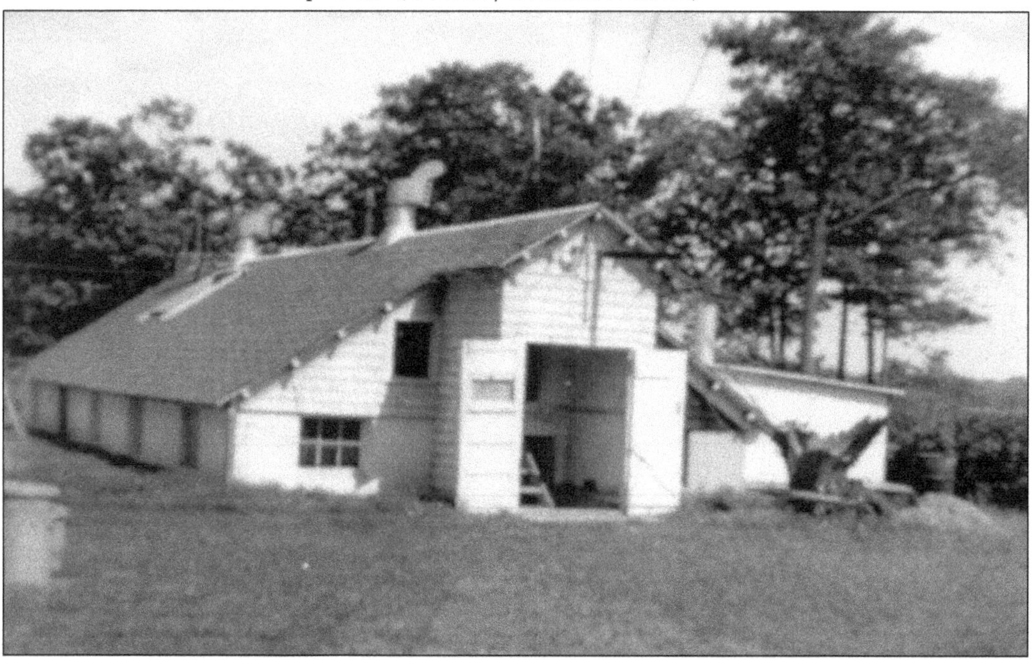

The Battery Room, Big Duck Ranch, Flanders, 1958. Baby chicks started out here in "batteries," or cells with feed on one side and water on the other. The floor was dug around 10 inches down to maintain a more consistent temperature. Attached on the far right was the generator shed with coal bin. (Courtesy Leonard Desson.)

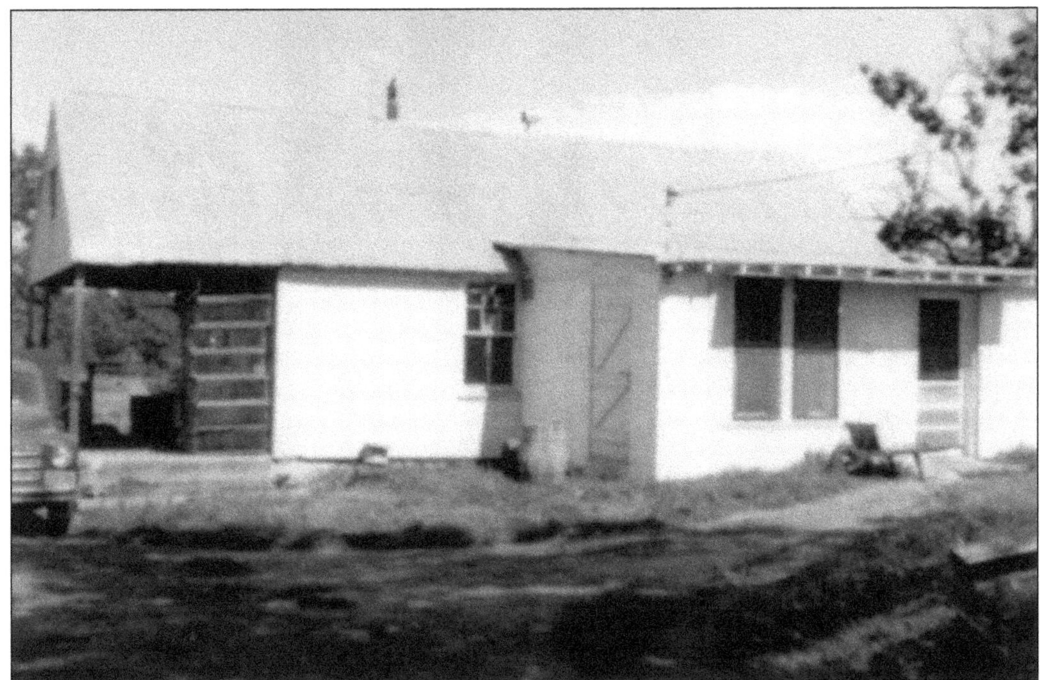

THE KILLING ROOM, BIG DUCK RANCH, FLANDERS, 1958. Chickens were killed Monday, Wednesday, and Friday and were cleaned Tuesday, Thursday, and Saturday. The wheelbarrow outside was used to cart the cleaned baskets of chickens from the refrigerator to the Big Duck to sell. The stacked chicken crates were used to carry the live chickens. (Courtesy Leonard Desson.)

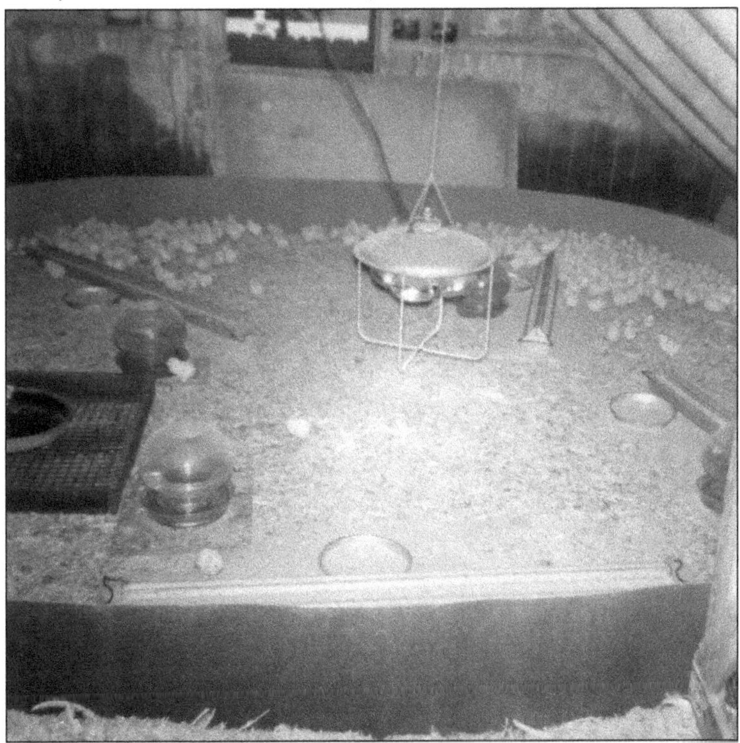

CORNISH GAME HENS ABOVE THE KILLING ROOM, C. 1958. The hens were enclosed by a cardboard circle to keep them close to their water, food, and heat. The bedding used in all buildings was shredded sugar cane. (Courtesy Leonard Desson.)

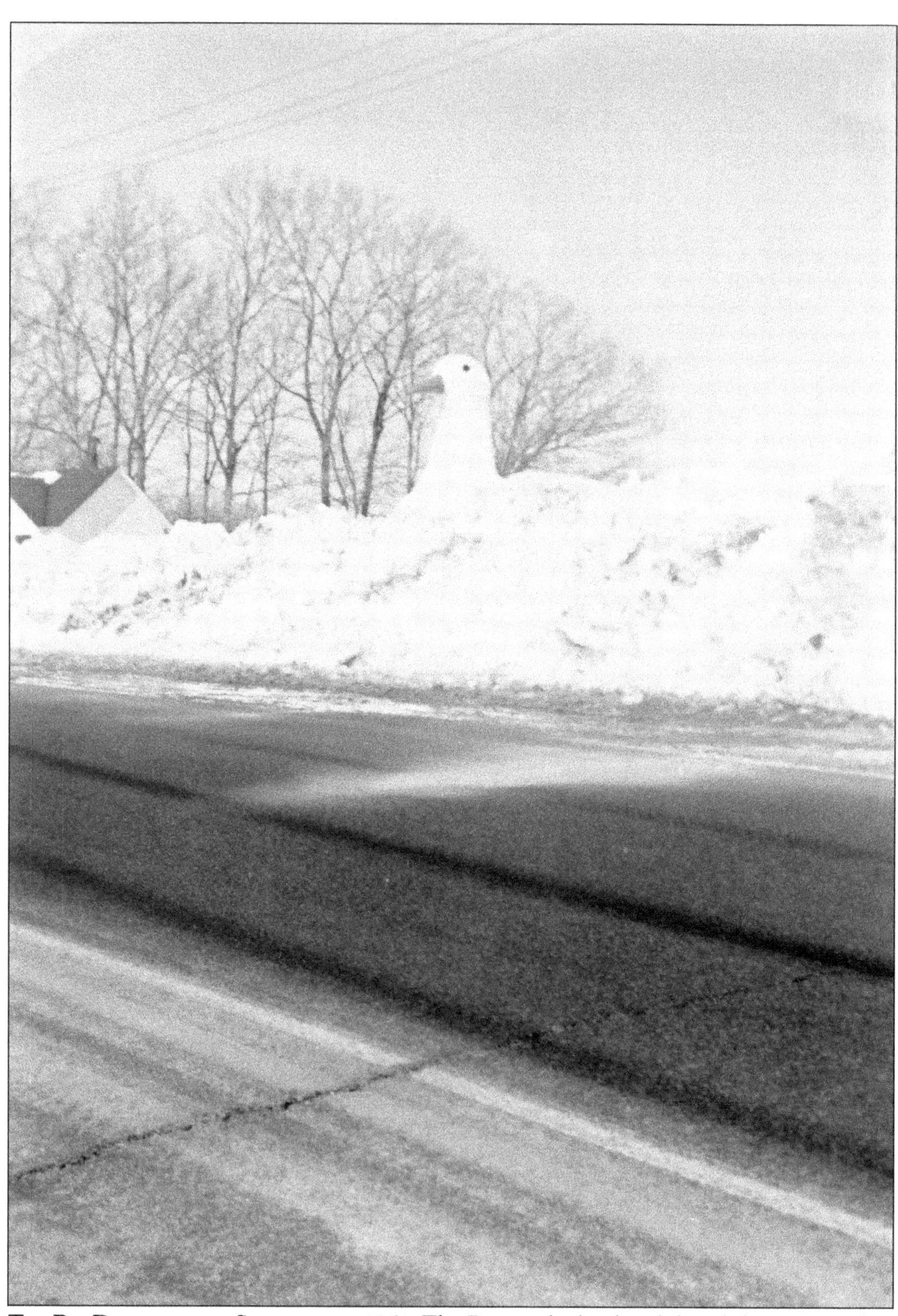

The Big Duck after a Snowstorm, 1961. The Dessons had to hand shovel the snow, as they did not have snowplows or a snow blower at this point. (Courtesy Leonard Desson.)

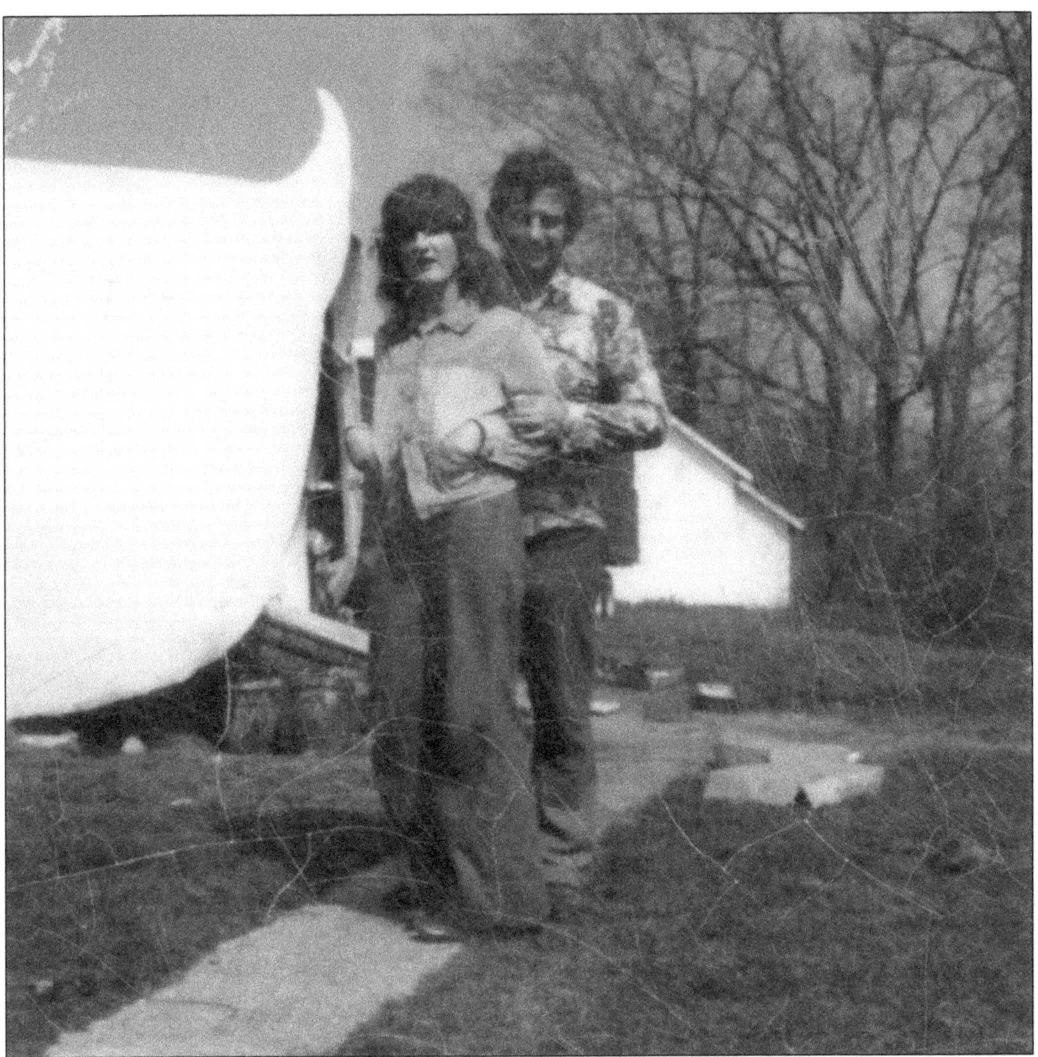

Jean and Mario Colombo in Front of the Big Duck, 1972. Jean (left) and Mario Colombo (right) purchased the Big Duck and Big Duck Ranch from the Dessons in 1971. Mario came from a cooking background and worked as a cook at the Ambassador Inn. They raised mostly chickens with a few turkeys, sheep, Muscovy ducks, and pigs and continued to operate the Big Duck, a shop where they sold rotisserie chickens. They made the building once known as the "tool shed" into an antique shop. They also transformed the building previously known as the "manure house" into a sandwich shop, followed by a "gingerbread house" that sold cookies. (Courtesy Dean Colombo.)

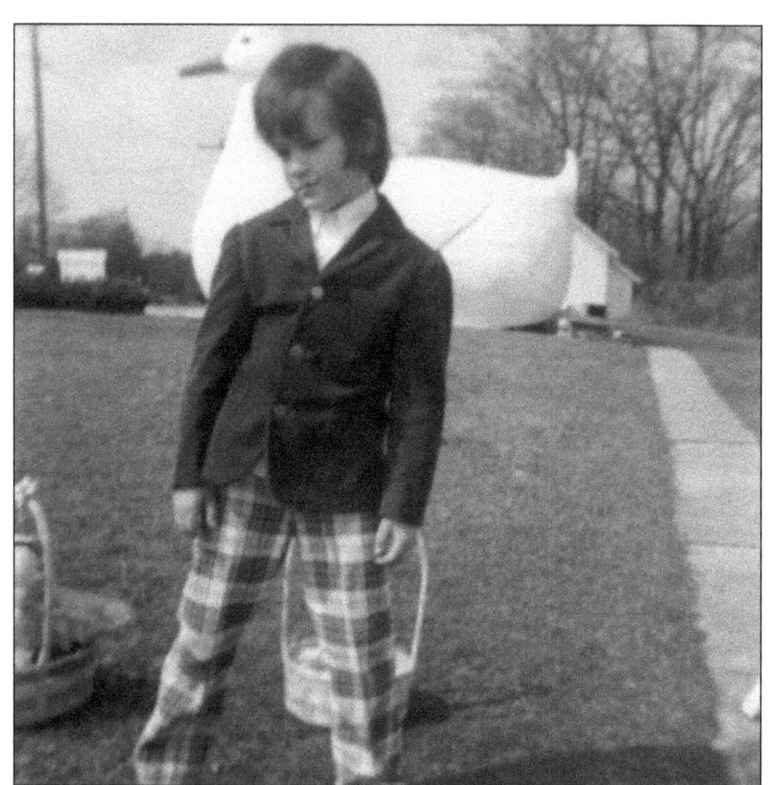

Dean and Denise Colombo, c. 1976. The Colombos had two children: Dean and Denise. Here, they posed in front of the Big Duck on Easter Sunday. (Courtesy Dean Colombo.)

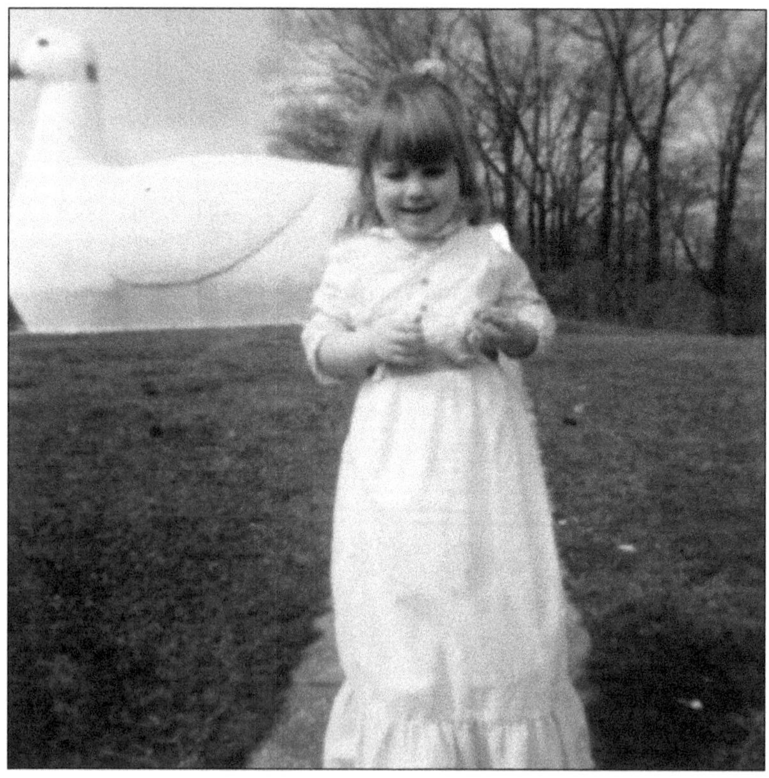

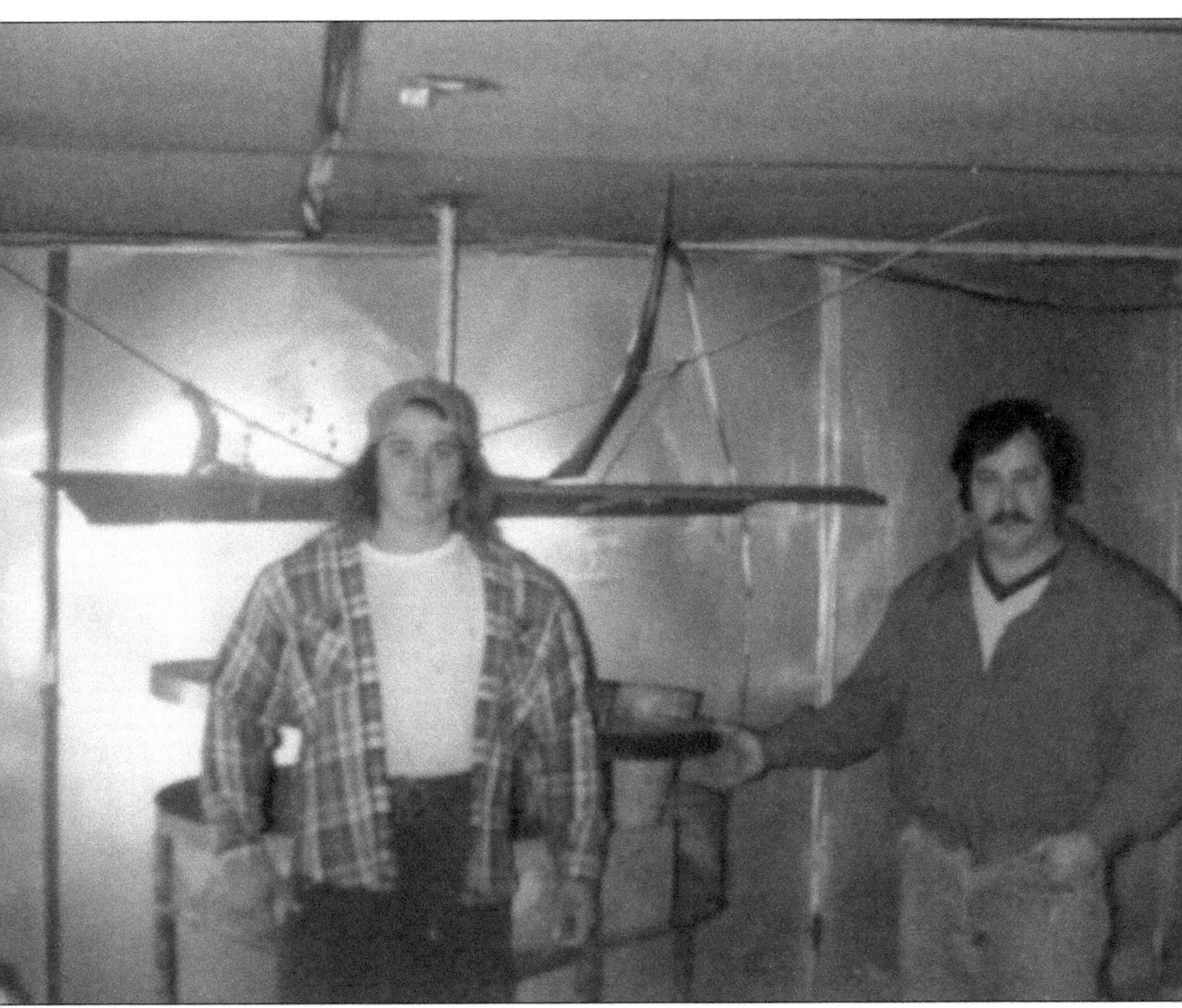

DEAN COLOMBO AND GLYNN GILLY GOSS IN THE KILLING ROOM (LEFT TO RIGHT). The Colombos would stick the chicken upside-down in the metal contraption in the background. They would cut the jugular, and the stock would bleed out into the circular bin underneath. (Courtesy Dean Colombo.)

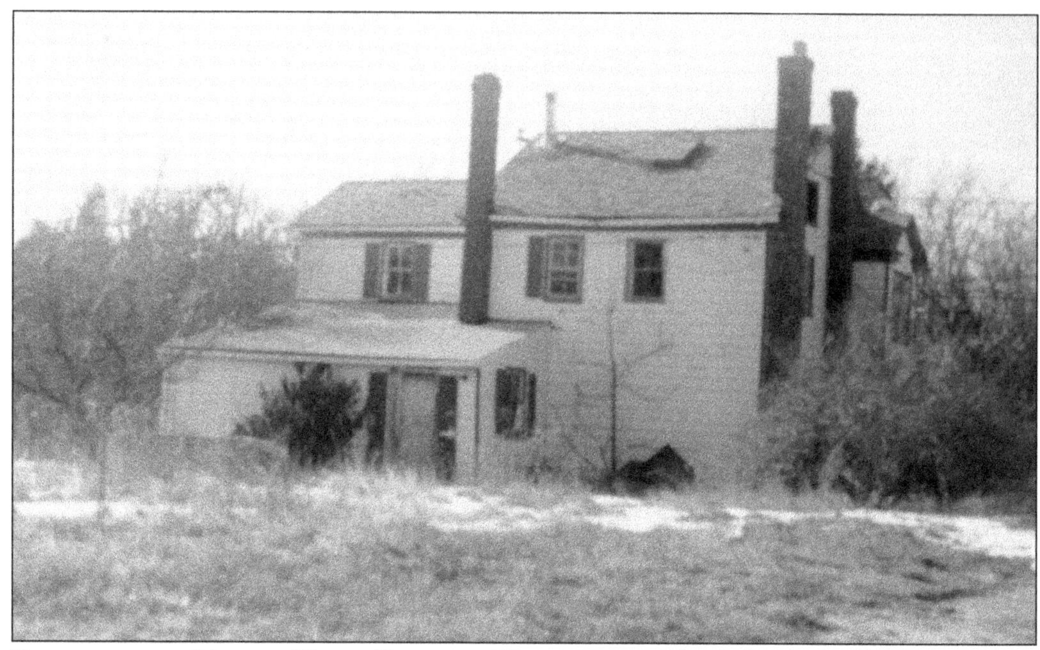

Farmhouse and Manure House/Sandwich Shop, c. 1987. The Colombos sold the property in 1982 to Kia and Pouran Eshghi, a couple who had emigrated to the United States from Iran in 1962. Kia, an accomplished sculptor and painter, and his wife, Pouran, hoped to transform the land into an artists' residence; however, the permits never materialized and the fate of the Big Duck became unclear. The farm sat unused from 1984 to 1987; in that time, the property became quite neglected and run down. (Courtesy Dean Colombo.)

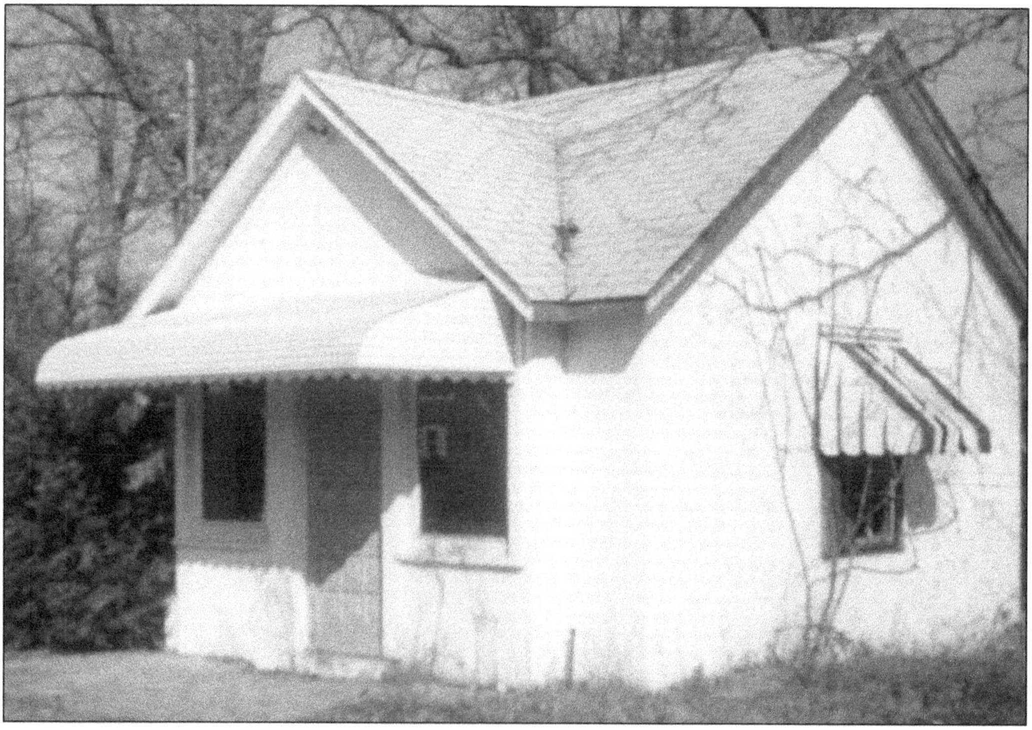

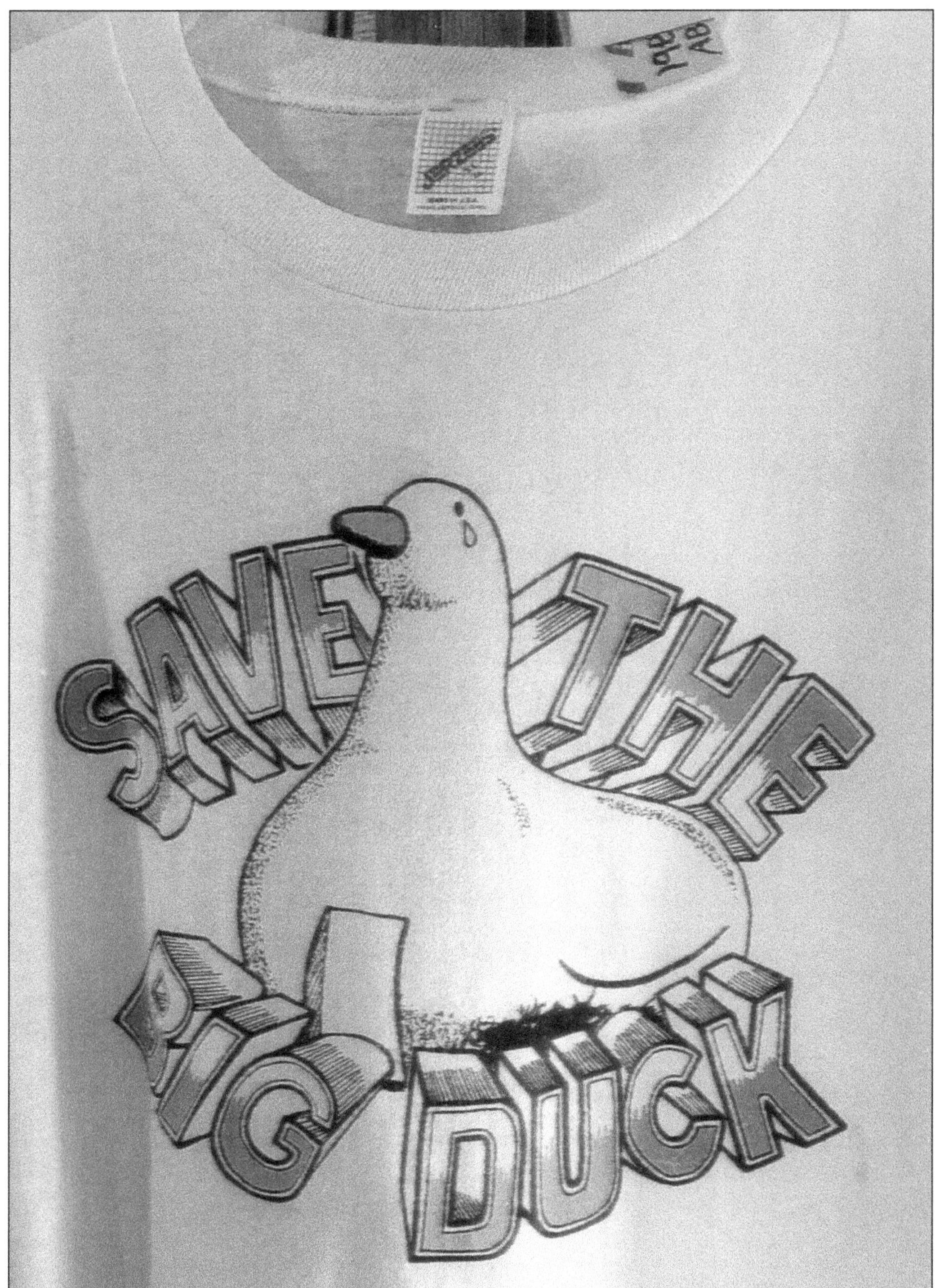

"SAVE THE BIG DUCK" T-SHIRT, 1987. A campaign to "Save the Big Duck" took shape. J. Lance Mallamo, director of Suffolk County Division of Historic Services, and Jerry Kessler, president of Friends for Long Island's Heritage, approached the Eshghis about donating it to Suffolk County. (Author's collection.)

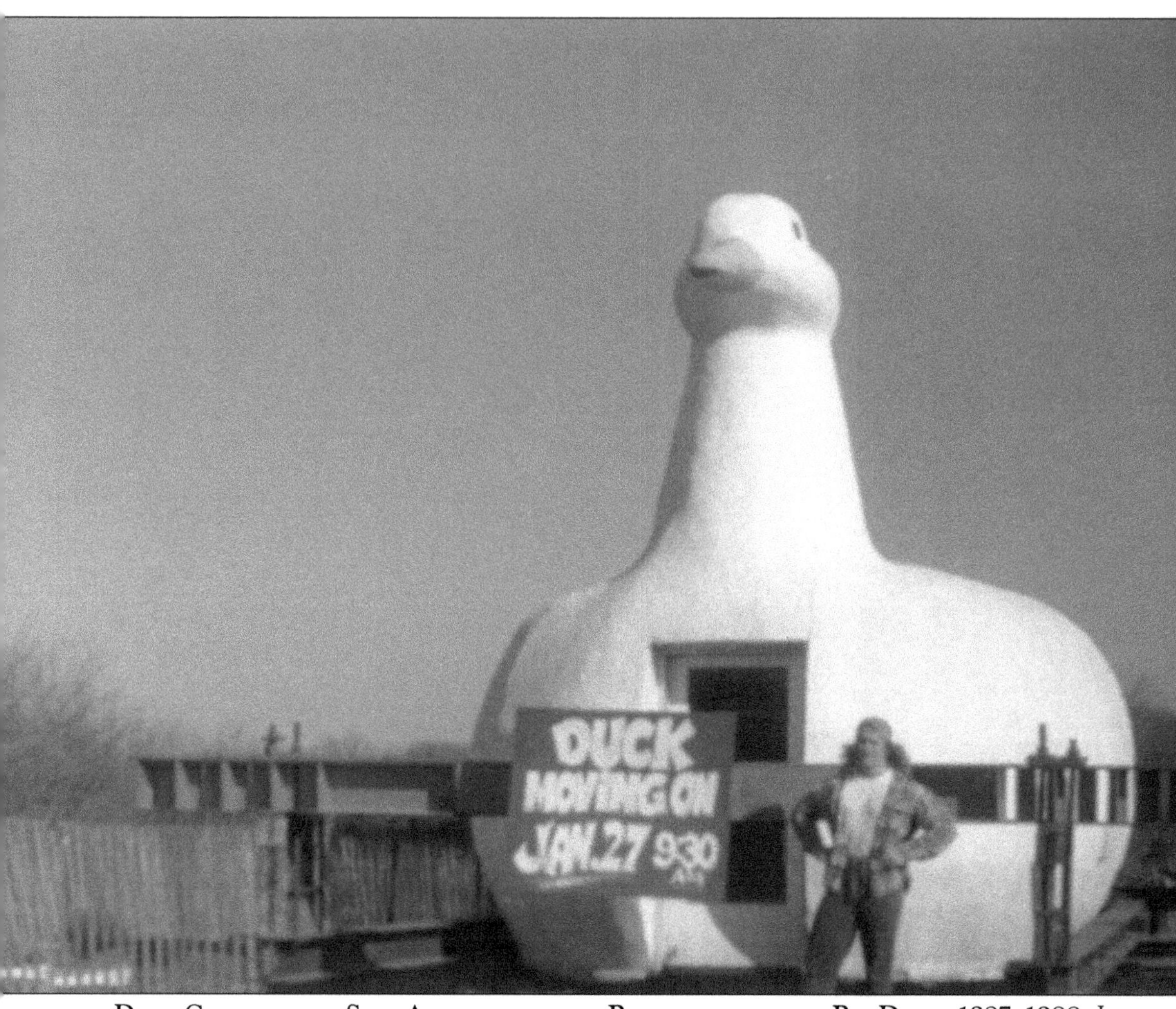

Dean Colombo and Sign Announcing the Relocation of the Big Duck, 1987–1988. In 1987, the Eshghis donated the Big Duck to Suffolk County on the condition that it would be moved from their property within six months; subsequently, they sold the land to a real estate developer, and Suffolk County decided to move the Big Duck to Sears Bellows County Park, a few miles southeast on Route 24. (Courtesy Dean Colombo.)

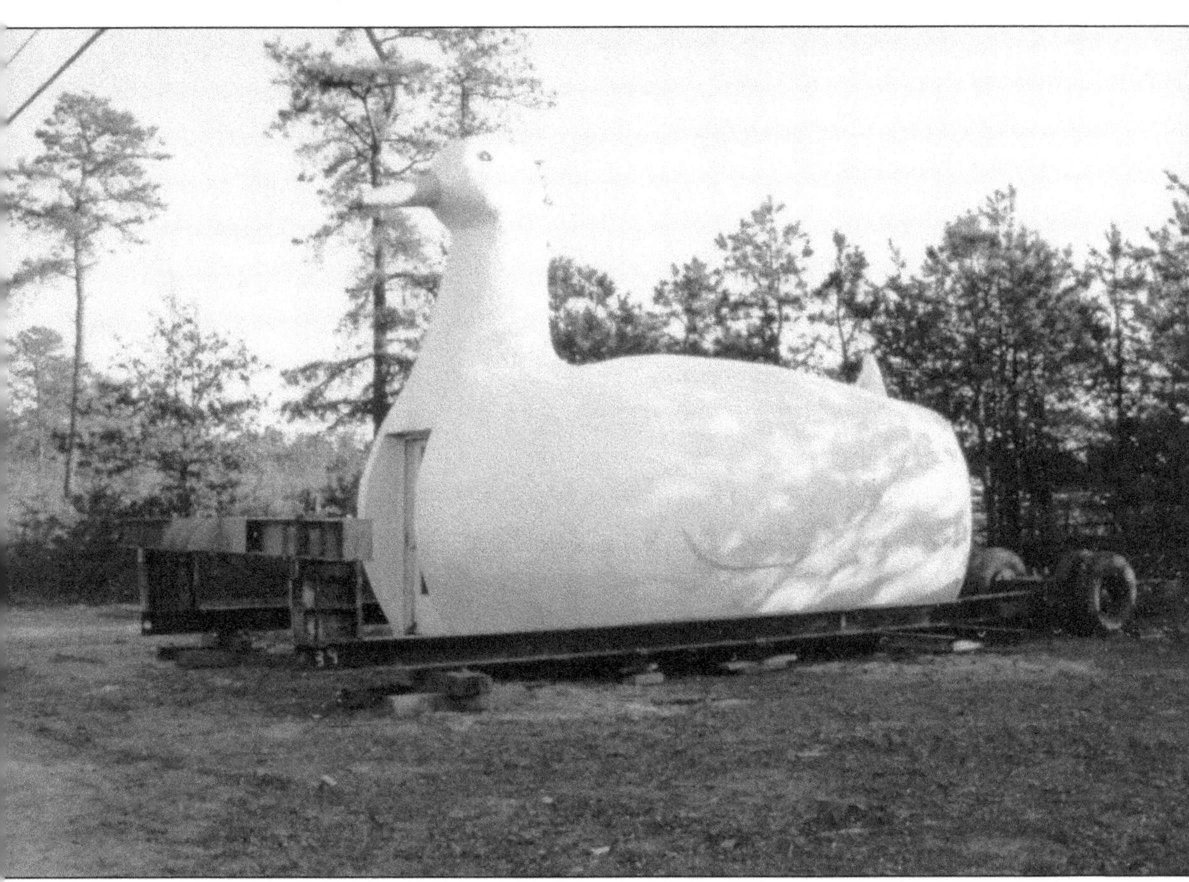

Moving the Big Duck, 1988. In 1988, Davis Brothers Building Movers of Blue Point, who donated their services for free, moved the Big Duck four miles to the entrance of Sears Bellows County Park on Route 24. The Big Duck was moved in one piece, first placed on flatbed rails. (Courtesy Suffolk County Parks.)

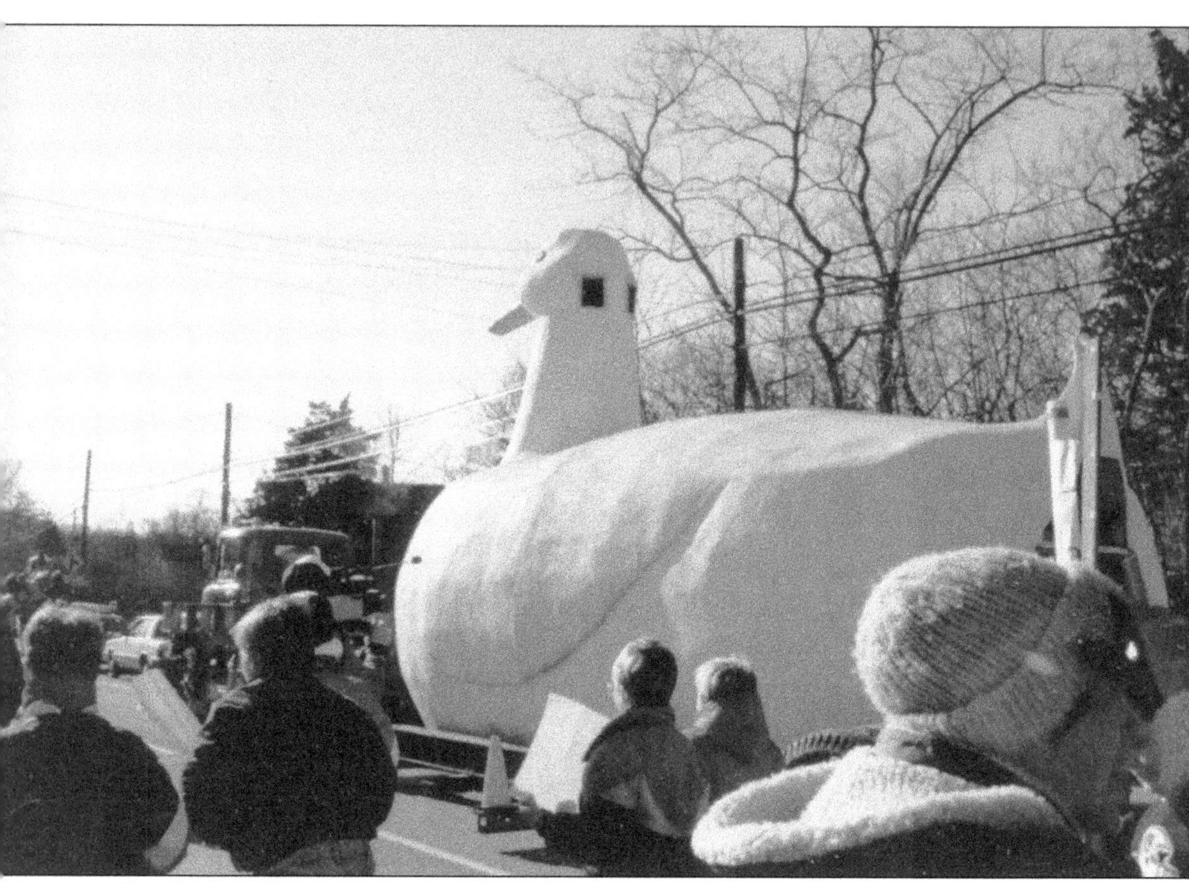

Big Duck on Route 24, 1988. The rails were attached to a truck, and the Big Duck was moved four miles on Route 24 to Sears Bellows County Park. Onlookers came to watch the fanfare, and volunteers escorted the Big Duck to make sure that it cleared telephone wires and tree branches. Once at Sears Bellows, it was given a new foundation and restored by monies raised by the Friends for Long Island's Heritage. (Courtesy Suffolk County Parks.)

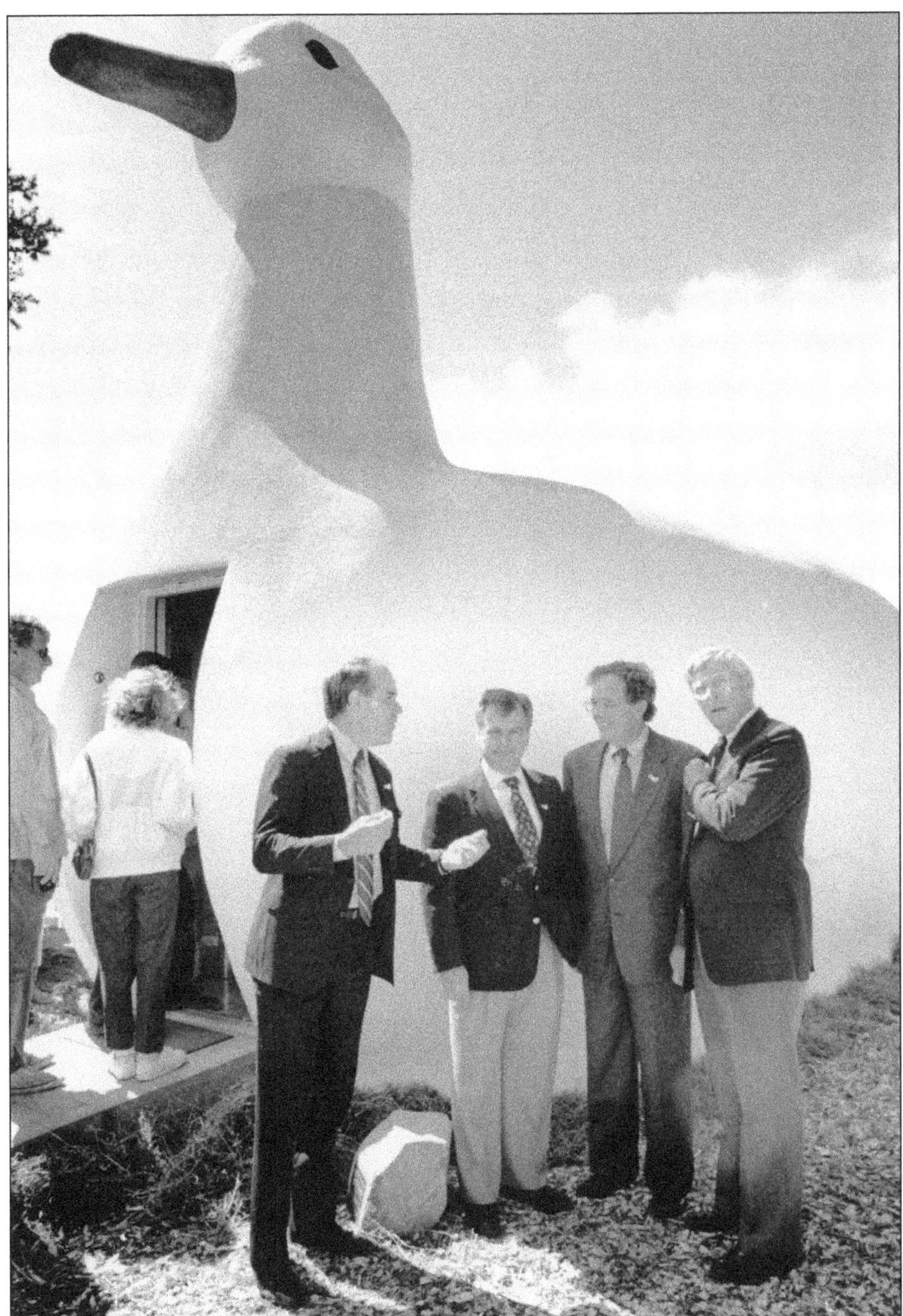

Reopening of the Big Duck at Sears Bellows County Park, 1993. J. Lance Mallamo, director of Suffolk County Division of Historic Services (far left), and Robert J. Gaffney, Suffolk County executive (second from right), pose in front of the Big Duck at the opening reception at Sears Bellows County Park in 1993. Four years later, the Big Duck was added to the National Register of Historic Places. Mallamo hoped to turn the Big Duck into the main attraction of a museum of roadside architecture but could not gain enough support for the endeavor. (Courtesy Suffolk County Parks.)

Dedication Plaque, 1993. The reopening of the Big Duck in its new location at Sears Bellows County Park in 1993 recognized the generosity of the Eshghis' gift and decision to donate the Big Duck. After realizing that the duck farms attracted a large immigrant worker population, their daughter Dana Eshghi believed that their purchase of the Big Duck was about "paying homage to the immigrant's pursuit of the American Dream." (Author's collection.)

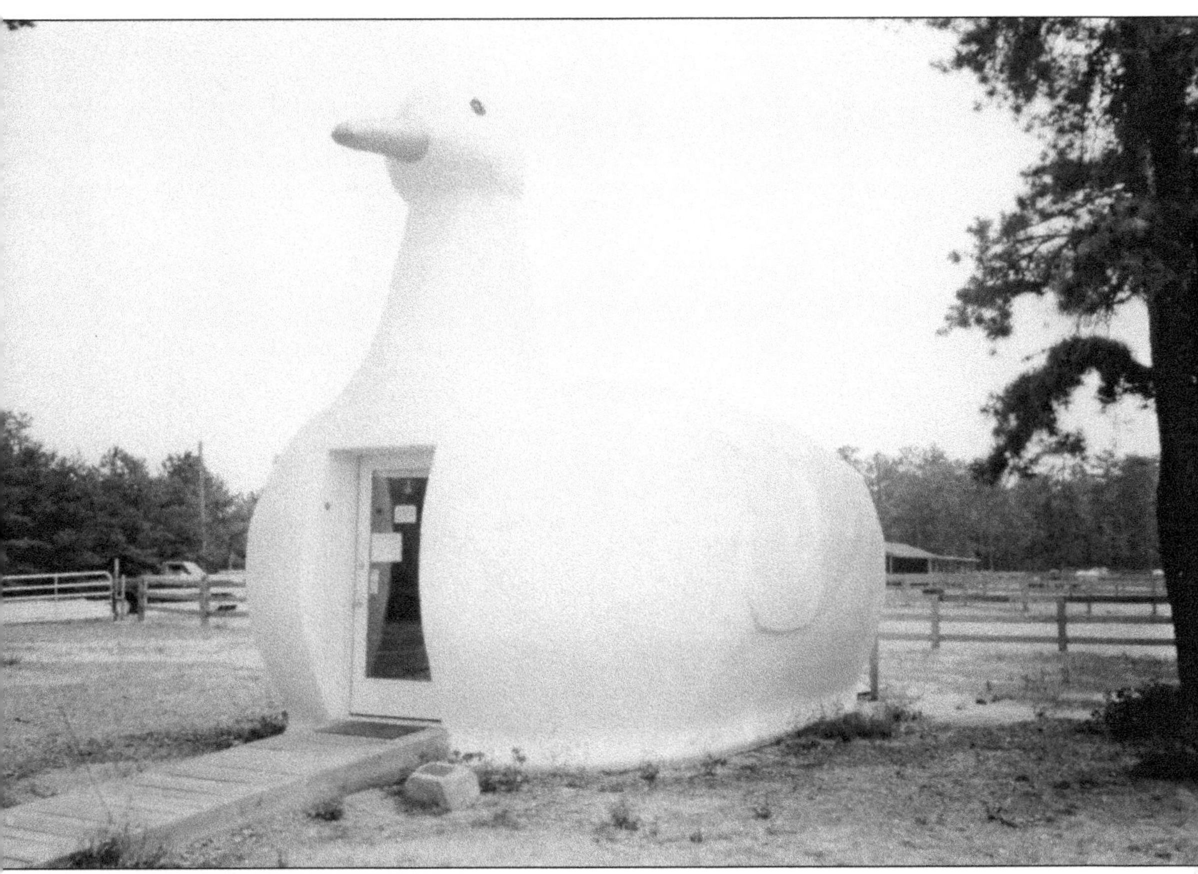

Big Duck Installed at Sears Bellows County Park, 1993. The Big Duck stood at the entrance of Sears Bellow County Park from 1988–2007. In 2004, there was a bid in a *New York Times* op-ed piece by the president of the Long Island Business Aviation Association to move the Big Duck to a more visible location at MacArthur Airport in Ronkonkoma, but it was met with opposition. (Courtesy Suffolk County Parks.)

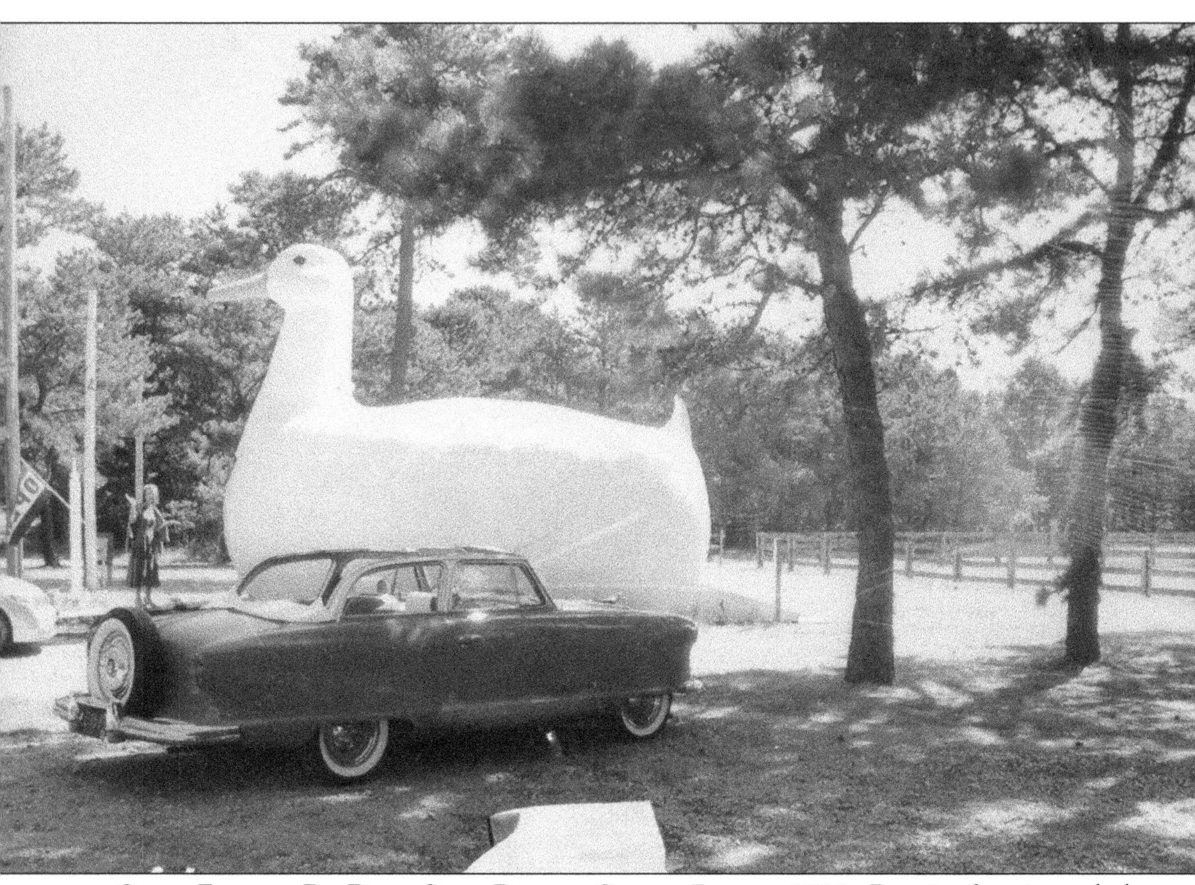

Car in Front of Big Duck, Sears Bellows County Park, c. 1990s. Drawing from its roadside architecture roots, from 1991 to 1992, motorists passing by could tune to radio station 88.3 to hear a pre-taped, two-minute message by supermodel Christie Brinkley as the voice of the Big Duck in order to raise money for the interior renovations that was spearheaded by the Friends for Long Island's Heritage. (Courtesy Suffolk County Parks.)

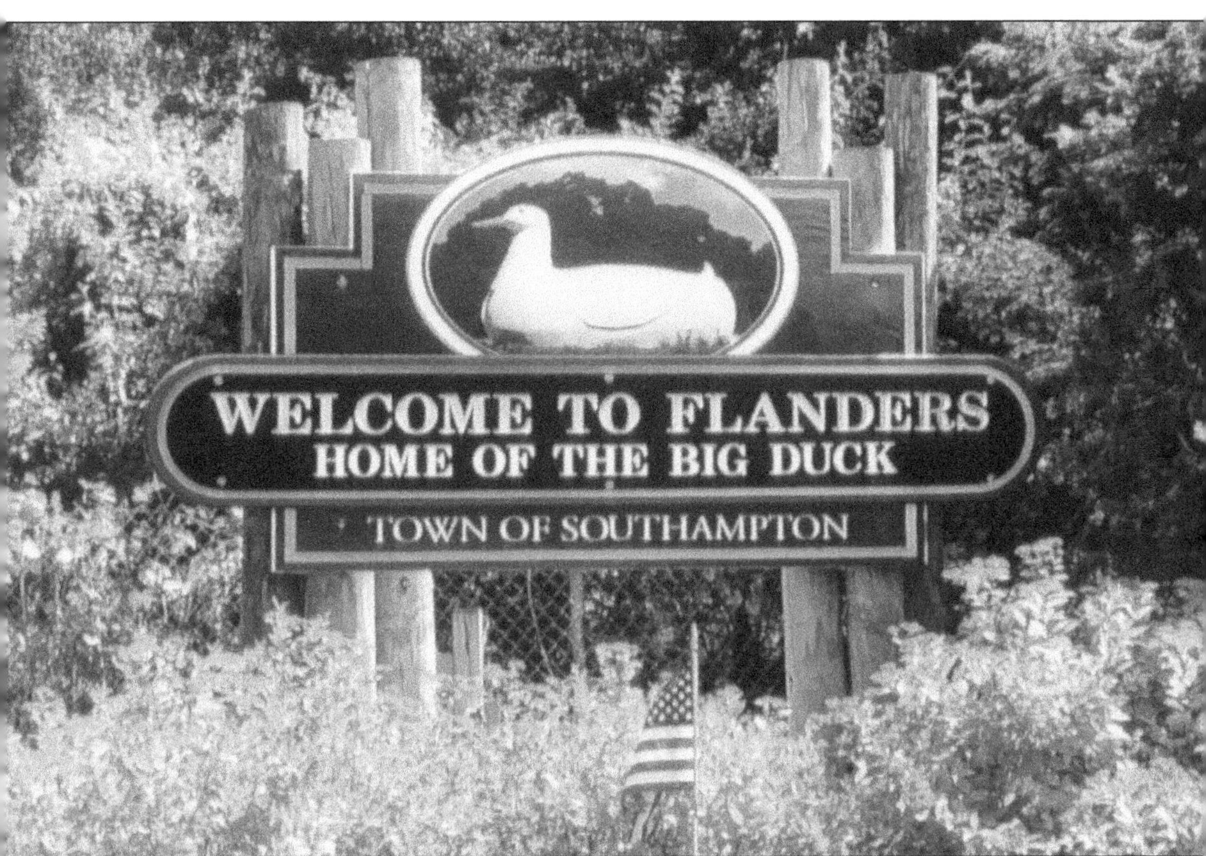

Flanders Sign, 2018. By 2001, the land of the second location of the Big Duck on Route 24 (where it stood from 1936 to 1988) was not developed, and the Town of Southampton purchased it. In 2007, the Big Duck moved a third time back to its second location. Davis Construction House and Building Movers in Westhampton completed the job free of charge. (Author's collection.)

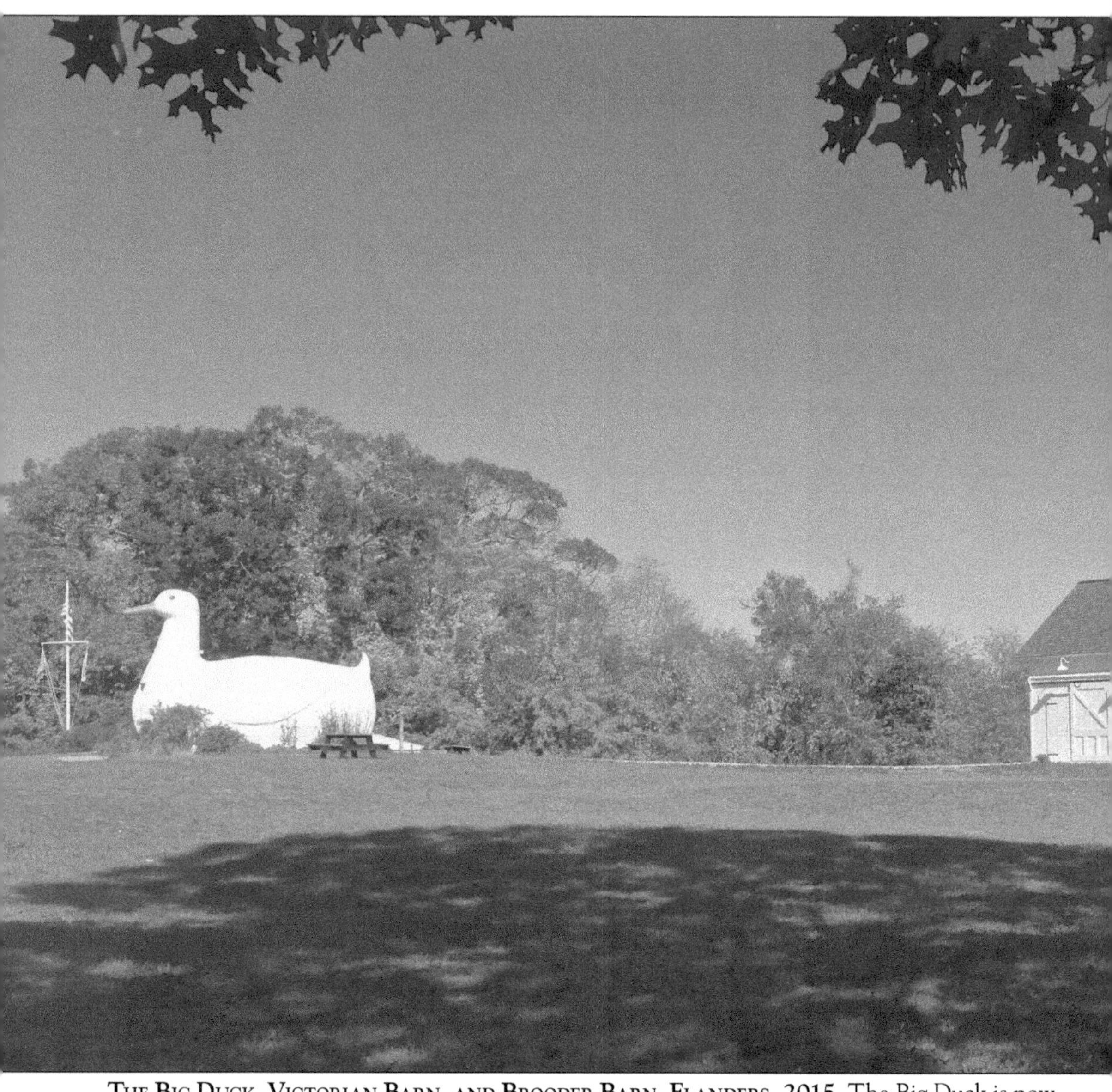

The Big Duck, Victorian Barn, and Brooder Barn, Flanders, 2015. The Big Duck is now owned and maintained by Suffolk County, the land is owned by the Town of Southampton, and the

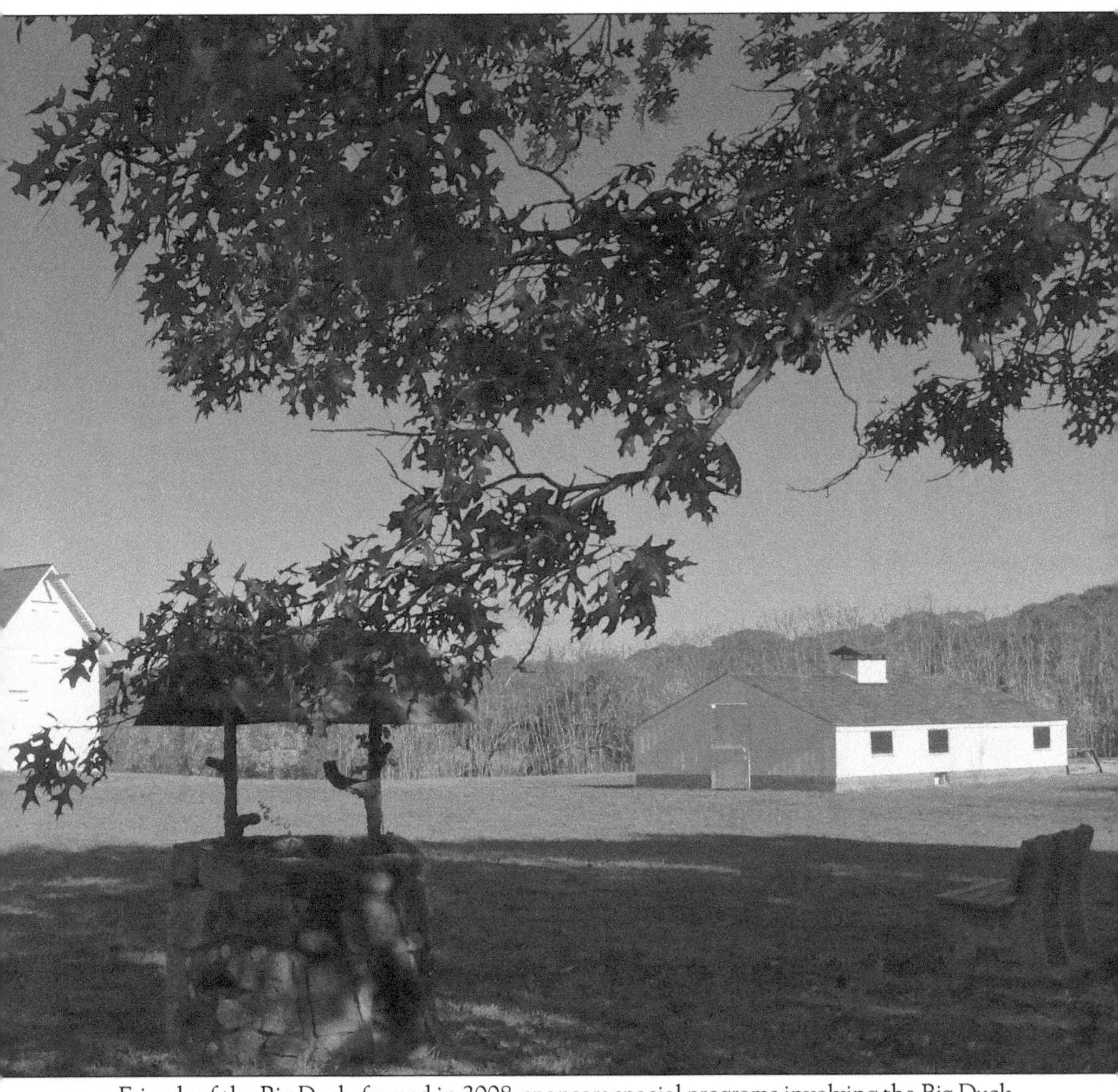

group Friends of the Big Duck, formed in 2008, sponsors special programs involving the Big Duck (which are highlighted in chapter four). (Courtesy Jeff Heatley, *Art and Architecture Quarterly*.)

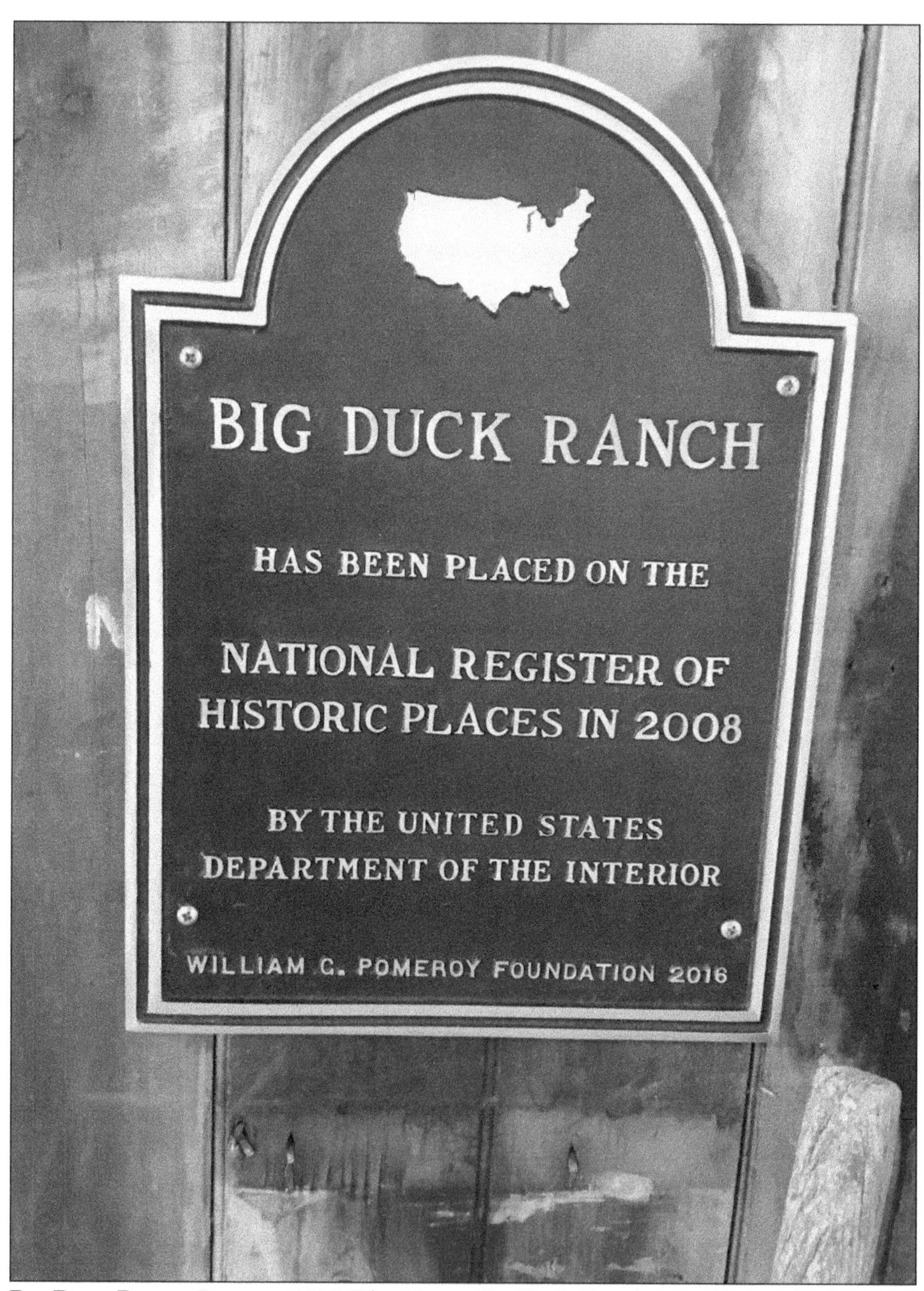

Big Duck Ranch Plaque, 2016. The 13-acre Big Duck Ranch was added to the National Register of Historic Places in 2008. The National Registry status of both the Big Duck and Big Duck Ranch affords them the privilege of having the Advisory Council on Historic Preservation weigh in on all projects affecting both entities. (Author's collection.)

Four

THE LEGACY OF THE BIG DUCK AND EASTERN LONG ISLAND DUCK FARMING TODAY

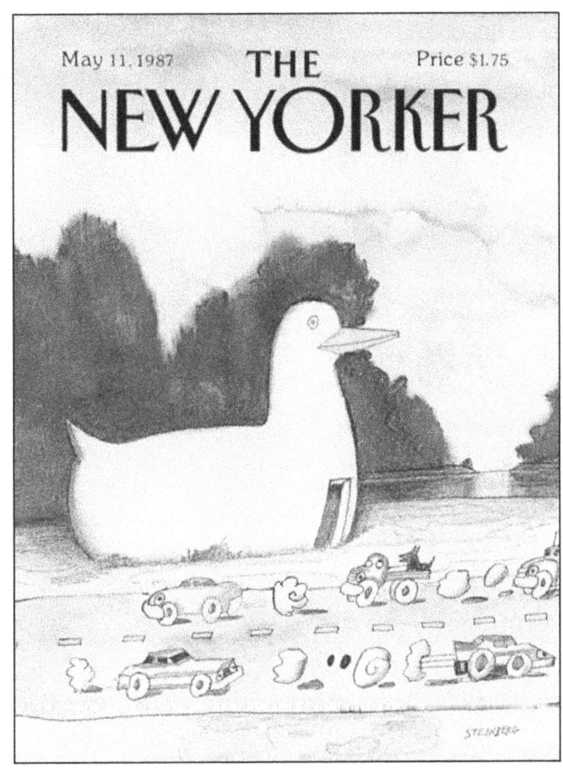

SAUL STEINBERG, COVER OF THE *NEW YORKER*, MAY 11, 1987. From 1979 to 1987, famed illustrator Saul Steinberg, who was a longtime resident of Amagansett, created several drawings of the Big Duck. This version was featured on the cover of the May 11, 1987, issue of the *New Yorker* magazine, showing a side profile of the Big Duck in front of Peconic Bay with one red eye visible and cars and trucks whizzing past it spewing exhaust into the air. (© The Saul Steinberg Foundation /Artists Rights Society [ARS], New York. Cover reprinted with permission of the *New Yorker* magazine. All rights reserved.)

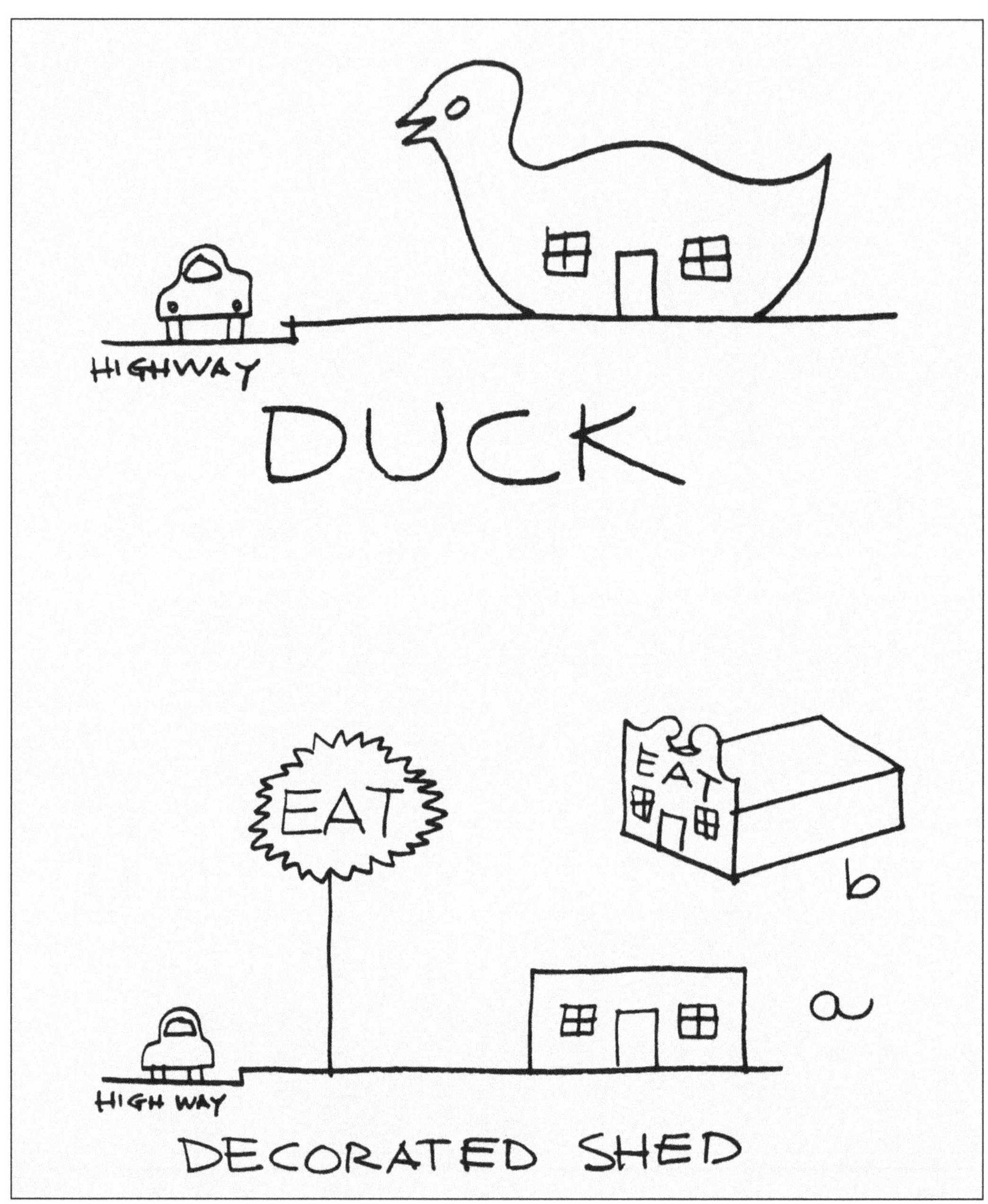

"Big Sign–Little Building or Building as Sign" from *Learning from Las Vegas* (1972). The Big Duck was famously praised by architects Robert Venturi and Denise Scott Brown in their influential 1972 book *Learning from Las Vegas*, in which they used Venturi's illustration of the Big Duck to introduce the term "duck" for any building that was a symbol that took the shape of its function, opposed to the more common "decorated shed" that "applies symbols" or required signage to determine function. As a result of their theorizing, no matter the shape, any building that takes the shape of its function is now called a "duck." Many photographic examples of "duck" architecture can be viewed on the interior walls of the Big Duck, such as the Big Apple in Ontario, Canada, that sells pies and the Hood Milk Bottle in Boston, Massachusetts, that sells ice cream. (Sketch by Robert Venturi, courtesy Venturi, Scott Brown and Associates, Inc.)

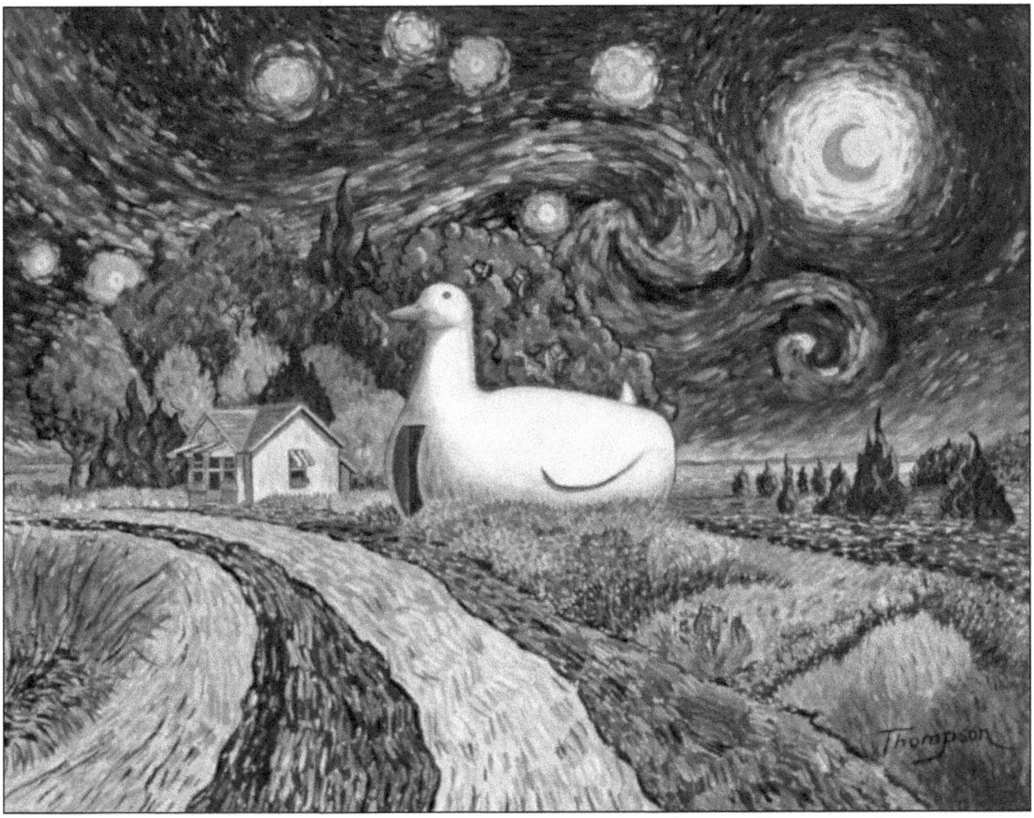

The Big Duck V.G., Flanders, Long Island, 2006. Local artist Elaine Faith Thompson's popular printed reproductions of the Big Duck incorporate the swirling night sky of Vincent van Gogh's *The Starry Night* (1889) into a landscape with the Big Duck and Big Duck Ranch. (Courtesy Elaine Faith Thompson.)

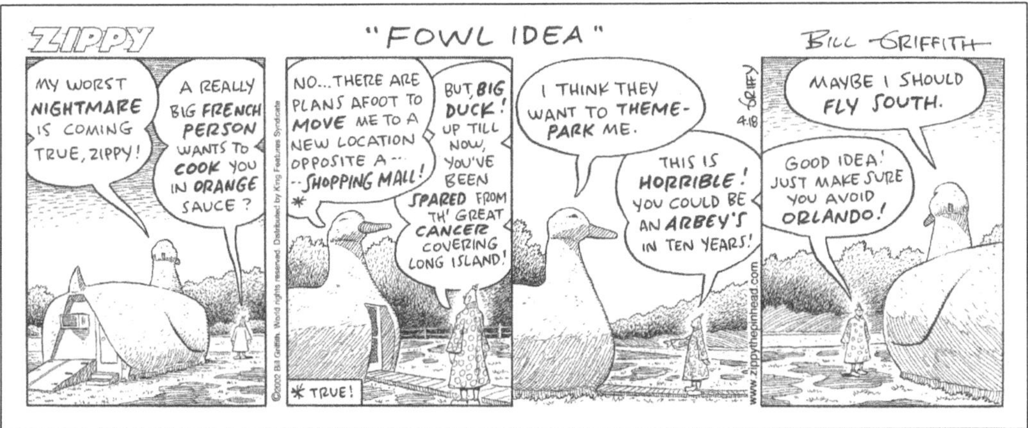

Bill Griffith, "Fowl Idea," *Zippy* Comic Strip, April 18, 2002. Bill Griffith, who is originally from Levittown, Long Island, is the creator of the *Zippy* comic strip that has featured the Big Duck on numerous occasions since the late 1990s. "Fowl Idea" references the rapid commercial development with strip malls and chain stores that have befallen areas of the East End and the Big Duck's close calls with being torn down. (Courtesy Bill Griffith.)

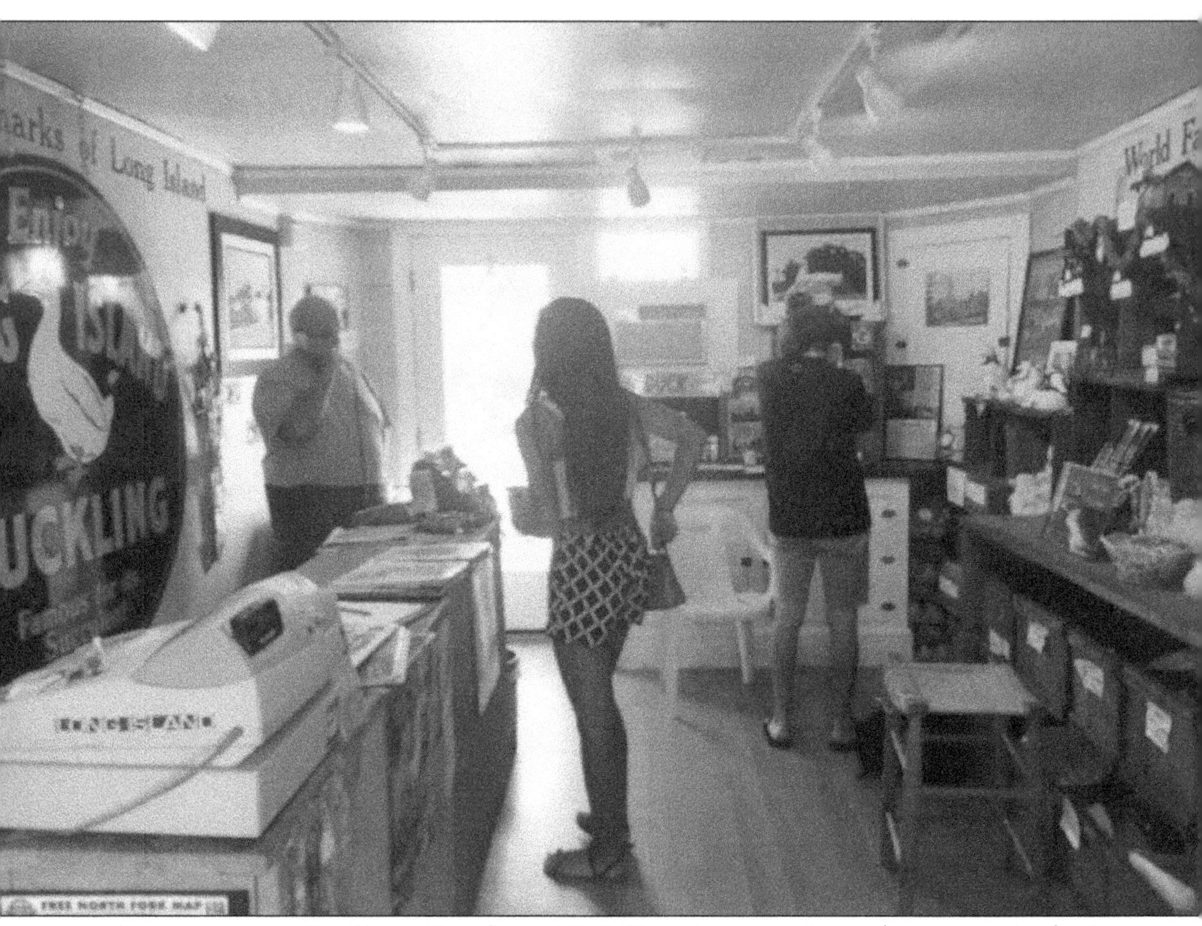

INTERIOR OF THE BIG DUCK GIFT SHOP, 2017. Since its restoration and reopening in the Sears Bellow County Park location in 1993 and then continuing in the Flanders location in 2007, the interior of the Big Duck has operated as a gift shop and East End Visitors Center and sells duck merchandise, or "duckabilia." (Author's collection.)

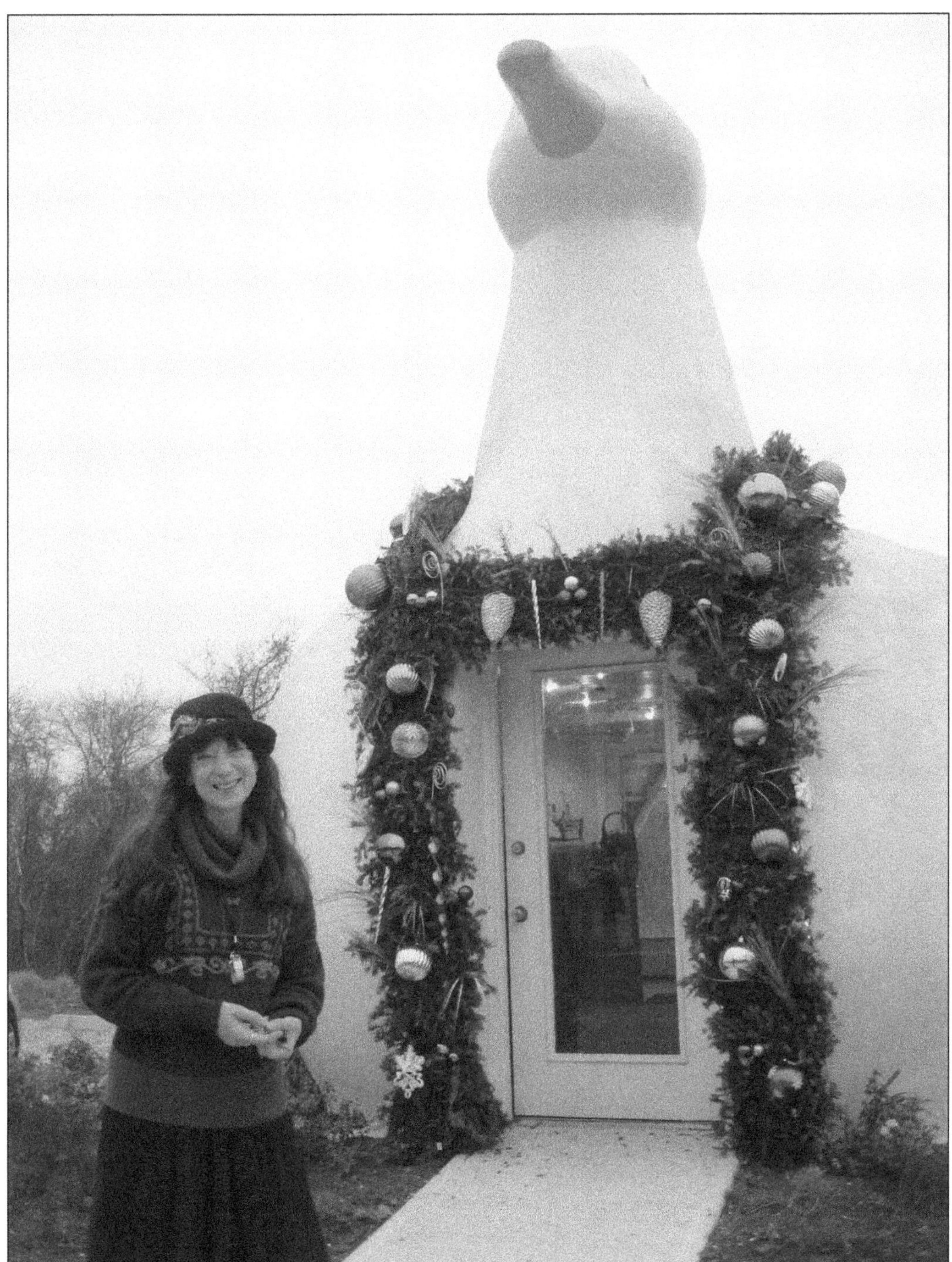

Big Duck Docent Barbara Bixby in Front of the Big Duck, c. 2015. Since operating the interior of the Big Duck gift shop since 1993, a group of loyal and knowledgeable docents have warmly welcomed visitors to the Big Duck. Barbara "Babs" Bixby, who referred to herself as the "duck lady," worked at the duck for 22 years. (Courtesy Janice Jay Young.)

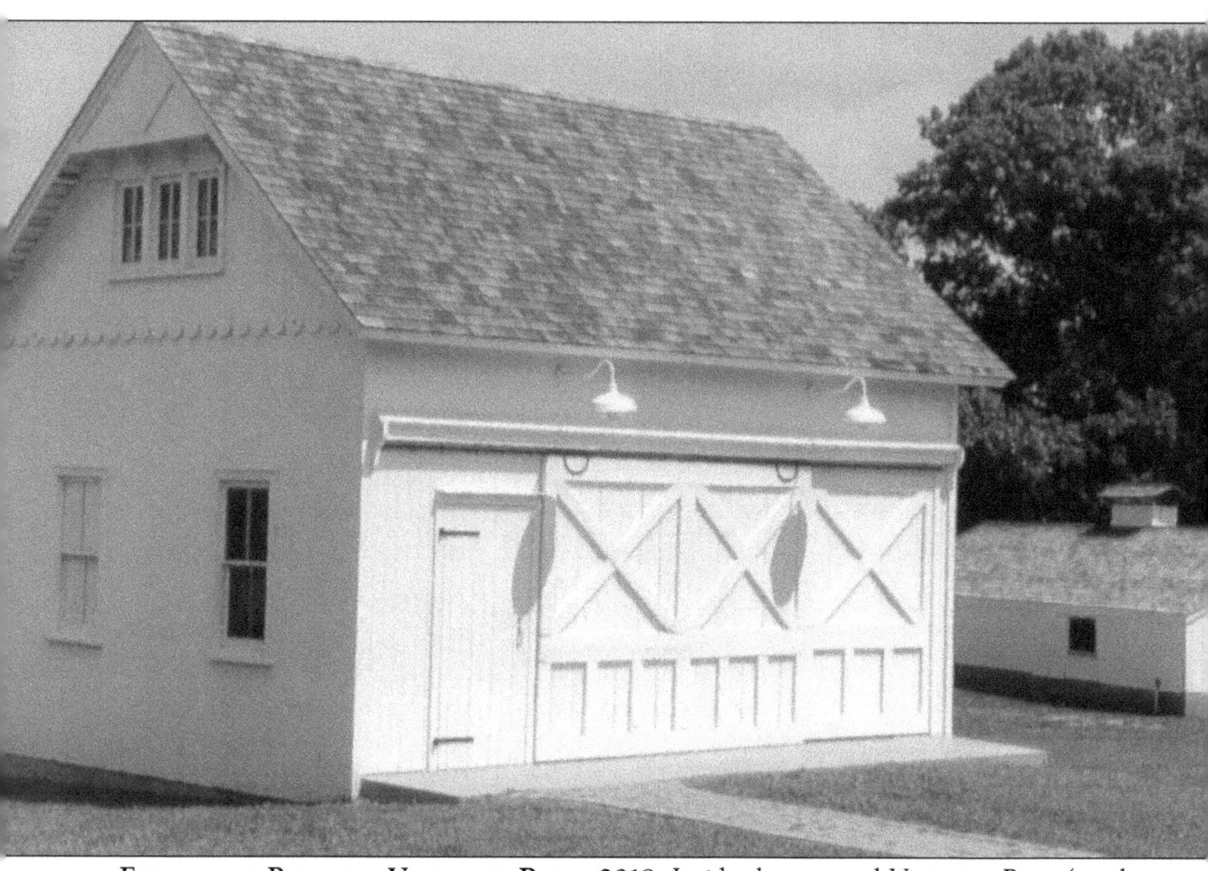

EXTERIOR OF RESTORED VICTORIAN BARN, 2018. Inside the restored Victorian Barn (on the site of the old tool shed), the Long Island Duck Farm Exhibit, co-curated by Lisa A. Dabrowski and David Wilcox Jr. (whose grandfather LeRoy Wilcox wrote the history of the Long Island duck farming industry in 1949), features objects and ephemera related to duck farming as well as educational text panels and videos. (Author's collection.)

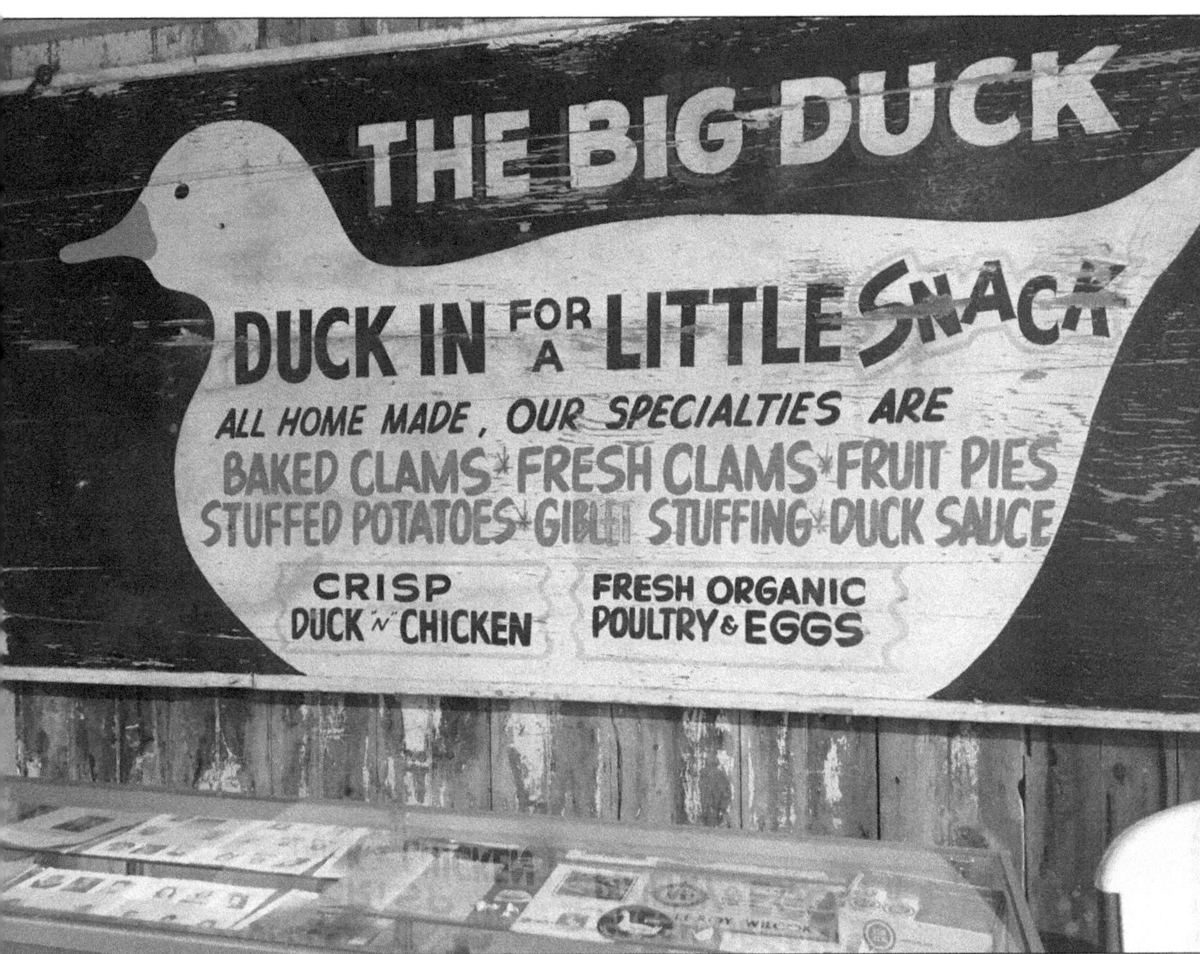

Wooden Sign, Long Island Duck Farm Exhibit, Interior of Victorian Barn, 2018. The wooden sign advertises foods once sold inside the Big Duck. Underneath, a glass case holds stickers, pamphlets, and books related to Eastern Long Island duck farming. (Author's collection.)

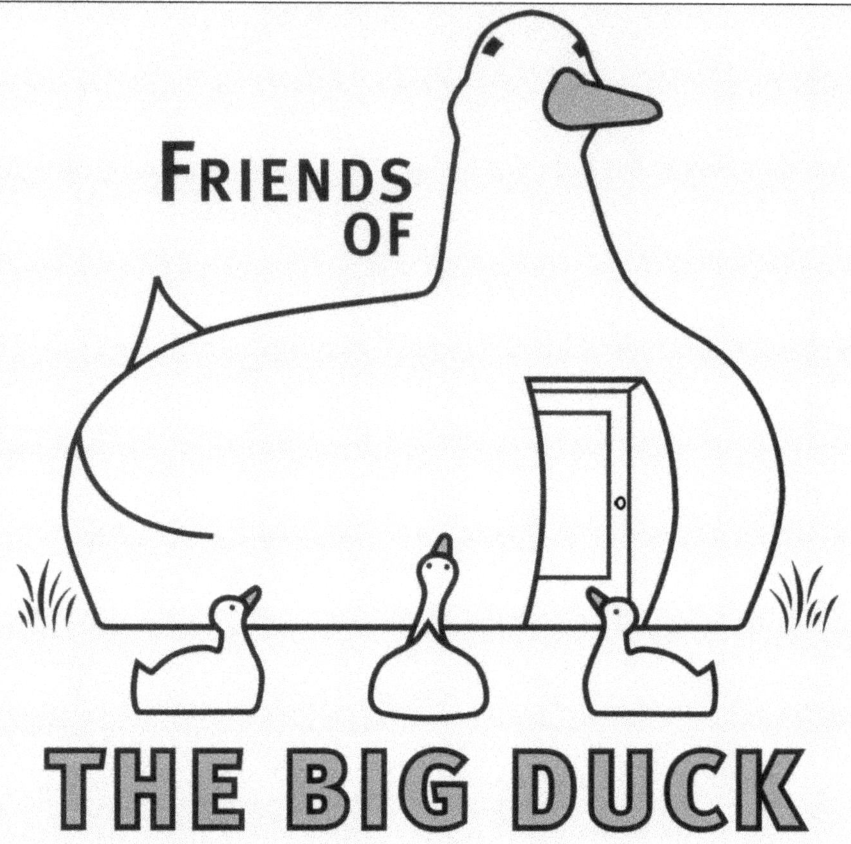

FRIENDS OF THE BIG DUCK, c. 2010s. The Friends of the Big Duck Group was formed in 2008 as a non-profit, volunteer-run organization to help preserve the history of the Big Duck, sponsor programs involving the famous landmark, and oversee the Long Island Duck Farming Exhibit. Special events sponsored by the Friends include the Big Duck Egg Hunt in spring, Rubber Ducky Race in August, and various craft fairs and festivals. Meetings are held on the first Tuesday of every month at the David W. Crohan Community Center in Flanders. (Logo by Neil B. Young, Resonant Handcrafts.)

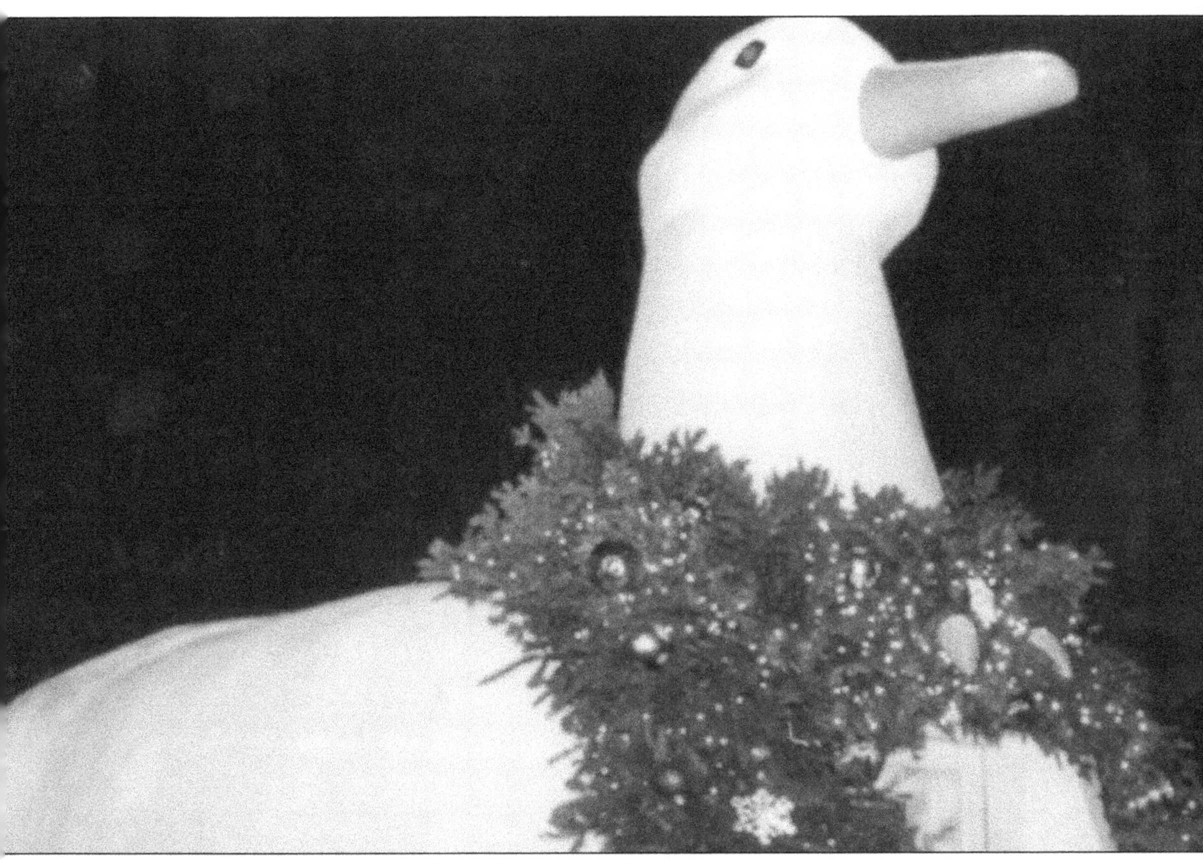

THE BIG DUCK LIGHTING, C. 2017. Dean Colombo first began to hang garland and lights around the Big Duck for the holidays in the 1980s. Suffolk County Parks has continued the tradition with the Annual Big Duck Lighting for the past 29 years on the Wednesday after Thanksgiving to kick off the holiday season. This popular community event includes the lighting ceremony, carolers singing "duck carols," and a visit from Santa Claus escorted by the Flanders Fire Department. (Courtesy Denise Civiletti, *Riverhead LOCAL.*)

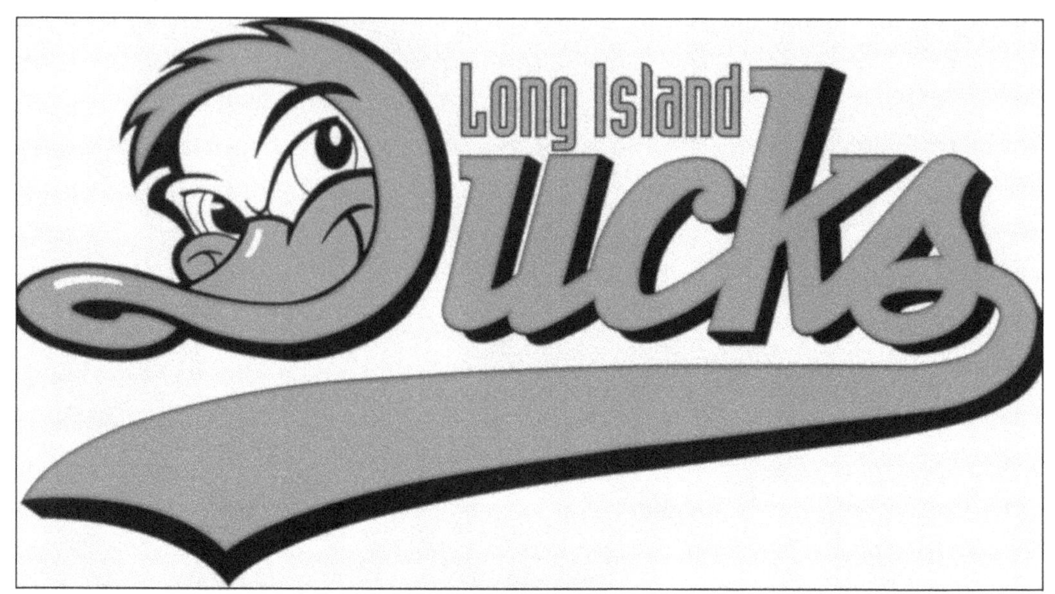

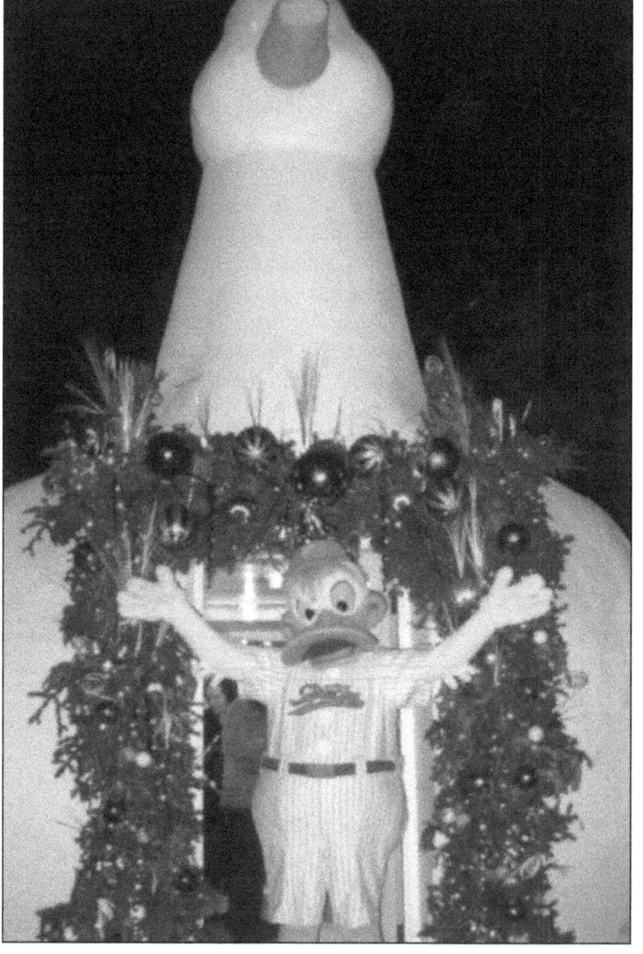

Long Island Ducks Baseball Team Logo, c. 2000. When Frank Boulton founded a Minor League Baseball team based in Central Islip in 2000, he named them the Long Island Ducks, paying homage to the history of duck farming and the Big Duck in Suffolk County. The championship-winning team (2004, 2012, and 2013) plays at Bethpage Ballpark. (Courtesy Frank Boulton.)

QuackerJack at the Annual Big Duck Lighting, c. 2017. The Long Island Ducks' mascot, QuackerJack, attends the Annual Big Duck Lighting Ceremony every year. (Courtesy Frank Boulton.)

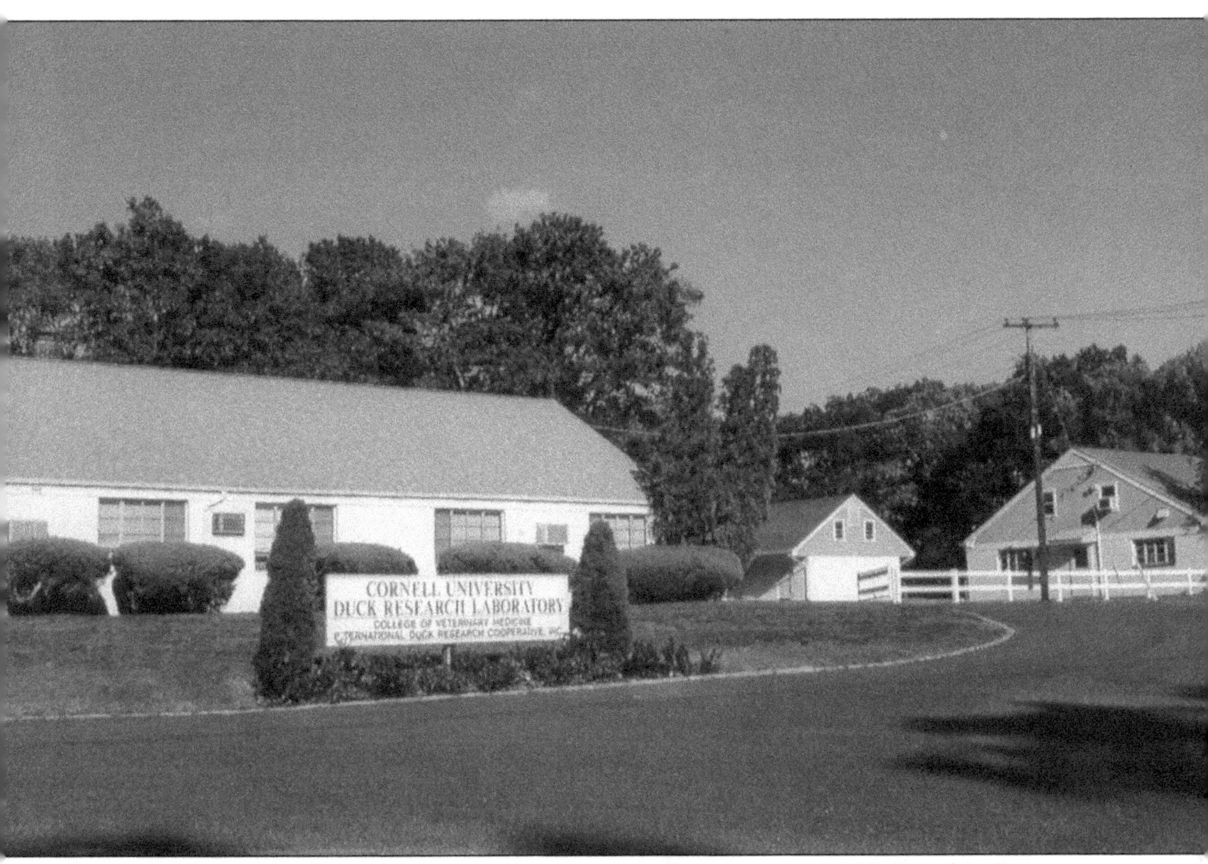

CORNELL UNIVERSITY DUCK RESEARCH LABORATORY, EASTPORT, c. 2007. Based in Eastport, the Cornell University Duck Research Laboratory is still in existence and has expanded to serve other regions outside of New York, causing them to change their name to the International Duck Research Cooperative in 1992. Their priorities include the vaccination, diagnosis, and treatment of diseases affecting ducks. (Courtesy Dr. William F. Dean.)

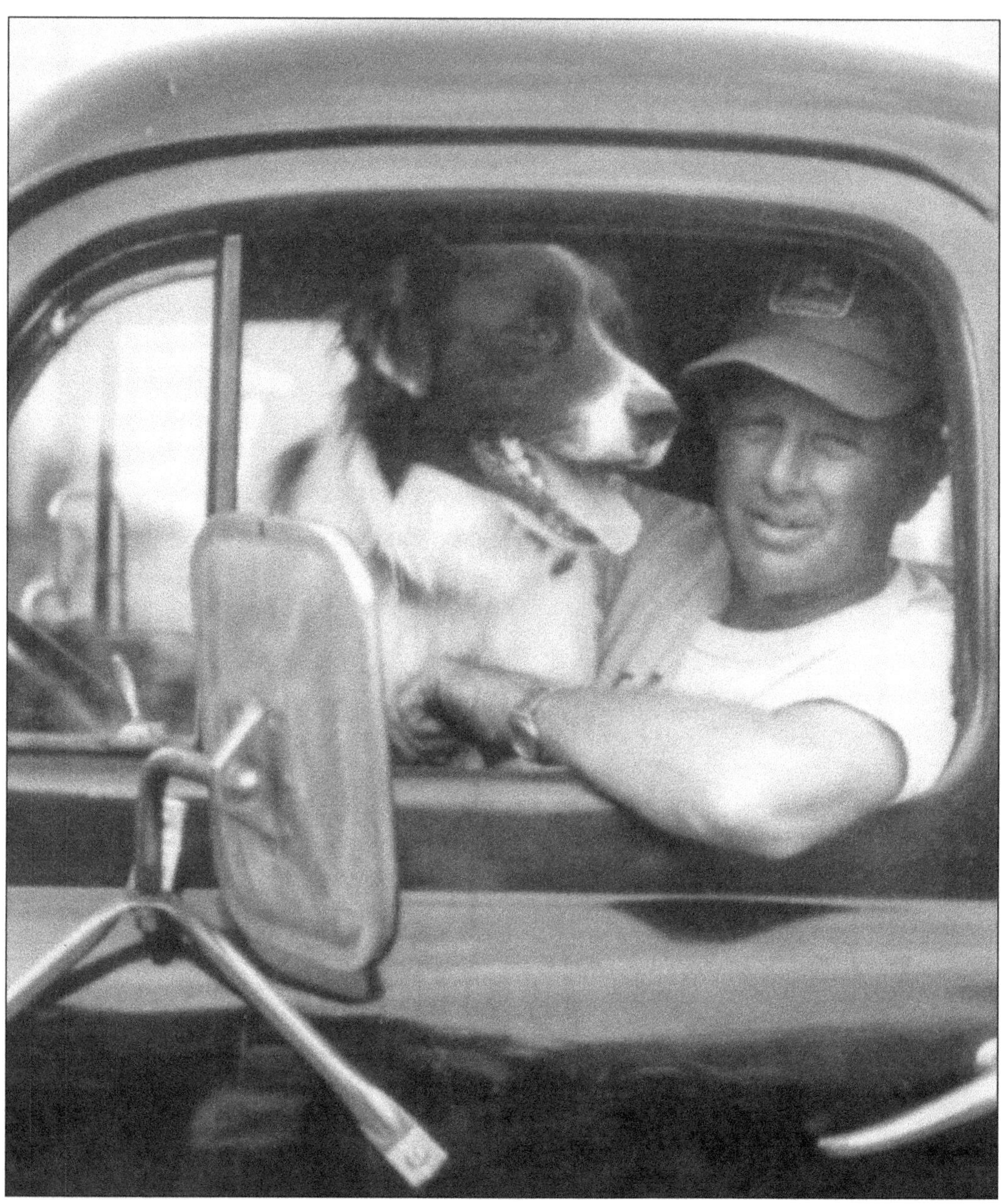

Ronald Bush, Bush Farm Museum, South Haven. Ronald Bush, a former real estate broker who now devotes his time to farming, has been collecting farm tools for the past 50 years and, in 1989, established a private farm and museum in South Haven that was once part of Robinson Duck Farm. The complex includes a two-story barn stocked with smaller hand tools, outbuildings with antique plows and tractors, a milk house, and the Brookhaven Railroad Station, which used to supply feed and materials to the surrounding duck farms and dairy farms before the intrusion of Sunrise Highway brought about their decline. (Courtesy Ronald Bush.)

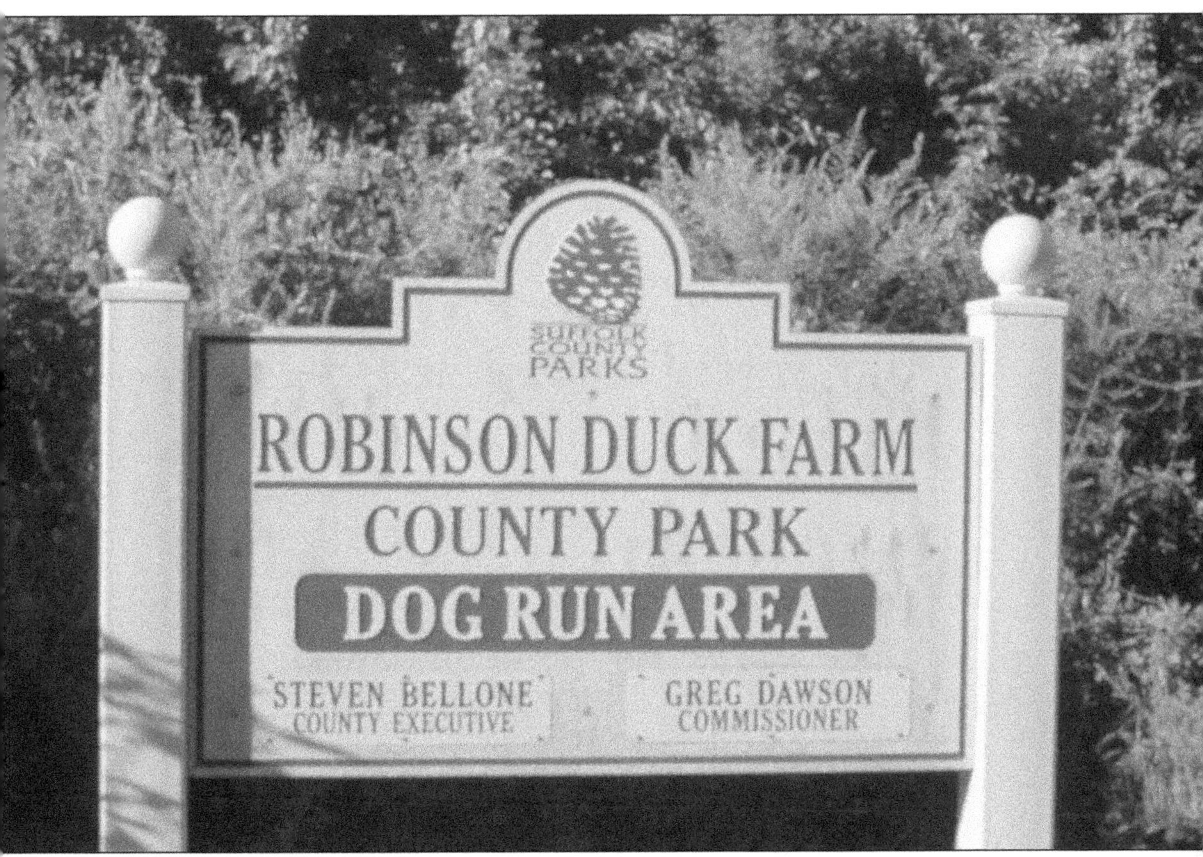

Robinson Duck Farm Dog Park, South Haven. Suffolk County has acquired numerous duck farms, and the Department of Planning has conducted complex environmental studies to rehabilitate the toxicity of the water and soil caused by the duck farms in order to transform them to be used for open space and recreational purposes. Such projects include Robinson Duck Farm Dog Park, former site of Robinson Duck Farm, in South Haven, which opened to the public in 2009 and the Mud Creek Restoration, an intended nature preserve, which was the former site of Gallo Duck Farm, in East Patchogue. (Courtesy Suffolk County Parks.)

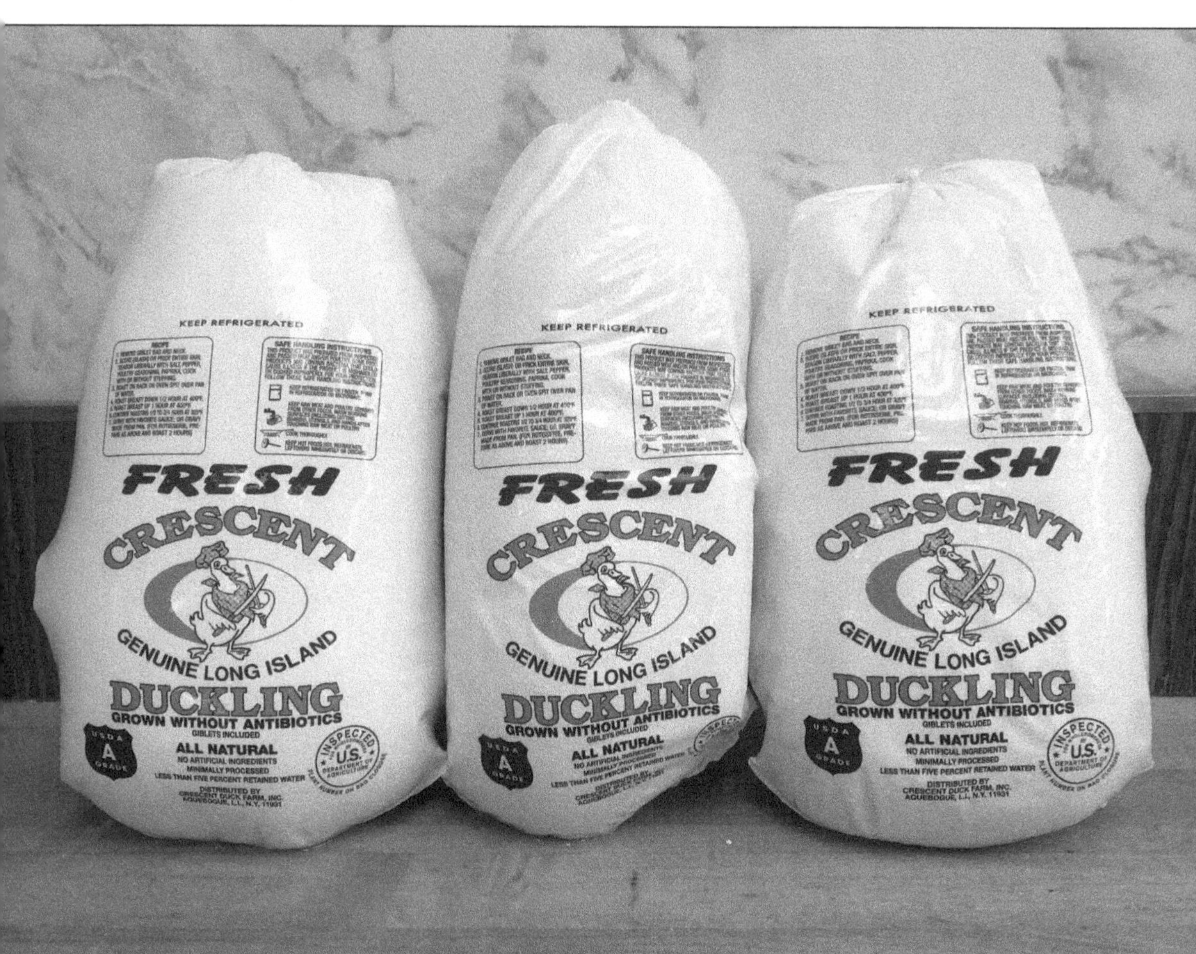

Crescent Ducklings, c. 2017. Crescent Duck Farm is the last remaining major duck farm on Long Island. In 2015, Crescent produced approximately one million ducks (four percent of the nation's duck supply) with the average six-pound Crescent duck selling for $2.20 a pound. Crescent's ducks are served in top-rated dining establishments such as Eleven Madison Park and the Four Seasons Restaurant. Pres. Douglas Corwin's sons, fifth-generation farmers, plan to keep the Long Island duck tradition alive for many years to come. (Author's collection.)

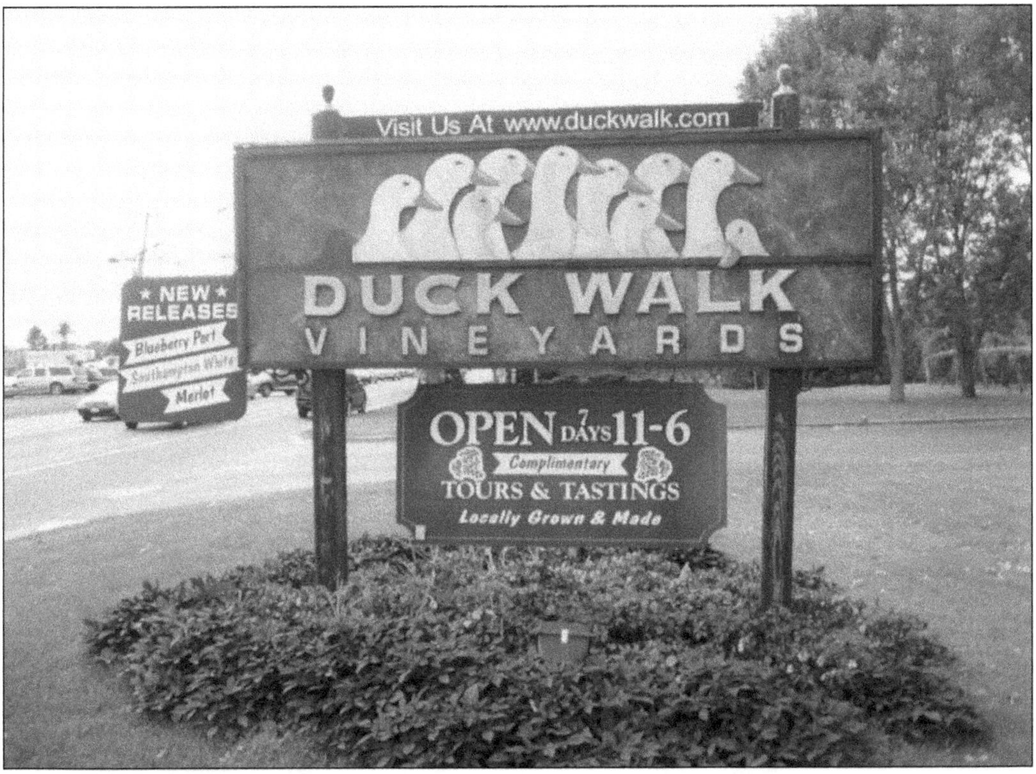

DUCK WALK VINEYARDS, SOUTHAMPTON, C. 2010S. In the past two decades, the East End of Long Island has become known for its wine production and vineyards. Duck Walk Vineyard was established in Southampton in 1994. When the owner, Dr. Damianos, discovered that the land had once been a duck farm in the 1940s, he decided to name it Duck Walk to honor the region's farming history. (Courtesy Duck Walk Vineyards.)

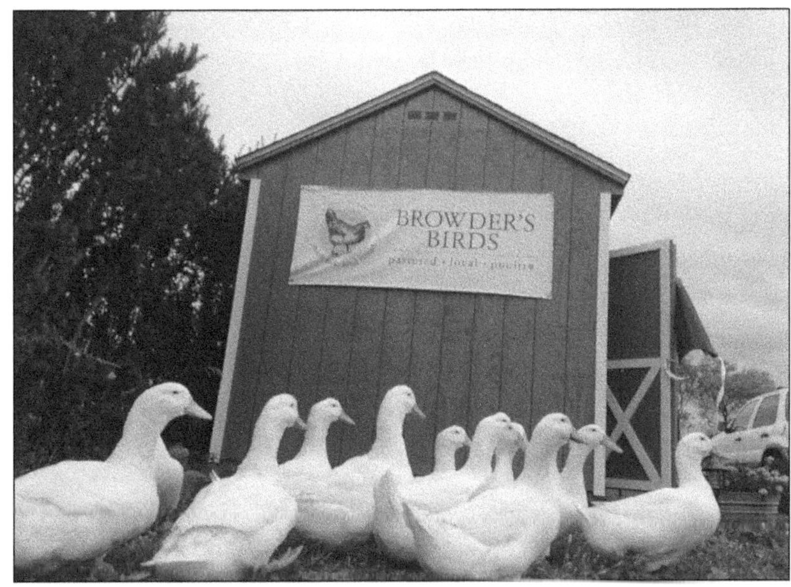

DUCKS, BROWDER'S BIRDS, MATTITUCK, C. 2015. In recent years, there has been an uptick in small, organic poultry farms on the North Fork of Eastern Long Island clustered between Riverhead and Greenport. One such farm is Browder's Birds in Mattituck that raises chickens, turkeys, ducks, and sheep. (Courtesy Chris and Holly Browder.)

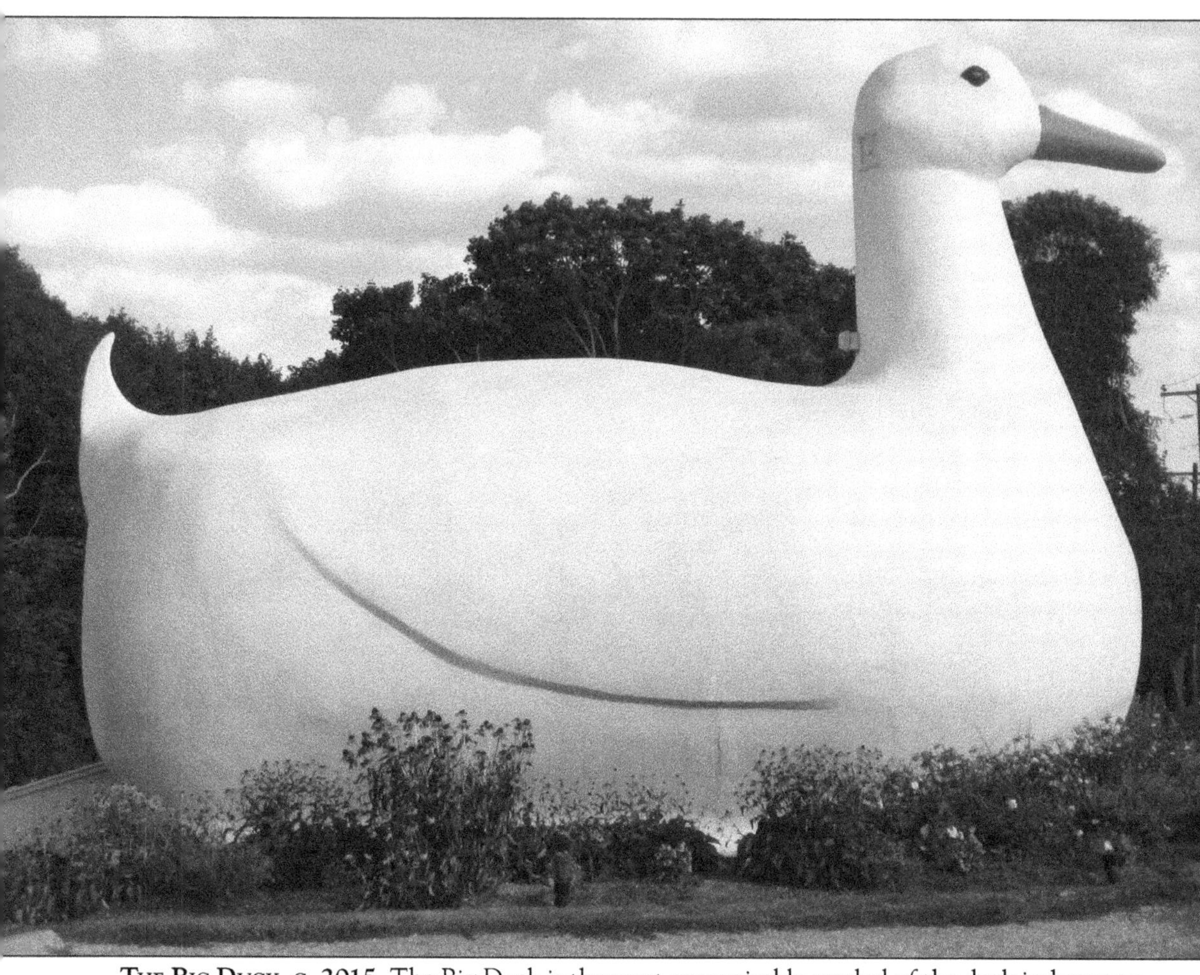

The Big Duck, c. 2015. The Big Duck is the most recognizable symbol of the duck industry on Eastern Long Island and Suffolk County Parks' most popular historic site. It receives more than 10,000 visitors a year. (Courtesy Janice Jay Young.)

Bibliography

Big Duck Ranch. National Register Nomination Application, May 2008.

Davies, Carolyn L'Hommedieu. "Creating a Landmark: Hatching the Big Duck." *Long Island Forum* 55. (Spring 1988): 66–70.

Flatow, George. "Famous Long Island Ducks, Where they Originated—How They are Hatched, Grown and Marketed in 12 Weeks." *Sunrise—The Magazine of Long Island*. (September 1929): 13–14.

Lamon, Harry and Rob R. Slocum. *Ducks and Geese*. New York: Orange Judd Publishing Company, 1922.

Naylor, Natalie A. "The Big Duck: From Ad to Icon." *The Nassau County Historical Society Journal*, 66. (2011): 29–34.

Venturi, Robert, Denise Scott Brown, and Steven Izenour. *Learning from Las Vegas: The Forgotten Symbolism of Architectural Form*. Cambridge: MIT Press, 1977.

Verbarg, Ronald. "Long Island Duck Farm History and Ecosystem Restoration Opportunities." Suffolk County Department of Planning. February 2009.

Wilcox, LeRoy. "Duck Industry," Chapter XVIII. In Paul Bailey, ed. *Long Island: A History of Two Great Counties, Nassau and Suffolk*, Vol. II, 439–458. New York, Lewis Historical Publications, 1949.

Yeager, Edna Howell. "The Big Duck." *Long Island Forum* 55. (May 1988): 66–70.

www.ingramcontent.com/pod-product-compliance
Lightning Source LLC
LaVergne TN
LVHW000624110826
845147LV00015B/930
9781467102827